Lord Bolingbroke

CONTRIBUTIONS TO THE
CRAFTSMAN

Lord Bolingbroke

CONTRIBUTIONS TO THE
CRAFTSMAN

Edited by
SIMON VAREY

CLARENDON PRESS · OXFORD
1982

Oxford University Press, Walton Street, Oxford OX2 6DP

London Glasgow New York Toronto
Delhi Bombay Calcutta Madras Karachi
Kuala Lumpur Singapore Hong Kong Tokyo
Nairobi Dar es Salaam Cape Town
Melbourne Auckland

and associates in
Beirut Berlin Ibadan Mexico City Nicosia

Published in the United States
by Oxford University Press, New York

© *editorial matter Simon Varey 1982*

British Library Cataloguing in Publication Data

Bolingbroke, Henry St. John, Viscount
Lord Bolingbroke: contributions to the Craftsman.
I. Title II. Varey, Simon III. Craftsman
824'.4 PR3324.B/
ISBN 0-19-822386-2

Library of Congress Cataloging in Publication Data

Bolingbroke, Henry St. John, Viscount, 1678–1751.
Lord Bolingbroke, contributions to the Craftsman.
Includes index.
1. Great Britain—Politics and government—
1727–1760—Addresses, essays, lectures. I. Varey,
Simon, 1951– II. Title. III. Title:
Contributions to the Craftsman.
DA500.B62 1982 941.07'2 81-22464
ISBN 0-19-822386-2 AACR2

Set by Macmillan India., Bangalore
Printed in Great Britain
at the University Press, Oxford
by Eric Buckley
Printer to the University

For C. A. V.

PREFACE

SOME of Lord Bolingbroke's contributions to the *Craftsman* were printed in David Mallet's edition of Bolingbroke's *Works* (1754), from which the nearest thing we have to a standard edition of the 'mercurial' Viscount is derived (*Works*, 1967, reprinting an edition of 1844). The fifty-one *Craftsman* essays printed there are mostly the well-known ones: the *Remarks on the History of England* and *A Dissertation upon Parties*, 'The First Vision of Camilick', 'An Answer to the London Journal', and six others. The present volume brings together Bolingbroke's other forty-nine contributions, which have remained unpublished since his lifetime. Of his original works, only three pamphlets are still unavailable in modern editions.

The *Craftsman* was recognized in its own time as a publication of considerable literary and political importance, partly because of Bolingbroke's involvement with the paper. Sir Robert Walpole, who was constantly attacked in the pages of the *Craftsman*, took its threat seriously enough to subsidize at least three papers opposing it, to block its circulation through the Post Office, and to send two King's Messengers to the printer's premises to seize all the documents they could lay their hands on. One might sympathize with the harassed printer, but the documents—which Walpole fortunately kept among his private files—provide a source of important and illuminating information about the *Craftsman*, though they are unluckily of very little help in identifying any of the contributing authors.

Attribution of authorship of essays in the *Craftsman* is beset by hazards, among them the firm hold that contemporary rumour and subsequent imprecise scholarship seem to have taken. At the beginning of this century, Walter Sichel attributed essays to Bolingbroke and the Scriblerians, but without any evidence, and for over sixty years his fallible judgements passed unchallenged. In 1963 Giles Barber's bibliographical work on Bolingbroke brought some much needed good sense to bear on the question of authorship of the *Craftsman*, and in 1976 Bertrand A. Goldgar concluded, in view of the absence of hard evidence, that the Scriblerians were distinctly unlikely to have contributed. But, also in 1976, I found that John Gay had contributed a previously unpublished fable to the *Craftsman* in 1731. Further investigation has not turned up any similarly definite evidence, but my interpretation of the evidence that remains suggests, contrary to Mr Goldgar's view, that the Scriblerians might, after all, have been closely connected with the *Craftsman*.

My reasons for attributing to Bolingbroke the essays assembled here include evidence that belongs to 'initialmanship', as Isaac Kramnick called it in 1968. He referred to initial letters printed at the end of each essay in a reprint edition of the *Craftsman* in the 1730s. Kramnick doubts the value of the initials at all, and while I too recognize the dangers of too heavy a reliance on them as evidence, I believe that those letters help to strengthen arguments for Bolingbroke's authorship of specific contributions.

I am most grateful to the Marquess of Cholmondeley for permission to consult and quote from the Cholmondeley (Houghton) Manuscripts, on deposit at the Cambridge University Library. These are Walpole's papers. I am also grateful to the Earl of Egremont, the British Library Board, and the Keeper of Western Manuscripts at the Bodleian Library for permission to draw upon manuscripts in their care or possession. I also want to express my thanks to Howard Erskine-Hill, who supervised my doctoral dissertation on the *Craftsman*, and whose influence extends to the pages of this book.

My wife, Carol, has given me the benefit of her untiring support and advice; she has discussed with me all the problems of bibliography, editorial method, and authorship, as well as adding her mathematical expertise to my naivety in calculating the circulation figures of the *Craftsman*. Obviously, I am very grateful to her.

I am grateful too for assistance from Nicholas Cox, Theo D'haen, Vanessa Hawkes, David Lightfoot, Jaquelin Nash, and James Woolley.

Any discussion of the authorship of the *Craftsman* owes a lot to Giles Barber's analysis of the problems and the evidence. Further, it was at his suggestion that I prepared this volume when he decided not to undertake it himself. He generously placed at my disposal his transcript of the text of most of the essays, and he has been kind enough to give me encouragement and wise advice. This book would have been impossible without him.

It remains to be said that none of these generous people should be held responsible for the mistakes and lapses, which are entirely my own.

CONTENTS

Introduction   xiii

Note on the Text   xxxv

ESSAYS   I

Explanatory Notes   208

Appendix   217

Index   221

INTRODUCTION

On 5 December 1726, William Pulteney and Henry St. John, Viscount Bolingbroke, launched the *Craftsman*, written by the pseudonymous Caleb D'Anvers of Gray's Inn, Esquire.[1] It was edited by Nicholas Amhurst, and 'published' by Richard Francklin, who soon printed it as well.

For six months, the *Craftsman* appeared on Mondays and Fridays as a foolscap half-sheet, printed in two columns on each side.[2] Major alterations took place in May 1727, when the journal began to appear as a newspaper and was, henceforth, printed on a crown sheet folded once, with three columns on each page. The political article was retained on the front page, news filled most of the second page, and the last two pages usually consisted of advertisements. The inner pages occasionally contained letters which merited no special prominence. The 'new' paper appeared only once a week, on Saturdays, and to identify itself more definitely with the country interest, the title was expanded to the *Country Journal: or, the Craftsman.*

No precise calculation of the circulation of the *Craftsman* has been made, though a figure of 10,000 is usually cited, but the Cholmondeley (Houghton) Manuscripts contain material on which a calculation can be based, since they include the printer's accounts for the first six months of the paper's existence.[3] The accounts reveal that the initial sales were fairly modest: 300 in December 1726, rising to 800 in the next two months, then settling to a steady 700 for the next ten weeks. At that point the paper changed format, and no further detailed balance sheets survive, but another manuscript contains a list of profits accrued from every four issues, from 13 May 1727 until 7 March 1730.[4] This revealing document does 'give an excellent picture of the growth of the paper',[5] and it can provide the means to estimate circulation statistics based on our knowledge of costs recorded in the earlier, detailed accounts. From these figures I calculate that the lowest likely circulation per issue had reached 5,000 by the end of 1727, increasing very slightly during 1728, rising to about 8,000 during 1729, and 9,000 in early 1730, but the circulation may very well have been larger. It seems certain that it was higher in 1731, for which year a government pamphleteer, acknowledging that the *Craftsman* was 'the most popular News-paper', calculated that 'their usual Number was not less than 12,000 or 13,000 for a long Time'. Even though the purpose of the pamphlet is to show how dangerous the *Craftsman* is by spreading so much false news, the pamphleteer shows that he is well informed, and therefore his figures are likely to be reasonable.[6] He goes on to say that by 1732 the *Craftsman* is in decline, citing a fall in sales from 13,000 to 9,000, with interest in the trial of Francklin in December 1731 having raised the sales briefly to 10,000. By the time Bolingbroke left for France in 1735, sales were possibly only as high as those of the paper's sole subsidized opponent, the *Daily Gazetteer*, which sold about 4,000. In late 1738 and early 1739 the circulation of the *Craftsman* was definitely in the region of 4,000.[7] In 1748 Thomas Cooke, then editor, described his annual profit as 'considerable', and in 1753 Arthur Murphy was earning, as editor, $1\frac{1}{2}$ guineas a week, suggesting a net circulation of perhaps 700.

Papers were frequently read aloud and passed around, but they were also reprinted, in monthly magazines and in the provincial press. The *Craftsman* found extra outlets this way, in York, Bristol, and Newcastle (to name three areas of solid support). In Berkshire the *Craftsman* was 'the chief support to our spirits'[8] and a Sussex man complained to the Duke of Newcastle in 1733 that 'the Craftsman is very industriously sent down to the Tory Coffeehouse every weeke'.[9] For some time at least before September 1730, fifty-nine MPs bought 766 copies of the *Craftsman* each week, presumably using their right of franking to distribute them without fear of the Post Office interference which Walpole authorized.[10]

Another indication of early popularity was the first reprint of the *Craftsman*, begun when the journal was only seven weeks old. This reprint took the form of a sequence of pamphlets, the first of which contained the essays from Nos. 1 to 9. The pamphlet was entitled *The Craftsman: Being a Critique on the Times*, and was printed 'for J. Smith, near the Royal-Exchange'.[11] It had been announced in No. 9 and advertised in No. 13. In folio form, the total sale of the first nine issues had been about 3,000; this first pamphlet was printed in 1,000 copies, but soon ran to a second printing of 750 copies, and then to a third, again of 750. Essays from the next nine issues (now bearing Francklin's name) were reprinted in a second pamphlet, which ran to two editions of 1,000 copies each. The third pamphlet (containing Nos. 19 to 27), the fourth (28 to 36), and the fifth and last (37 to 44) were printed in 1,250 copies each. All five pamphlets were on sale at a shilling each by May 1727, and altogether 4,750 had been sold by August of the same year.[12]

The five pamphlets were later sewn to form a single volume, the first of a two-volume set under the same title. One thousand copies of volume ii (Nos. 45–85) were printed in March 1728 and put on sale on 11 May, and 650 were quickly sold.[13] The set was reprinted three times.

This form of reprint was discontinued, and no further reprinting took place until 2 June 1731, when Francklin published seven duodecimo volumes, containing the political articles from Nos. 1–255, under the title *The Craftsman*.[14] Seven further volumes appeared in 1737, continuing the series from No. 256 to No. 511. In this combined fourteen-volume edition, several papers were omitted (some for legal reasons), some rephrasing is evident, and several pamphlets originating from the *Craftsman*'s authors or its printer were included as appendices. 'Caleb D'Anvers' promised more volumes if these were favourably received, but there has never been any other collection or selection of the *Craftsman*.[15]

Since Bolingbroke broke his connection with the *Craftsman* in 1736, it is less important for the editor of his essays to consider in detail problems of authorship after that date, but the subsequent progress of Bolingbroke's journal is of interest. The identities of the editors only (as distinct from other contributors) are known after 1736.[16]

Nicholas Amhurst, editor from the start, appears after 1737 to have been the principal, perhaps the only author, according to the implication of a pamphlet by Henry Haines.[17] Haines had been Francklin's journeyman, but took over the printing of the *Craftsman* when Francklin was imprisoned in December 1731. Francklin's heavy fine had reputedly been paid by Bolingbroke and Pulteney, and the nervous Haines, fearing prosecution, wanted some sort of assurance. He was told that 'a *Set of Gentlemen* of GREAT FORTUNES [who] supported the Paper' would pay any fine and offer him compensation if he was imprisoned.[18] But when Haines was prosecuted for printing a libel in 1737, he received no financial aid from anyone until Francklin reluctantly paid some of the bail. The poor printer's pamphlet sought to expose the disgraceful treatment he had received through the negligence and malevolence of Francklin and Amhurst. Haines speaks of Amhurst as the author of the weekly essay, making money from the *Craftsman* at Haines's expense, until the end of his pathetic complaint, when he implies that Amhurst had little or nothing to do with the paper. If Amhurst was still drawing money from the *Craftsman* during the last few months of his life, he cannot have kept much, for he died in poverty, on 12 April 1742. Not even his own paper gave notice of its former editor's death.[19]

The next editor was Thomas Cooke, a strange successor since he had been an outspoken supporter of Walpole and opponent of the *Craftsman*.[20] Joseph Mawbey, writing in 1792, thought that Cooke took over from Amhurst 'a little while before the retreat of sir *Robert Walpole* from administration', that is, before 28 January 1742.[21]

It is not certain when Cooke left the *Craftsman*, nor when Arthur Murphy took over, nor whether any other editor came between them. Cooke was still in control in 1748, and signs of Murphy's involvement are evident near the end of 1751. The journal originally conceived by Bolingbroke and Pulteney came to an end when Murphy killed off Caleb D'Anvers on 21 October 1752 and changed the paper's title to *The Craftsman, or Gray's Inn Journal.* Eventually he dropped 'Craftsman' too, in 1753, but a journal called the *Craftsman* may have existed continuously from 1753 to 1810.[22]

In trying to establish the identities of contributors to the *Craftsman* during the period of Bolingbroke's involvement we have two kinds of evidence: that of contemporary attribution and that of the *Craftsman* itself. The folio issues did not contain signatory letters, as the *Spectator* had done, nor did the early pamphlet reprints, but in addition to the usual pseudonyms and initials of correspondents the fourteen-volume reprint included, at the end of each contribution, one letter, or occasionally two.[23] The six signatory letters have caused some controversy.

Bolingbroke and Pulteney made no secret of their prominence among the contributors, nor that Amhurst was their editor, but the identities of other contributors have remained uncertain. Contemporary attributions are relatively scarce, and later commentators have nominated particular writers on the basis of little or no evidence.

Of the plausible candidates for authorship, Lord Carteret and Sir William Wyndham can be discounted on the reliable authority of Lord Hervey: 'The first would not, the last could not.'[24] Of the other prominent opposition politicians, William Shippen, although reported to be closely allied with the *Craftsman*, almost certainly did not contribute, firstly because he poured scorn on the *Craftsman* in Parliament, secondly because his name is not on the list of subscribing MPs, and thirdly because he was a professed Jacobite.[25]

Lords Chesterfield and Lyttelton are occasionally named as contributors, although both were sympathetic to the ministry during the paper's earlier years. Chesterfield was said, by Joseph Mitchell, to be politically aligned with Pulteney in 1729, and before that, in November 1727, the *Craftsman* published a verse reflecting favourably on him, but Robert Halsband says that Chesterfield was still a supporter of Walpole in 1731.[26] The Speaker of the House of Commons, Arthur Onslow, recalled the popular assumption that Chesterfield 'furnished the weekly paper of the Opposition with the most poignant pieces it had',[27] but this may have referred to *Common Sense*, a paper run by Chesterfield and Lyttelton from 1737 to 1739 as a friendly rival to the *Craftsman*. Lyttelton, writing probably in 1729, 'speaks with disapproval of the *Craftsman* and other "disaffected papers", which misled foreign ministers into believing that the English nation would not support the court'.[28] Lyttelton was generally 'supposed' to have contributed to the *Craftsman* before *Common Sense*, but Robert Phillimore, editing Lyttelton in 1845, could not prove it.[29] One pamphleteer quite rightly charged Lyttelton with the authorship of the 'Persian' letter in *Craftsman* No. 459 (19 April 1735), but the letter was quoted; in No. 458, four more letters had been quoted from Lyttelton's recent and well-received *Persian Letters*, but mere quotation need not mean that he was the contributor to this or any other *Craftsman*.[30]

Another prominent member of the opposition commonly associated with the *Craftsman* is William Pulteney's cousin Daniel Pulteney. Thomas Newton, whose evidence is discussed below, stated that Daniel was one of William's 'able coadjutors', though even this phrase does not say specifically that Daniel was a regular contributor.[31]

The more unexpected names begin with that of Eustace Budgell. 'Theophilus Cibber' said that 'In the year 1730 and about that time,

[Budgell] closed in with the writers against the administration, and wrote many papers in the Craftsman.'[32] This ascription seems to be based on two pamphlets addressed to the *Craftsman*,[33] on '*several extraordinary Epistles*' printed not in the main part of the paper, but among the news items, and on three letters to Caleb D'Anvers sent by 'E. B.' In reply to the *British Journal* of 15 June 1728 Budgell denied any connection with the *Craftsman*, but he later wrote—and signed with his full name—a letter to Mr D'Anvers, printed in No. 207 (20 June 1730), acknowledging that the first pamphlet, *A Letter to the Craftsman*, was his, but he said he had nothing to do with the publication of the *Second Letter*, although it was a compilation of some of his earlier writings. The initials 'E. B.' were omitted from all reprints of the *Craftsman*, and in *A Letter to the Craftsman*, Budgell professes total ignorance of the meaning or significance of 'E. B.'[34] Characteristically perhaps, Budgell set about dissociating himself from the *Craftsman*, paradoxically, by writing to the editor. It is possible, though not probable, that he was a regular contributor.[35]

The government press had information that Samuel Strutt was the author of three letters to Caleb D'Anvers on the freedom and independence of Parliament (No. 427, 7 September, 428, 14 September, and 429, 21 September 1734). Strutt was a controversialist whose theological pamphlets were condemned as irreligious. When Walpole's journalists noticed that Strutt's three essays were omitted from the 1737 reprint of the *Craftsman*, the *Daily Gazetteer* quickly accused Caleb D'Anvers of cowardice.

The next unexpected name is that of Thomas Tooley. This little-known man himself acknowledged authorship only of pieces springing from 'an unaccountable contempt of all Ministers, whether Ecclesiastical or Civil', many of which 'are to be met with in Weekly Journals',[36] but Mark J. Simmonds goes farther, and claims that 'Tooley also wrote' for the *Craftsman*.[37] Since Tooley and Amhurst were both Merchant Taylor Fellows at St. John's, and both were expelled from Oxford in 1721, it is possible that they knew one another and therefore that Tooley contributed, but the only other evidence is No. 964 (15 December 1744), which contains an inscription referring to 'the new-built Parsonage-House at Kilmarsh in Northamptonshire' where Tooley was rector. Tooley wrote the inscription, and he might therefore have contributed it.

Two essays published in the *Craftsman* in 1735 were attributed at the time to the Chancellor of the Exchequer during the South Sea crisis, John Aislabie.[38] In No. 484 a series of essays began attacking The *Daily Gazetteer*'s defence of Walpole (and correctly ascribing to him the authorship of *Some Considerations Concerning the Publick Funds*).[39] In this paper there is a quotation from Aislabie's speech in the House of Lords in which he dissociated himself from the responsibility of '*those two Bubbles*, which were established to raise a supply for the Support of the *Civil List*'. The next issue, No. 485, defends Aislabie, but Caleb D'Anvers owns that he is 'no Advocate for Mr. *A———bie*, to whom I am utterly unknown'. Popular rumour also said that Walpole retorted with a reply to Aislabie in the *Gazetteer*, but there is no independent evidence to support a case for Aislabie's authorship of these two *Craftsman* essays.

Of the Scriblerians, Arbuthnot is listed in the *New Cambridge Bibliography of English Literature* as a contributor during 1726 and 1727; he is specified by W. T. Laprade as the author of No. 85 (17 February 1728), and S. W. Jackman and P. K. Elkin list him among regular contributors, but on what evidence we are not told.[40] Arbuthnot was certainly close to the *Craftsman*: a draft, though not in his hand, of a verse by him was among the papers seized during the raid on Francklin's shop on 3 September 1730.[41] Charles Kerby-Miller very reasonably thinks it probable that Arbuthnot and Pope 'contributed quietly', and Lester M. Beattie strikes the right note in recording the inadequacy of the evidence.[42]

It is certain that Gay made one contribution, to No. 237 (16˙ January 1731), in which his fable 'The Dog and the Fox' was first published.[43] Like the other Scriblerians, Gay was, as W. H. Irving says, 'near *The Craftsman*', and his 'friends on *The Craftsman* gave him plenty of publicity' with their essays on the political implications of *The Beggar's Opera*,[44] but there is no evidence that Gay was a regular contributor save a statement (whose tone is far from easy to identify) made by Arbuthnot in a letter to Swift, 19 March 1729: 'The inoffensive John Gay is now become one of the obstructions to the peace of Europe, the terror of Ministers, the chief author of the Craftsman & all the seditious pamphlets which have been published against the government.'[45] This remark may be calculatedly jocular, but we cannot assume that it is without foundation. However, without any corroboration it is impossible to establish definitely that Gay made any more than his one known contribution.

Swift presents a different kind of problem.[46] One of Swift's poems, his 'Epistle to a Lady' (1734), suggests at least some sort of kindred involvement with the *Craftsman*:

> If I can but fill my Nitch,
> I attempt no higher Pitch.
> Leave to D'ANVERS and his Mate,
> Maxims wise, to rule the State.
> POULTNEY deep, accomplish'd ST. JOHNS,
> Scourge the Villains with a Vengeance.
> Let me, tho' the Smell be Noisom,
> Strip their Bums, let CALEB hoyse 'em.
> Then, apply ALECTO's Whip,
> Till they wriggle, howl, and skip.[47]

But stronger evidence for Swift's authorship is our knowledge that Bolingbroke invited him to contribute to the *Craftsman* in 1727 during his stay in England, and that Swift responded with an essay. Bolingbroke, however, rejected it, writing on 6 June:

I return you the papers which I have read over twice since you was here. they are extremely well. but the Craftsman has not only advertis'd the publick that he intended to turn Newswriter. he has begun, & for some weeks continu'd to appear under that character. this consideration inclines me to think that another turn might be given to the introduction, and perhaps this would naturally call for a fourth letter from the occasional writer, to account for his silence, to prosecute y^r argument, to state the present disputes about political affairs, & in short to revive & animate the paper war.[48]

Contemporaries were clearly willing to assume that Swift and Pope contributed to their friend's journals, and Swift did indeed have something to do with another of Bolingbroke's journals, the *Occasional Writer*: Bolingbroke told him, three weeks before writing this letter 'to insinuate' in his 'Epistle, a part of which you shew'd me . . . that the only reason Walpole can have had to ascribe' the *Occasional Writer* to Bolingbroke 'is the authority of one of his Spies. . . . I had a hint or two more for you, but they have slipp'd out of my memory.'[49]

The *British Journal* No. 231 (25 February 1727) told Bolingbroke that Pope could have made a better job of the first two issues of the *Occasional Writer*, but more tangible evidence than that can be found to support a case for Pope's authorship of contributions to the *Craftsman* (one issue, No. 496, containing the remark that '*P–pe* was never Friend to Thee' [Walpole]). In a pamphlet by Atex. [*sic*] Burnet, *Achilles Dissected* (1733), Pope is made to say 'Envy'd I've always liv'd *among the Great*/ Tho' I've been Pimp, and often *Spy of State*' (p. 28). These lines merely parody a couplet from Pope's epistle to Fortescue (*Imitations of Horace, Satire* II. i. 133–4), but they are footnoted 'For Mr. P——–—y; and wrote the Character of a *Norfolk-Steward* in the *Craftsman*'.[50] There is no other evidence that Pope ever 'spied' for Pulteney: they did, at least, collaborate on the writing of two or three ballads.[51] *The History of the Norfolk Steward* was written in three parts. The first formed the leading article of *Craftsman* No. 61 (2 September 1727). The second and third parts were published together as a sixpenny pamphlet early in 1728, and were reprinted as an appendix to the third volume of the *Craftsman* of 1731. The first part discusses, in a thinly veiled allegory, Walpole's many alleged impositions on the British public, and accuses him of eight different crimes, mostly concerned with misappropriations of public money. The second instalment contains 'an Account of [the steward's] private character' and the third deals with his management. If Burnet's charge is as precise as it sounds, he is naming Pope as the author of the second part of the Norfolk Steward satire. More than a year earlier, 'Orator' Henley had written: 'We are told, that Mr. *P—e* wrote the Poem call'd Dawley Farm, and the *Norfolk Steward*, besides several Letters in *Fog* and the *Craftsman*',[52] and five years later he wrote: 'A. POPE is known to be an odd kind of Monster, a *Republican Papist*, and that he has written ten *Fogs*, and *Craftsmen*, is not to be doubted, by those, who remember the *Norfolk Steward* in *Fog*, *&c.*'[53] The last words weaken Henley's point, since the *Norfolk Steward* was not printed in *Fog's Weekly Journal*, but Henley was certainly insistent in trying to pin the authorship of that satire on Pope.

Henley is not especially likely to be reliable, and he may have been doing no more than gathering contemporary gossip to fill his journal. That, perhaps, lies behind his summary list of Caleb D'Anvers's 'Help-Mates and Yoke-Fellows in the good Work of joyning the People in a Scheme of Division': '*Jonadab Swift, Jeroboam Arbuthnot, Nebuchadnezar B——–—e, Achitophel P——, Rabsakeh Blocksem, Esau Budgel . . . Doeg* FIELDING, &c.'[54] Henley's reference to Fielding as a contributor (the only such ascription I have found anywhere) seems likely to be wide of the mark in 1731, for Caleb D'Anvers and the Scriblerians were satirized in Fielding's imitation of the *Dunciad*, written in 1729,[55] and late in 1730 the *Craftsman* itself scornfully noticed the encouragement given to Fielding by Walpole.[56]

If any of these men did in fact write essays for the *Craftsman*, they must have been careful to cover their tracks. The author of the *Flying Post*, 15 June 1731, simply gave up trying to identify individual contributors, and in 1733 James Bramston could write, 'But who puts *Caleb*'s *Country-Craftsman* out / Is still a secret, and the World's in doubt.'[57]

Caleb D'Anvers himself refers in No. 73 (25 November 1727) to some writers who 'have gone so far in their Attempts to destroy my Reputation, as to deny my very *Being*, and to represent me as an *imaginary Person* only, or a meer *fictitious Name*, made use of to screen the Performances of Men in the dark'. He then says that he has 'been set forth to the World' as 'a noble Lord' (Bolingbroke), 'a discontented Courtier' (Pulteney), 'an ecclesiastical Dignitary' (Swift), 'a learned Physician' (Arbuthnot), 'a celebrated Poet' (Pope), 'an expell'd Academick' (Amhurst), and 'a Grub-street Garreteer' (Budgell, possibly, among numerous candidates). If this list has a value, it is that we learn from it what Caleb D'Anvers found to be contemporary rumour, but alas, he just declines to discuss it.

In any attempt to determine authorship of individual essays, the most helpful clue, and at the same time the most frustrating, is the use of the capital letters A, C, D, N, O, and R, appended to the contributions reprinted in the 1731 and 1737 editions. The letters do not correspond to contributors' names where those are independently known; and where, for instance, Addison's signatory letters had spelled the name of his muse, the *Craftsman*'s letters spell nothing, unless it be CANDOR. Further, the letters first appeared in an edition printed when the journal had been in existence for nearly five years: they were therefore hardly likely to be useful as a screen against Walpole's discovery of the authors' identities, nor against possible litigation.

Each of the initial letters has been used at least once by the beginning of the second volume of the 1731 printing, where 'R', the last to appear, follows the essay in No. 46. If they actually correspond to the authorship of the weekly contributions, the letters indicate that each author began contributing before May

1727 and continued until late 1735.[58] Archibald S. Foord thinks the methods of identifying contributors too 'haphazard' to be reliable, and Isaac Kramnick finds the 'game of "initialmanship"' pointless.[59]

I think it is likely that the initial letters were used consistently, in accordance with occasional earlier practice, so that each letter represents one particular author.[60] The most plausible explanation of the existence of the initial letters is that Francklin, as printer and publisher, may have thought of the possibility of his reprinting contributions from some of the authors. He certainly thought he had a proprietary right to Bolingbroke's works in 1754, when he contested Mallet's right to print any of Bolingbroke's *Craftsman* essays.[61] The relative dearth of contemporary ascriptions seems to show that readers were largely ignorant of the authors' identities (but usually guessed that the Scriblerians had a hand in the paper), and this in turn suggests that it was pointless to obscure the secret any further with confusing initials.[62]

There is absolutely no doubt that Amhurst was the paper's editor. In addition to several contemporary statements to this effect, papers among the Cholmondeley (Houghton) Manuscripts confirm his function: editorial alterations to an essay printed on a proof sheet of No. 218 are in Amhurst's hand, which is not the hand that wrote the manuscript of the essay (upon which Amhurst also made a few alterations).[63] Thomas Newton ascribed to Amhurst all the contributions marked 'A', but the essay printed in No. 218 is marked 'A', and that was only corrected by Amhurst. It seems likely that Newton remembered the wrong letter, perhaps associating 'A' with the initial letter of Amhurst's name. Newton's statement must weaken the remainder of his evidence unless we can believe that his memory was at fault in a particular detail, not in the general case, and there are good reasons to suppose that this was so. In his memoirs, Newton says that William Pulteney was 'not only a most excellent speaker, but also a very fine writer, of which there are abundant proofs in The Craftsman and other papers and pamphlets. . . . His own papers were marked with the letter C. Those marked with CA were written by him and Amherst jointly, or by Amhurst from his dictation.'[64] Having once ascribed 'A' to Amhurst, he would clearly give the same letter to represent Amhurst's part in a collaboration, but the number of essays marked 'C. A.' is scarcely memorable—a mere three.[65] However, Newton was in a good position to know about Pulteney, who, upon his creation as Earl of Bath in July 1742, appointed Newton his chaplain. This must give weight to Newton's statements, and strongly suggests that Pulteney's contributions were marked 'C'. As for Amhurst, it would be reasonable to expect the editor to make the largest number of contributions, as Giles Barber argues,[66] for in the words of James Ralph, it would inevitably fall to the editor to supply 'Materials when none was communicated'.[67] By far the most frequently used letter is 'D', which appears on its own 193 times: no other letter is used even 100 times. If Newton actually had in mind a relatively substantial number of essays marked with two letters, he would probably have remembered the commonest combination, 'C. D.', which occurs twenty-four times.[68] I consider 'D' to have been Amhurst's signatory letter.

It was Newton who first attributed a letter to Bolingbroke's contributions, which, he said, 'were distinguished by the letter O', an ascription that is not difficult to justify.[69] In his will, Bolingbroke acknowledged authorship of several essays which had first appeared in the *Craftsman*.[70] The object of acknowledging them was to bequeath the publishing rights to David Mallet. Bolingbroke listed specifically 'The Vision of Camilick' (No. 16), 'An Answer to the London Journal' (No. 131), *Remarks on the History of England*, and *A Dissertation upon Parties*. The *Remarks*, serialized in twenty-four parts in the *Craftsman* in 1730–1 over the pseudonym of Humphrey Oldcastle, were reprinted in the 1731 edition, all with the letter 'O' (except for two without any letter), and it has been thought that 'O' stood for Oldcastle. Similarly the *Dissertation*, which consists of nineteen essays, was reprinted in the 1737 edition over the letter 'O' (also containing two unsigned essays). Only two papers confidently attributed to Bolingbroke were reprinted in 1731 or 1737 over a letter other than 'O'. The first is the long essay in No. 131, which Bolingbroke acknowledged and Mallet therefore printed. This paper had been marked 'C', Pulteney's letter, and rumour in the Commons at the time said that Pulteney had written it.[71] Barber argues that the evidence of the will (and Mallet's acceptance of it) probably indicate that 'C' was a misprint for 'O' in this case.[72] The other attribution of this sort is No. 252, containing the essay published separately as *The Monumental Inscription on the column of Blenheim-House*. Pope told Joseph Spence unequivocally: 'Lord Bolingbroke wrote the long inscription on the column set up in honour of the Duke of Marlborough at Blenheim',[73] and Pulteney wrote to Sarah, Duchess of Marlborough, telling her that it was written by Bolingbroke.[74] In the 1731 reprint No. 252 is marked 'D', perhaps another misprint.

In all, Bolingbroke acknowledged his authorship of works constituting forty-four separate contributions to the *Craftsman*. One is marked 'C', four are not marked at all (but these belong to the two large sequences), and the remaining thirty-nine are all marked with letter 'O'. Ten other *Craftsman* essays printed by Francklin in 1742 in *A Collection of Political Tracts* by Bolingbroke had all been marked 'O'. This is all reasonable justification to conclude that 'O' indicates a contribution by Bolingbroke, that forty-two other contributions marked 'O' are his, and that the three essays marked 'A. O.' (No. 142), 'D. O.' (No. 225), and 'O. D.' (No. 264) indicate participation by Bolingbroke, in conjunction with another author. With the exception of Nos. 131 and 252, the criterion for inclusion of a contribution in the present volume is the signatory 'O' in the collected *Craftsman* of 1731 and 1737.[75]

A *Craftsman Extraordinary* of 30 June 1734 contained a memoir of the Duke of Berwick. No copy of this paper has been found, but a French translation appeared in the *Mémoires du Maréchal de Berwick*, where it is ascribed to Bolingbroke: I see no reason to doubt this ascription and I include as an appendix the text of the French translation.[76]

Apart from a group of four essays published in April 1736, it is improbable that Bolingbroke contributed any essays after his departure for France in 1735. In June 1735 Walpole had transferred his subsidy of his three main journals to just one, the *Daily Gazetteer*:[77] this looks like a gesture of contempt towards both the *Craftsman* and Bolingbroke, whose credibility Walpole had practically destroyed in the House of Commons.[78] On 29 November 1735 Bolingbroke told Wyndham, 'my part is over, and He who remains on the stage when his part is over, deserves to be hissed off it',[79] and on 27 March 1736 the author of the *Gazetteer* could say that it had been 'an Honour' over the years 'to wrestle a Fall' with Bolingbroke, but now he had gone. A further indication, if any were needed, that his contact with his journal was at an end is his not coming forward with financial help for Henry Haines in 1737. Extracts of Bolingbroke's *Idea of a Patriot King* were printed in the *Craftsman* in June, August, and September 1749,[80] but soon after his death the *Craftsman* contained two sneers at him.[81]

If 'O' indicates Bolingbroke's contributions to the *Craftsman* up to 1736, 'C' Pulteney's, and 'D' Amhurst's, what of 'A', 'N', and 'R'? We have a specimen of A's handwriting (the manuscript for No. 218) but it belongs to none of the likely candidates, nor indeed to anyone named in this discussion of authorship. Gay's one definite contribution in 1731 was marked 'R', but if the letters indicate actual authorship week by week, no letter would be exclusively Gay's, since all the letters continue to be used under essays written after his death in 1732. This complication may appear to negate arguments based on the signatory letters, but it is possible that 'R' had been responsible for inserting Gay's fable in No. 237, if it was not Gay himself. So who was 'R'? If there is any weight to Burnet's evidence that Pope 'wrote the Character of the Norfolk Steward', 'R' would look like Pope, since the 'Character'—the second of the three parts of the satire—was marked 'R'.

Attribution on the evidence of style or range of subjects is likely to prove unrewarding, for as Pope remarked, 'There is nothing more foolish than to pretend to be sure of knowing a great writer by his style.'[82] Many of the essays confirm Kramnick's belief that the *Craftsman* reflects Bolingbroke's ideas, but it is not true of all of them.[83] The prose style of the *Craftsman* tends towards uniformity and allows few personal habits of style to intrude.

Since Amhurst, Arbuthnot, Gay, Pope, the Pulteneys, and Swift (when in England) were frequent visitors to Bolingbroke's farm at Dawley, it is likely that a gathering of some of these men could sometimes produce the substance of the next *Craftsman*. When a 'club' has ideas, and one member gives them their final expression, we cannot confidently put a name to the author on the evidence of style. Pope, Swift, and Gay had distinctive enough voices, but much Scriblerian work cannot be attributed to any one of them. Much the same is true of the authorship of the *Craftsman*.

The few hard facts that present themselves suggest that Pope was close to the *Craftsman*, and that Arbuthnot, Gay, and Swift had something to do with the paper. If Newton's evidence is good, as I think it must be, it is probable that Daniel Pulteney, too, made occasional contributions at least, but he died in 1731, so that initial letters are unlikely to indicate his contributions. Further evidence is needed before attributions can be made with complete confidence.

Whoever the authors were, they were highly respected, for the

Craftsman enjoyed a reputation in its own day as the most prominent and distinguished paper in circulation. It drew forth comment from George II and his court,[84] from MPs, from writers of pamphlets, newspapers, broadsides, poems, novels, and plays. And it provoked Walpole to try to suppress it.[85] Walpole, of course, was the paper's central target, and Bolingbroke his most committed enemy.

Bolingbroke's miscellaneous essays demonstrate his passionate concern to preserve the balance of power in Europe, usually through maintaining free and healthy trade, and his desire to rid the major trading companies and, by implication, also Walpole's administration, of corruption. Bolingbroke's essays are nearly always characterized by clear, eloquent argument, but he was quite capable of departing from the logical exposure of Walpole's restrictions on trade to write slapstick satire (e.g. No. 167, or 'The First Vision of Camilick' in No. 16); satire directed against the legal interpretation of innuendo (No. 319), or satire on both Handel's oratorio and the Excise Bill (No. 353). His *History of England* papers are simultaneously historical and defiantly satirical. Like most of the essays in the *Craftsman*, Bolingbroke's contributions show the skill of a rhetorician needing to appeal to a diversified audience.

The paper's literary quality led Lord Hervey, a regular reader and opponent of both the *Craftsman* and Bolingbroke, to judge that 'All the best writers against the Court were concerned in the *Craftsman*, which made it a much better written paper than any of that sort that were published on the side of the Court'.[86] In 1753 'Theophilus Cibber' wrote that at its peak the *Craftsman* 'was more read and attended to than any political paper ever published in England',[87] and Goldsmith, in 1770, thought the *Craftsman*'s essays had been 'written with great spirit and sharpness'.[88] Thomas Newton's view, noted in his memoirs in 1782, was that 'The Craftsman may be said without exception to consist of some of the best political papers that ever were published . . . And the manner of writing was as excellent as the matter, with all the beauties and graces of language, some of the first and ablest pens in the kingdom being employed besides [Pulteney's].'[89] If that seems a little too adulatory, the final eighteenth–century judgement should belong to that often judicious historian, William Coxe, who thought that the *Craftsman* 'always contained the strength of the arguments urged against the measures of government, detailed with great eloquence and wit'.[90]

The subsequent reputation of the *Craftsman* and Bolingbroke has been mixed. The paper was often neglected altogether or summarily dismissed in histories of the press or politics. Despite Burke's questions, 'Who now reads Bolingbroke? Who ever read him through?',[91] Bolingbroke *has* continued to be read, but his *Craftsman* generally has not, until quite recently. In 1968 Isaac Kramnick used the paper extensively in his excellent account of Bolingbroke's political philosophy, and since then Maynard Mack and Howard Erskine-Hill have demonstrated the significance and value of the *Craftsman* for our appreciation and understanding of Pope's major poetry of the 1730s.[92] The *Craftsman* played an important role in moulding opinion during the Walpole regime, in a world whose political writing contained substance as well as cant. If it still appears that the *Craftsman* is more referred to than read, perhaps one should remember William Pulteney's advice to Francis Colman, telling him that Samuel Gumley 'will give you a set of the "Craftsman," which you must put, like the monks, into that part of your library which they call *l'Inferno*; and be sure, like them, to read these books more than any in the rest of the library . . .'[93]

NOTES TO THE INTRODUCTION

1. The name did have some significance and was related to the aims of the journal. Briefly, 'Caleb' indicated Caleb the son of Jephunneh, one of the leaders of the Israelites sent into the promised land as a scout, and 'D'Anvers' (as was said in No. 28) indicated attachment to the cause of the Emperor—because he held the town of Anvers—and therefore opposition to the Pretender.

2. No. 1 had been slightly different, consisting of a single sheet attached to the front of a larger, folded sheet, making three leaves in all.

3. Cambridge University Library, Cholmondeley (Houghton) Manuscript P74, f. 28 hereafter cited as C (H) MS.

4. C (H) MS P74, f. 7.

5. M. R. A. Harris, 'Figures Relating to the Printing and Distribution of the *Craftsman* 1726 to 1730', *Bulletin of the Institute of Historical Research*, xliii (1970), 237. The relevant accounts are printed in this article.

6. *The Danverian History of the Affairs of Europe* (1732), pp. 67–80.

7. Henry Haines, *Treachery, Baseness and Cruelty Display'd to the Full* (1740), p. 27; and *Craftsman* No. 746, 18 October 1740.

8. William Stratford to Edward Harley, 29 May 1728, *Historical Manuscripts Commission: Portland MSS* (1901), vii. 464.

9. T. Ball to Newcastle, 4 November 1733, British Library Add. MS 32689, f. 9.

10. C (H) MS, P74, f. 72 is a subscription list containing the names of the MPs. P75, f. 19 is a memorandum to 'put a Stop at the Secretary's Office & at the Post Office to the Circulation of the Craftsman, Fogg's Journal, The London Evening Post, and Daily Post'. A further attempt to block the *Craftsman*, as No. 82 reported, was a letter sent to 'our Readers in all Parts of the Kingdom' saying that the paper would '*be sent* no longer' and telling people to order a different paper in future.

11. J. Smith's name appeared in the colophon of each of the first fifteen issues of the *Craftsman*. The next two were printed 'for T. Warner', and after that for Richard Francklin. The printer of the first seventeen was Samuel Aris (C (H) MS P74, f. 12). Francklin seems to have been involved from the start, since the accounts are in his hand throughout, and since he was detained while Aris, Warner, and Amhurst were released after all four had been charged with 'publishing' the allegedly libellous No. 16. 'J. Smith' could have been a fictitious name to cover a printer reluctant to attach his own name.

12. C (H) MS P74, ff. 13, 28.

13. C (H) MS P74, f. 12.

14. Francklin wanted Bolingbroke's *History of England* papers to be together in a continuous sequence in one volume, so he rearranged the order of essays in volumes vi and vii, without rearranging numbers and dates. A full table of the original and revised orders is printed by Herbert Davis, 'Reprinting *The Craftsman*', *The Book Collector*, ii (1953), 279–82.

15. Some of Bolingbroke's contributions were reprinted in selections of his works, in the case of his two series of essays (the *History of England* and *A Dissertation upon Parties*), in separate editions. For details see Giles Barber, 'Some Uncollected Authors XLI: Henry St. John, Viscount Bolingbroke', *The Book Collector* xiv (1965), 528–37.

16. During 1739 and 1740, two rival papers called the *Craftsman* existed. The authors of the paper not associated with Amhurst *et al.* were Benjamin Norton Defoe and Denis de Coetlogon. See Simon Varey, 'Printers as Rivals: *The Craftsman*, 1739–40', *Library*, 6th series, ii (1980), 220–2.

17. *Treachery, Baseness and Cruelty Display'd to the Full*, p. 8.

18. Ibid.

19. Richard Rawlinson's information was that the cause of Amhurst's death was 'his immoderate drinking of Geneva', and one enemy had noted that '*Nick* drinks hard'. Legend said that he died of a broken heart (Mark J. Simmonds, *Merchant Taylor Fellows of St. John's College, Oxford* (Oxford, 1930), p. 55; *A Political Conversation* (1733), p. 9; James Ralph, *The Case of Authors by Profession or Trade, stated* (1758), p. 32). Negative evidence that Amhurst died in poverty is that the Prerogative Court of Canterbury proved wills or granted administrations when goods of more than £5 worth were left in more than one diocese of the Province, or in both Provinces. There is no will in Amhurst's name, nor any record of an administration of his goods: if he did die in poverty he would have warranted no record under the PCC's jurisdiction (information from Mr Nicholas Cox).

20. Cooke wrote a column as 'Atticus' in the pro-Walpole *London Journal* in 1728–9. See also C (H) MS Corr. 1997.

21. *Gentleman's Magazine*, lxi (1792), 26.

22. Simon Varey, 'The Publication of the Late *Craftsman*', *Library*, 5th series, xxxiii (1978), 230–3.

23. Seventeen poems and twelve other contributions were printed without any letter, fifty-eight were marked with a pair of letters, and 513 with one letter.

24. *Some Materials towards Memoirs of the Reign of King George II*, ed. Romney Sedgwick (1931), p. 263 (hereafter cited as *Memoirs*). Carteret is named by Archibald S. Foord, *His Majesty's Opposition 1714–1830* (Oxford, 1964), p. 143, and by Charles Kerby-Miller, *Memoirs of . . . Martinus Scriblerus* (Yale, 1950), pp. 325–6. David H. Stevens, *Party Politics and English Journalism 1702–42* (Menasha, 1916), p. 126, names Wyndham as a contributor.

25. *An Epistle to W. S. Esq;* (1728), pp. 6–7; see also W. T. Laprade, *Public Opinion and Politics in Eighteenth Century England* (New York, 1936), pp. 350–1; *Historical Manuscripts Commission: Diary of the Earl of Egmont* (1920–3), iii. 331; and C (H) MS P74, f. 72.

26. [Joseph Mitchell], *Poems on Several Occasions* (1729), ii. 62; *Craftsman* No. 73 (25 November 1727); Robert Halsband, *Lord Hervey, Eighteenth-Century Courtier* (Oxford, 1973), p. 116.

27. *Historical Manuscripts Commission: Earl of Onslow* (1895), p. 472. Hervey's reference to Chesterfield's anti-Walpole activity is ambiguous (*Memoirs*, p. 263). P. K. Elkin lists Chesterfield as a contributor (*The Augustan Defence of Satire* (Oxford, 1973), p. 120).

28. Rose Mary Davis, *The Good Lord Lyttelton* (Bethlehem, Penna, 1939), p. 33, citing Hagley MS, I, ff. 53–6, and Lyttelton, *Works* (1774), p. 681.

29. *Memoirs and Correspondence of George, Lord Lyttelton from 1734 to 1773* (1845), i. 47. Such a 'supposition' seems typical of 19th-century rumour that often passed for evidence. One such supposition is that Gabriel Johnston (while Professor of Hebrew at St. Andrews) contributed between 1728 and 1734. This is confidently reported in the *Dictionary of American Biography*, citing a range of 19th-century sources, though I can find no supporting evidence. I am grateful to Mrs Jaquelin Nash for bringing this to my attention.

30. *The Crafts of the Craftsmen* (1736), pp. 10–11.

31. Thomas Newton, *The Works of the Right Reverend Thomas Newton, D. D. With Some Account of his Life, and Anecdotes of Several of his Friends, Written by Himself* (1782), i. 72 (hereafter cited as *Life*).

32. *Lives of the Poets of Great Britain and Ireland, to the Time of Dean Swift* (1753), v. 11.

33. *A Letter to the Craftsman* (1729), and *A Second Letter to the Craftsman, relating to the Case of Eustace Budgell, Esq.* (1730).

34. *A Letter to the Craftsman*, p. 16.

35. Budgell has been named as a regular contributor subsequently by the somewhat unreliable Nathan Drake, *Essays . . . Illustrative of the Tatler, Spectator and Guardian* (1805), iii. 14; also by Stevens, *Party Politics*, p. 93, and by Harold Herd, *Seven Editors* (1955), p. 13. Two contemporary authors were less certain: see *Discontent; or, An Essay on Faction* (1736); [Robert Moncrieff], *Magnanimity. A Poem* (1735).

36. Bodleian Library, MS Rawlinson J, fol. 5, leaf 144^v.

37. *Merchant Taylor Fellows*, p. 55.

38. John Carswell, *The South Sea Bubble* (1960), p. 206.

39. See J. H. Plumb, *Sir Robert Walpole* (1956–60), i. 326, 343, 352.

40. Laprade, *Public Opinion*, p. 309; Jackman, *Man of Mercury* (1965), p. 41; Elkin, *Augustan Defence*, p. 120. The two last also list Pope and Swift.

41. The manuscript is now C (H) MS P74, f. 29, where it is entitled 'The Triple Alliance': the verse appeared in the 'last' volume of the Pope–Swift *Miscellanies* in 1727 as 'Ay and No'. It has been attributed to Gay, but on thin evidence. Arbuthnot's authorship is attested by the Earl of Oxford (British Library, Lansdowne MS 852, f. 228; see Vinton A. Dearing and Charles E. Beckwith (eds.), *John Gay: Poetry and Prose* (Oxford, 1974), ii. 628).

42. Kerby-Miller, *Scriblerus*, p. 177; Beattie, *John Arbuthnot: Mathematician and Satirist* (Cambridge, Mass., 1935), p. 316.

43. Simon Varey, 'John Gay: A Contribution to *The Craftsman*', *Études Anglaises*, xxix (1976), 579–82.

44. W. H. Irving, *John Gay: Favorite of the Wits* (Durham, NC, 1940), pp. 231, 256. Stevens, Jackman, and Elkin all list Gay as a regular contributor.

45. *The Correspondence of Jonathan Swift*, ed. Harold Williams (Oxford, 1963–5), iii. 326 (hereafter cited as *Corr.*).

46. Jackman, *Man of Mercury*, p. 41, and Stevens, *Party Politics*, pp. 122–3, favour a case for Swift's authorship.

47. *The Poems of Jonathan Swift*, ed. Harold Williams (2nd edn., Oxford, 1958), ii. 635.

48. Swift, *Corr.*, iii. 212.

49. 18 May 1727; *Corr.*, iii. 211–12.

50. See J. V. Guerinot, *Pamphlet Attacks on Alexander Pope 1711–1744* (1969), p. 224.

51. Joseph Spence, *Observations, Anecdotes, and Characters of Books and Men*, ed. James M. Osborn (Oxford, 1966), i. 152 (item 341).

52. *Hyp-Doctor*, 9 November 1731. 'Dawley Farm', a panegyric on Bolingbroke, appeared in *Fog's Weekly Journal*, 26 June 1731.

53. *Hyp-Doctor*, 17 June 1736.

54. *Hyp-Doctor*, 22 June 1731. I take '*P––*' to be Pope, and '*Rabsakeh Blocksem*' could be Pulteney, in the character of a blasphemer who seeks to stir a public revolt (2 Kings 18: 17–37; Isaiah 36).

55. Isobel Grundy, 'New Verse by Henry Fielding', *PMLA*, lxxxvii (1972), 213–45.

56. No. 220, 19 September 1730. It is possible that Fielding contributed to the *Craftsman*, as a forthcoming article by Martin C. Battestin will argue. I am grateful to Professor Battestin for allowing me to read a draft of his article.

57. *The Art of Politicks* (1733), p. 11.

58. 'R' was the first to be discontinued, making its last appearance in No. 488, but 'D. R.' was used for the last time in No. 490 (22 November 1735).

59. Foord, *His Majesty's Opposition*, p. 143; Kramnick, *Bolingbroke and His Circle: The Politics of Nostalgia in the Age of Walpole* (Cambridge, Mass., 1968), p. 274.

60. This had been the practice of the *Spectator*, though prior to the

Craftsman there had been no exactly identical arrangement of signatory letters in a collected edition of papers that had printed no letters in folio form.

61. Francklin, *A Short State of the Case with Relation to a Claim on David Mallet* (1754).

62. Newton, *Life*, i. 72, recorded that 'several excellent letters were sent with the signature of Walter Raleigh, the author whereof [Pulteney] never knew, nor could ever discover', but Francklin must have known, because he offered, provided certain conditions were satisfied by the Crown, to disclose the identity of the author of the allegedly libellous No. 160, signed by 'Raleigh' (Lawrence Hanson, *Government and the Press 1695–1763* (Oxford, 1936), p. 67). The paper was marked 'A' in the 1731 printing. The case against Francklin was dropped, and he was not obliged to reveal his special knowledge.

63. C (H) MS P74, ff. 2, 28, 64.

64. *Life*, i. 72.

65. Contributions to Nos. 92, 125, and 506 were marked 'C. A.', and those in Nos. 28 and 77 'A. C.'

66. 'A Bibliography of Henry Saint John, Viscount Bolingbroke' (University of Oxford B. Litt. thesis, 1963), p. 90.

67. *A Critical History of the Administration of Sr Robert Walpole, now Earl of Orford* (1743), p. 507.

68. 'D. C.' was appended to six further contributions. The other combinations were: 'D. R.' (12), 'R. D.' (2), 'R. A.' (3), 'C. A.' (3), 'A. C.' (2), and 'A. N.', 'A. O.', 'C. N.', 'N. R.', 'D. O.', and 'O. D.' once each. Altogether 'A' appeared independently 80 times, 'C' 36, 'N' 46, 'O' 90, and 'R' 67.

69. Newton, *Life*, i. 72.

70. *The Last Will and Testament of the Late Rt. Hon. Henry St. John, Lord Viscount Bolingbroke* (1752), pp. 8–9.

71. *Historical Manuscripts Commission: Diary of the Earl of Egmont* (1920–3), iii. 331.

72. Barber, 'Bibliography', p. 123.

73. Spence, *Anecdotes*, i. 120 (item 272).

74. David Green, *Blenheim Palace* (1951), p. 174. See note 1 to No. 252, below.

75. Dependence on these letters naturally means that some contributions cannot be ascribed to anyone without further evidence: those included in the 1731–7 printing but not marked with a letter are parts of Nos. 123, 125, 181, 207 (reprinted as 206), 292, 446, 478, 499, and

the poems appended to volume v, which were also published separately. Several papers or parts of papers were omitted in the reprinting: Nos. 63, 295, 297, 310, 323, 354, 392, 401, 427–9, 432, 434, 458, 460, 463, and 504.

76. *Mémoires du Maréchal de Berwick, écrits par lui-même* (Paris, 1778), i. ix–xvi. A few errors in that text have been corrected in my appendix.

77. *The London Journal* continued independently until 1738. The other two (the *Free Briton* and *Daily Courant*) stopped in 1735.

78. H. T. Dickinson, *Bolingbroke* (1970), p. 243.

79. West Sussex Record Office, Petworth House Archives, 19, f. 35.

80. These were partially reprinted in *Mitre and Crown* (2 vols., 1750). No copies of the *Craftsman* from January 1745 to September 1749 are known to have survived.

81. 21 December 1751 and 11 November 1752.

82. Spence, *Anecdotes*, i. 171 (item 392).

83. Kramnick, *Bolingbroke and His Circle*, p. 274.

84. Hervey, *Memoirs*, p. 501.

85. See above, p. vii.

86. *Memoirs*, p. 263. See also ibid., pp. 260–1.

87. *Lives of the Poets*, v. 337.

88. *Collected Works*, ed. Arthur Friedman (Oxford, 1966), iii. 466.

89. *Life*, i. 71.

90. *Memoirs of the Life and Administration of Sir Robert Walpole, Earl of Orford* i (1798), xx.

91. *Reflections on the Revolution in France* (New York, 1955), p. 101.

92. Kramnick, *Bolingbroke and His Circle*; Mack, *The Garden and the City: Retirement and Politics in the Later Poetry of Pope, 1731–1743* (Toronto, 1969); Erskine-Hill, *The Social Milieu of Alexander Pope: Lives Examples and the Poetic Response* (New Haven and London, 1975).

93. 12 June 1731. Richard Brinsley Peake, *Memoirs of the Colman Family*, i (1841), 23.

NOTE ON THE TEXT

THERE is one example of the transmission of a small part of the text of a *Craftsman* essay from manuscript to proof, proof to folio, and folio to reprint (C (H) MS P 74, f. 2; *Craftsman* No. 218, reprinted in 1731 as No. 211). Collation of the three versions reveals that Amhurst initially adapted an occasional point of style, and that he regulated some of the accidentals, but that the printer was responsible for the uniformity of accidentals in the newspaper. The reprint contains some further alterations which are more likely the work of the editor or author than a compositor, and that final text is far from the manuscript. Although revealing, the evidence of this part of an essay is too slight to form the basis of a reliable hypothesis about the transmission of texts in the *Craftsman*. No manuscript of any other contribution printed in the *Craftsman* is known to have survived. According to Francklin (perhaps indulging in his customary disingenuousness) 'the Copy always went to the Press in [Amhurst's] Hand, nor did Lord *Bolingbroke* ever send a single Line to the Printer of those Papers in his own Hand-writing'. Mallet was obliged to admit that he had no manuscripts of Bolingbroke's *Craftsman* essays.[1]

As a business venture, the *Craftsman* belonged to Amhurst. It is not probable that he would waste his time and money having the several authors supervise the reprinting of their essays. Further, Francklin would surely not have sent bundles of proofs to Bolingbroke in France in 1736, and Pulteney's attitude was to leave the final wording of many of his contributions to Amhurst for their first printing. I see no reason to suppose that Amhurst treated the authors' manuscripts with any more reverence when he had them reprinted.

I have selected the folio sheets as copy-text for this edition, which therefore represents the first printed text of Bolingbroke's essays, quite possibly edited by Amhurst. For the reason suggested above, I doubt if the printings of 1727–8, 1731, and 1737 have authority, but I have recorded substantive variants from those printings, and I have adopted readings from them where they supply alternatives to readings in the copy-text that make no sense, and where they correct obvious errors of the press. Eighteenth-century spellings are retained, as are instances of inconsistent spelling. The later editions contain scores of variants of punctuation and capitalization, and rather fewer of italicization and spelling, but a record of such a quantity of accidental variants from texts of doubtful authority could be nothing more than a distraction, and I have therefore made no attempt to list them. All departures from the copy-text are recorded, except corrections of the following: turned letters, two separate words printed together, one word split into two parts, repeated letters, and omitted full stops in places where no other punctuation could have been intended.

An apparent inconsistency is my adoption of different forms of presenting Bolingbroke's quotations. He indifferently used quotation marks or italics (or sometimes both) to indicate quoted material; in print, quotation marks would normally be run down the margin and italics printed simply as one would expect. I have modernized his use of quotation marks, and have not supplied them where the copy-text used only italics.

In dating the first three contributions, I have discarded the clumsy form used while the *Craftsman* was appearing twice a week, and I have adapted throughout the form used in all issues from 13 May 1727. Errors in dating and numbering are silently corrected, and, where relevant, dates are cited as if the new year began on January 1 and not as with the Old Style of the Julian Calendar, on March 25.

In the textual notes, the following abbreviations are used:

A: *The Craftsman, being a Critique on the Times* (2 vols., 1727–8).

B: *The Craftsman* (14 vols., 1731–7).

fol.: *The Craftsman*, later *The Country Journal, or the Craftsman*, folio.

NOTE TO THE NOTE ON THE TEXT

1. See *A Short State of the Case with Relation to a Claim on David Mallet* (1754).

ESSAYS

No. 25. Friday, 3 March 1727.

As it is my Design, in the Course of these Papers, to pay the utmost Regard to all the kind assistances of my Correspondents, as far as it shall be consistent, in any measure, with the original Intention of this Undertaking,[1] so I must rely on the good nature of these Gentlemen, who will, I hope, indulge me in some Liberties, that it will be necessary for me to take with their Letters, by *adding* or *retrenching*, where I see occasion for so doing, as well as in the publication of them,[a] which it will not always be proper to do in[b] the same order of Time in which I receive them. On the other hand, I am ready to assure them, that I will never presume to take any Wanton, or Officious Freedoms of this sort, by making any Alterations, but where I think it absolutely necessary or expedient for the better carrying on this Design; nor will I use any partiality in preferring one Letter to another, any farther than[c] it conduces to the same end; so that every Gentleman's[d] Thoughts may appear in their proper place, at the most seasonable Time, and consequently to the best Advantage.

I hope this general Apology will satisfy all persons, who shall please to favour me with their Correspondence, and that it will, in particular, excuse me to that[e] Gentleman, who obliged me with the following Letter, as well as those, whose Thoughts have not yet seen the Light.

To CALEB D'ANVERS, *Esq:*
SIR,[f]

WHEN your UNCLE died, he was possessed of several *Plantations* in the *West-India* Colonies, which are now vested in you, among[g] his other Estates, by virtue of his last *Will* and *Testament*. They were then in good order, and in flourishing Circumstances; for as he was sensible of their Value, and how beneficial they were to his Estate in *Stafford-shire*, he wisely encouraged his *Tenants* to improve them: But alas! how have they since gone to decay, through the *Rapacious* temper of some of your *Stewards*, and the *Ignorance*

---

[a] them,] them, in *A, B*.   [b] to do in] for me to observe *A, B*
[c] than] than as *B*.   [d] Gentleman's *A, B*; Gentlemans *fol*.   [e] that] the *B*.
[f] SIR,] *A*; SIR *fol*.   [g] among] amongst *B*.

of *others*, who had the care and management of them! by which means, many of your *Tenants* have been obliged to remove, and 'tis[a] thought that others will follow, to the great Detriment, if not the utter Ruin, of those Estates. Good[b] Mr. D'ANVERS, make some Enquiry into those affairs, before it be too late; consider the Consequence to your own Interest, as well as to them; should they continue under the same or any other Discouragements, how will you be able to vend many Commodities that[c] are produced from your Estate in *Stafford-shire?* has not the[d] Estate been improv'd from twenty to thirty Years purchase, since those *Plantations* have been in your Family? and will[e] it not be affected in proportion as they decline? how will you cultivate those Lands, or procure new *Tenants*, should the present Possessors quit their Leases? it is high time, to look into the Conditions granted by your *Uncle*, which encourag'd them to go over (at the hazard of their Lives and Fortunes) to settle those Lands and to see them punctually perform'd; and since such great advantages arise, from the Labour of those industrious people, it is certainly your Interest rather to Augment than Diminish their Privileges, as it may induce others to go over, and by that[f] Means the Value of your *Estates* will be increased proportionably.

The world is perfectly convinc'd of your humane and compassionate Temper, of which the Appointment of your *Stewards*, from time to time are certain Demonstrations; but then your own Interest and the Ease and Satisfaction of your *Tenants*, seem to have been very little, if at all, consider'd.

I am informed that one of your *Plantations* will admit of very great Improvements, having some thousand Acres of manurable Land, belonging to it, which has hitherto been neglected and uncultivated; is it not your Interest to send over an *able, judicious* Person to manage it? One, who[g] understands the Nature of the[h] Soil; who has some Knowledge in Trade, and will be at the Pains of looking into former Mismanagements, and rectify them; one, that[i] considers Mankind as his *Fellow-Creatures*, and though he has a Superiority over your *Tenants*, yet will not treat them as his *Vassals*, or[j] invade their just Rights and Properties, in manifest breach of the laudable precepts of *your Family*.

[a] 'tis] it is *B*.   [b] Good] *A, B*; Good, *fol.*   [c] that] which *B*.
[d] the] that *A, B*.   [e] and will] Will *B*.   [f] that] those *B*.
[g] who] that *B*.   [h] of the] of *A*.   [i] that] who *B*.   [j] or] and *A, B*.

It is reported, that some of your *Tenants* had taken a Resolution of acquainting you with their *Grievances*, which were become almost insupportable; and accordingly wrote you a *Letter*, in the most humble and submissive Terms; but notwithstanding the fair Speeches of *one* of your Servants, and his promises to deliver it, there are some Grounds to believe that it never came to your hands; for it was soon after taken up dirty and torn in St. *James's-street*, where he either designedly or carelessly drop'd it.

A NEIGHBOURING GENTLEMAN, who is of *French* Extraction,[2] has two or three *Plantations*, at no great distance from yours; it is almost incredible, what vast Improvements he has made thereon[a] within a few Years; for however strictly he persues the rigid maxims of his *Prædecessors*, yet he justly considers, that the only way to make them flourish, is to grant his *Tenants* and *Servants* such privileges as may induce them to go over and settle there: By such like methods his *Plantations* thrive to that degree, that wanting more Land, he makes no scruple of running out to his next Neighbour, who is his UNCLE; and 'tis thought that in Time he will jostle him out of the whole. If he uses so near a *Relation* after that manner, what may you expect, whenever it is convenient for him, or he has it in his Power? for, whatever *Professions* he makes[b] you, may be only *Grimace*; very few of your Friends imagine him to be *sincere*, or that he has any *real Value* for you. In short, Mr. D'ANVERS, I don't like the *principles* of that *young Gentleman*, who has made such early discoveries of the same Temper and Disposition which his *Grandfather* was of, who[c] was so *litigious* an old Gentleman, that 'tis well known he was all his Life at *Law* with his *Neighbours*; that he seldom had less than *two* or *three Suits* at a time, upon his hands, and sometimes *seven* or *eight*;[3] and that he bore an *implacable Enmity* to your UNCLE, who had the goodness to support *those*, who were not otherwise able to go to Law with him, in Defence of their just *Rights* and *Properties*.

As I have been at his *Plantation* as well as yours, I intend hereafter, if I find it will be acceptable, to give you some other hints, which may be useful; for I have reason to believe[d] you have very imperfect Notions of them, as well as your *domestick Servants*, under whose particular Province they are; either through the Multiplicity of other affairs, which engrosses so much of their time,

---

[a] thereon] on them *B*.   [b] makes] makes to *B*.   [c] who] and He *B*.
[d] believe] believe that *B*.

that they cannot give the Attention which is necessary, or the false *Representations* of your *Stewards* abroad, to cover their own *sinister Designs*; it is no new or uncommon thing, when they find their *Schemes* for enriching themselves, at any rate, meet with opposition, to load your *Tenants* with terms of reproach, such as *seditious, turbulent Spirits, Jacobites*, and other such[a] opprobrious names, as they imagine will render them obnoxious to your *self* or your *Domesticks*: notwithstanding this, I dare venture to affirm, that no part of Mankind can be more steadily and heartily attached to your *Person* and *Interest* than they are; nor are they wanting, in such demonstrations as are in their power, or, their remote Situation will admit of: They are, indeed, tenacious of their *Rights* and *Liberties*; but, as they claim no other Privileges, than what they enjoy'd in their *native Country*, and pay the Obedience, which is due to you as their rightful and lawful LANDLORD, it cannot be supposed that their insisting upon what they are intitled to by *Birth*, will be disagreeable, when it is understood, that this is their only aim and design, and that they contend for nothing more.

I am, with the utmost Submission,
SIR, *Your most Obedient, and*
most Faithful Servant
WILL. BRITON.

Hampstead,
Jan. 3, 1726.

No. 30. Monday, 20 March 1727.

To CALEB D'ANVERS, *Esq*;

Sir,

    Though you have not published, according to your promise, *An account of the whole Affair relating to*[b] *your Man ROBIN*,[1] *and the Motives which induced you to proceed, in a gentle manner, with so ungrateful and refractory a Servant*; yet, it is very pleasing to your friends, That they can now communicate[c] their thoughts, since you have ordered your Letters to be taken in by your Bookseller:[2] Indeed, Mr. *D'Anvers*, it was no small grievance to have them intercepted, and stifled, as they were before very frequently;[d] for,

---

[a] such as . . . other such] as . . . such other *A, B*.   [b] relating to] of *B*.

[c] now communicate] now safely communicate *A, B*.

[d] before very frequently] very frequently before *A, B*.

6

how shall your poor *Tenants* and *Servants* be redress'd, when they are injured, if The *Channel*, through which Their Complaints are to be convey'd, is interrupted or stopped up?

To give you an[a] Instance of the Candour of your *Servants*, and Their regard to the Interest of your *Tenants*, among[b] many others, which may be enumerated; They were often applied to, in relation to some *Acts of Violence*, committed by the Count PHILIPEAUX'S Servants,[3] without receiving any manner of satisfaction, except fair speeches, and promises, which they are very bountiful in bestowing; yet, I am inform'd, that they have *since* made use of those very *complaints*, upon some other differences, between you and that Gentleman, which is[c] like to End, in a troublesome and expensive *Law-Suit*: not that Those unhappy People will be in any wise the better for it; but it serves a turn at this present juncture; had they advised you to resent Those abuses in time, it might have prevented some other injuries, which you have sustain'd; for *Mankind are apt to impose on those, who will either bear it, or make the least Concession.*

It has often grieved me, when I was at one of your *Plantations*, which is esteem'd the most considerable of Them all, to see the ruinous condition it was in, and the little care, that was taken to improve, or keep it in order; for it was over-run with weeds, and the Enclosures were all broken down, so, that no Man's property[d] could be distinguish'd, or asserted; the Neighbour's cattle ranged in the corn-fields, and meadows; and your *Tenants* were daily insulted, nay plunder'd, without being able to obtain any kind of redress; your *Stewards* and *Servants* at home, as well as those abroad, were too intent upon Their own *private affairs*, to have any regard to Those oppressions, or indeed to your honour and interest, which were affected thereby:[e] And how can it be otherwise, when your *Plantations* are generally under the direction of *Indigent* and *Ignorant* persons? Can you reasonably expect to be better served by such Men, or that your interest, in those parts, can be improved, or even preserved from distruction, unless more care is taken of them? What Complaints are daily made of the *insolent* behaviour of some of your *Domesticks*, and the *corrupt* practices of others? If They, who are under your Eye behave in that manner, does it not argue,

<hr/>

[a] an] one *B*.   [b] among] amongst *B*.   [c] is] are *B*.
[d] property] *A*, *B*; property, *fol*.   [e] thereby] by them *B*.

that there is a necessity for Those to be laid[a] under a greater restraint, who are at a distance, and vested with powers, too extensive, to be reposited in the hands of any Mortal; *The generality of mankind being Tyrants in Their Nature, and not to be trusted with an unlimited Power?*

I could wish, *Sir*, that you would now and then, of an Evening, come *incog.* to the publick *Coffee houses*, as some of your Predecessors have done; for then you will be truly informed, of the Opinions and Sentiments of Mankind, who cannot be suspected of any sinister designs, since you will, by *those*[b] Means, be unknown to them.

It was pleasant enough, the other day, to hear one of your *Menial Servants*, a creature of ROBIN'S, after many invectives, and base insinuations, assert, with a confident air, that you are not the Author of the *Craftsman*, but that those papers are written by some of your *discarded Servants*, to vent their *Spleen* and *Malice*, and that they impose upon the World, by prefixing your Name to them; Nay, He had the assurance to mention some particular persons, who are not only incapable of any Low designs, but are as eminent for Their *wit* and *fine* parts, as for their *probity* and *untainted virtue.*

I can't help making one observation more. Since you appointed Dr. *King* Physician to your family, and recomended his *Nostrums* to the World, your *Servants*, and some of your *Tenants* in *Staffordshire* are so wonderfully fond of his prescriptions, that they look on those, who are not of so happy a constitution, as to be able to swallow or digest them, either disaffected to your person, or to be in an ill habit of body; for my part, Though I have a personal very great[c] regard for you, and perhaps may allow the *Doctor* to be an ingenious Gentleman, yet methinks, 'tis very hard, that a man must be abused, or suffer in his Character, because he has not the same opinion of your *Operator.*[4] It is certain, whatever improvements he has[d] made, he does not pretend that those *Nostrums* are his own, but that he learnt them of the famous *Dr.* CATILINE; nor indeed, are they *infallible* remedies, for they only *patch* and *palliate*, and have not been known to perfect any one cure; This is evident from the continual *supplies*[e] which he is obliged to furnish his Patients with, fearing they will[f] otherwise relapse into their former distempers.

---

[a] does it not . . . be laid] is it not reasonable to lay Those *B.*   [b] *those*] that *A.*
[c] personal very great] very great personal *A, B.*   [d] has] hath *B.*
[e] *supplies*] *Supplies*, with *B.*   [f] with, fearing they will] lest They should *B.*

Now, *Sir*, give me leave to make some mention of my self, and to
desire a favour of you; I was once a very active Man, and have been
in several parts of the World; but as I am advanc'd in Life, I feel
some of the infirmities of old age creeping upon me, *viz.* a strong
propensity to getting of[a] Money, and to Living[b] in a sedentary way;
I should therefore be glad of a *Place*, that will bring in *much*, and
require *little* to be done for it; several of my Neighbours, by your
bounty, enjoy themselves after that manner; which makes me
desirous of doing the same. What I am most inclined to, is a good
Benefice; for I am informed that you have several in your Gift; I am
not, indeed, in *Orders*; but why may not I act *by* a *Deputy*, as well as
another? I am sure, it is altogether as *reasonable*, and may as justly
be *dispensed* with, as many things which are tolerated *by your
favourite Servants*, whom you confide in.[c] I must own my self
defective in some fashionable Qualities, and that I am one of those
unfortunate fellows, who dare not act repugnant to *Reason*, or the
dictates of my own *Conscience*; It is likewise a Misfortune to me,
that I am not *Allied* to, nor even acquainted with any of your
Domesticks, and therefore I might probably fail of obtaining their
favour and Recomendation, though I was Master of the *Necessary
Talents* of *Lying*, *Pimping*, &c. but, notwithstanding these
discouragements, I have hopes of overcoming them, if you are
disposed; for I am Master of some *Arguments of such weight*, as
seldom fail to convince Men of their reason and understanding:
nay, rather than be disappointed,[d] I will allow them one *half* of the
profits, as I am told many others do; for certainly there is a good
deal of reason and truth in an old *English* proverb that, *half a Loaf is
better than no Bread.*

I am, Sir,
Your most Obedient
and most Humble Servant.
WILL. BRITON.

Hampstead,
March the 2d. 1726–7.[e]

No. 35. Friday, 7 April 1727.

The Port and Town of *Gibraltar* being become the subject of
most Conversation, and its Preservation the Object of every honest

[a] getting of] get *B*.   [b] Living] live *A, B*.
[c] whom you confide in] in whom you confide *B*.
[d] disappointed] *A, B*; disapointed *fol.*   [e] I am . . . 1726–7] *omitted A, B*.

man's hopes and wishes, the great Consequence thereof[a] to this Kingdom never more justly deserved our attention that at this Time, if consider'd only in two points; *first*, as it preserves to us the Conveniency, Protection and Security of our Trade to the *Streights*, above that of all other Nations; more especially in Regard to the *Algerines* and *Sallee-men*,[1] who are influenced by it to continue their *Treaties* made with us, which they never do longer with any other nation than till they find it their Interest to break them; *secondly*, in Respect to the great Advantage, which the Possession of that place hath already given us, when in War with *France* and *Spain*, and consequently will always give us again on[b] the like occasions, whilst we continue to keep it.

First, in Respect to our *Trade*; for as it commands the Passage or Entrance of all our Navigation into the *Mediterranian*, both in Peace and War, so it is equally necessary and as much our Interest to keep it ourselves, as it is for any Gentleman to keep possession of the Gate, which leads to his own House, it being in the Power of Those, who possess this Port, at all Times to interrupt, annoy or hinder whom they shall think fit in their Trade, by keeping only *two* or *three* Ships of War constantly on that Station, in the same manner almost as the *Danes*, by the Possession of *Elsineur*, command the passage into and out of the *Baltick*; so that if this Port were in the hands of any other Nation, it would be in their power likewise either to permit us to navigate or trade within the *Streights*, or not, as they should think fit, unless a very strong Squadron were constantly kept at the Entrance of the *Streights-mouth* to secure the Passage, and to be relieved from Time to Time by fresh Ships; which would put us to a much greater Expence than what we are now at in keeping the Place in Dispute.

Before *England* was in Possession of *Tangier*, on the opposite side of the *Streights*, we were never able to deal with the *Algerines* and other *Turkish Rovers*, who, for near an hundred years, had carried on a successful *Piratick* War against the Commerce of this Nation, and never could have been[c] reduced, till, by the situation and our possession of the abovementioned Place, we distressed them so much, not only by taking their Ships going in and coming out of the *Streights*, but also by retaking such of their Prizes, as they had taken in the Ocean, that at last they were forced to be content with such a

---

[a] thereof] of it *B*.   [b] on] upon *B*.   [c] have been] be *B*.

Peace as we would give them; the continuance whereof[a] is now owing to nothing so much as to our having been, for many years past and at present, in the same Condition to chastise those *Rovers*, by the possession of *Gibraltar*, as we were before by the possession of *Tangier*.

The security of our *Italian*, *Turkey*, and *Fish* Trades intirely depends on our Possession of this Place; and should we ever lose it or part with it, it is very reasonable to believe that both the *Algerines* and *Sallee-men* would soon break with us again; so that, in such a case, the above-said Branches of Trade would almost wholly fall into the Hands of our Rivals the *French* from *Marseilles*, who by their situation are always ready at hand to furnish those Markets; as soon as they are in want; while we, on our part, shall be obliged to carry on that Trade by the tedious Methods of *Fleets* and *Convoys*, and at last, perhaps, come long after the Market is supplied by our *Rivals*. Besides all this, the Article of *Insurance*, which would certainly run much higher than usual under these Circumstances, would prove an[b] heavy charge on our Goods, more than on those of other Traders, which would thereby very much affect those Branches of our Trade and Navigation.

Nay, the Mischief would not stop here; for as the *Algerines*, of late years, cruize in Summer Time at the Mouth of our Channel (where they lately took a very rich *Ostend East-India* Ship) and as some of them have also come into our very Ports two or three years successively, so it is possible that, if we should lose *Gibraltar*, they may become, being so well acquainted with our Channel, a much more dangerous Enemy to us, than ever they were formerly, and may attack all our Trade in general, as the St. *Malo* Privateers did in the late Wars when ever they shall find that they can carry home their Prizes without Interruption; which is not to be done, unless we should be dispossessed of *Gibraltar* and thereby[c] the Bridle, which hath[d] hitherto restrained them, should be taken[e] out of their Mouths.

Secondly, in respect to our Neighbours, *Gibraltar* is situated in such a manner, that it is in the power of the present Possessors to cut off any naval Communication, between one Port and another of each of those Two very powerful Kingdoms, with which we have had such frequent occasions to be at War for almost these forty

---

[a] whereof] of which *B*.   [b] an] a *B*.   [c] thereby] thereby take *B*.
[d] hath] had *B*.   [e] should be taken] *omitted B*

years past; who would soon turn the Tables upon us, if they should recover this Place out of our Hands, especially in Times of any Rupture between us; nothing being more self-evident than that it gives to those, who are Masters of it, the Sovereignty and Command of the Commerce and Navigation of the *Mediterranean* Sea, and makes it impracticable for any other Nation to trade there without their Leave. And farther, by our possession of this Place, all Nations within the *Mediterranean* will be obliged to court our Friendship or fear our Power, particularly the *Piratick* States, who beholding vengeance so near at hand, will be thereby deterred from attempting to interrupt our Trade, while they are destroying that of all others.

Neither is this Advantage all that we reap from the Possession of *Gibraltar*; for it hath put into our hands almost all the *Freight-Trade* into the *Mediterranean* for many years past, especially that of the *Hamburghers* and *Hollanders*, who have made use of *British* Bottoms only to carry on their Commerce in those Seas, till very lately, when the *Dutch* obtained a Peace with the *Algerines*, as it is said by *our means*; whereby we are likely to lose one of the greatest Advantages at present belonging to the Navigation of *Great Britain*, which we before enjoy'd, whilst those Merchants made use of *English* Ships, finding it dangerous to venture their Estates in any other.

But, laying aside all other Considerations, there cannot be a stronger proof of the Importance which the Possession of this place hath been to us, than that it hath in a manner destroyed the naval Power of *France* from the Hour of our taking it to the conclusion of the second *French* War; nor indeed could they ever send any Naval Stores round about into those Seas, without an apparent Danger of their falling into our hands, in going through the *Streights*; so that the greatest part of their Fleet hath become useless ever since and never appeared at Sea again, but lay rotting in their Harbours.

It would be needless to inforce this Argument with many other Instances, which might be given of the Advantage of this Port; only it must not be forgot that its Proximity to *Cadiz*, the great Mart and Center of almost all the Riches of *America*, gives us the greatest opportunity of commanding that Port, and the Trade frequenting it from the *West-Indies*, which, in time of a[a] War with *Spain*, may be reckon'd of no small Consideration or Importance.

[a] of a] of *B*.

Whether therefore we look on *Gibraltar* either in a *mercantile* or a *political* Light; *first*, as it not only secures all our own Commerce to *Italy*, *Africa*, and the *Levant* from the Insults and Annoyance of those terrible Enemies the *Algerines* and other *Turkish Rovers*, but also helps us to the *Carriage Trade* of several other Nations; or, *secondly*, as it cuts off all communication between the Ports of our most formidable Rivals, and thereby renders their naval Force very precarious and inconsiderable; the possession of this Place seems to be of such Importance, that I am at a Loss to guess what *Equivalent* could be given us for it; I am sure at least, that any one of the foregoing Considerations, taken singly, would more than over-ballance all the Expence, which the Nation at present feels on that Account.

But once more, and to conclude; as the Advantages of *Gibraltar*, which result to this Kingdom from the foregoing particulars, are fully confirm'd and demonstrated by the Experience of many years past; so the preservation of it at this Time is of much *greater Importance* than it ever was before, as will appear by considering the present State of affairs, that Manufactures are springing up in most parts of *Europe* and that several powerful States are endeavouring to vye with us in *Commerce* and a *maritime Force*; which ought to put us on the strictest Guard, and determine us not to part with a Place, which is manifestly of so much Advantage, by securing and improving our own Trade and Navigation, as well as by defeating the Attempts of our *Enemies* and *Rivals*.

No. 52. Saturday, 1 July 1727.

The Race *is not to the* Swift, *nor the* Battle *to the* Strong; *nor yet* Power *to Men of* Understanding, *nor* Favour *to Men of* Skill.

Solomon.[1]

To CALEB D'ANVERS, *Esq*;

SIR,

SINCE you allow *Translations* a place in your Journal, I hope the following Extracts out of a favourite Piece of the celebrated Monsieur BALSAC, intitled ARISTIPPUS or of the COURT, will not be unacceptable; especially since you have already published some observations on the subject of *lucky Incidents* and *fortuitous Events*.

This penetrating Author begins his *second discourse* of the *Court* by observing that *Princes* cannot live without *Favourites*, any more than they can without *Ministers*, and apologizes for them by the Practice and Authority of the best and wisest of Princes, such as *Augustus* and *Antonine*, who had an esteem for some *Persons* more than for *others*; nay he does not scruple to strengthen his Argument, by quoting the Example even of *God Almighty* and our *blessed Saviour* themselves, as having some *particular Affections* to particular Persons; but being apprehensive that such arguments may be thought to border on *Prophaneness* or to be urged with too much *Freedom*, I have for that Reason omitted them in the following Abstract, which I have made as short as possible, and tho' I have not always scrupulously adhered to the *Letter*, yet I think that I have no where varied, at least not materially, from the sense[2]—He goes on thus;

"Since then the *Author* and *Finisher* of *Virtue*, as well as *Faith*, had these particular *Regards* and *Partialities*, and gave way to the calls of innocent *Nature*; Princes may, upon the authority of this high and incontestable Example, have their particular *Confidents* and *Favourites*.

"It must be own'd indeed, that the case of *earthly Princes* and that of the *Prince* of *our Salvation* is vastly different; the divinity of our blessed Saviour could search the inward parts of the *Ministers* of his Kingdom and could either discern them to be at first inclined to be faithful in their office, or powerfully dispose and influence them to Habits of virtue and integrity. But the case of earthly Princes is very different; the *Favourites* and *Creatures* of their *Confidence* are but as *Clay* in their Hands, of which they are the *Artificers*. They may indeed make it more *beautiful*, but cannot make it a jot intrinsically the *better*. They may mould it into a more agreeable *outside* and *figure* than they found it in at first; but cannot give it any *inward goodness*. They may indeed make it an *Idol*, a *false God*, but cannot improve it into a *living, Thinking, rational Man*.

"Such *Idols* as these often meet our Eyes even in *Christian* Countries. We almost daily see Instances of Men, who are *unworthily* Great and *unjustly* buoy'd up by the favour of their Prince. Thus the *Ægyptians* (as wise and learned a People as they were) placed *Beasts* upon their Altars, and, notwithstanding their

Imperfection and *Deformity*, paid them the highest duties of Prayer and Adoration.

"Behold the good works of *Fortune*! Behold likewise the extravagant Caprices of that Goddess, without Eyes and without Judgment! To whom antient *Rome* gave so many different Names and dedicated so many Altars. You have often heard of melancholy, giddy-headed Queens who have fallen in love with *Dwarfs, Blacks* and *Monkies. Fortune* seems to be of the same humour with these foolish Princesses, often courting to her Embraces the most *unworthy* and *undeserving*, and, in the Election of a *Prætor*, preferring the villainies of a *Vatinius* to the virtues and publick spirit of a *Cato*. It is to this injudicious *Beldame* that the *Creatures* of the greatest Princes owe their rise and grandeur and the vast returns of their Rapine and Oppression. And as their rise and beginning was a *luckey hit* and a kind cast of *Fortune*, so they govern by the Influence and wanton motions of that blind *Goddess*, at hazard and adventure. They make themselves meer *Phaethon*'s[a] in their Administration, and for want of Judgment to manage the Province, which they have undertaken, dispense unequal Light and Heat in the World, *scorching* up part of it and leaving the other to starve with *Cold*. Such ignorant *Administrators* are scared at their own *Blunders,* They daily run the fortune of that unhappy Youth, just mentioned, being perpetually alarmed at the impending Ruin of their Country, involved in their own; and when they have somewhat refined their *ignorance* and steeled[b] their sense of *Reflection,* by a constant attendance at Court as well as by the servile Fawnings and Applauses of a croud of Flatterers, and when one or two *luckey hits* (the Effects of the provident and watchful Genius of their Nation) have given them a good opinion of themselves, they boast of what they received, as if they received it not, and place all their *fortunate accidents* to their own *foresight* and *Sagacity*.

"All their Actions are out of season; they are *false Measures* from a *false Rule*. Instead of acting in the article of opportunity, so much observed by all wise men, and so necessary for the perfection of Affairs, they pass it by, or cannot come up to it; they are always either *before*, or *behind*. One day they declare *War* in Pett, and the next sue for Peace out of Cowardice and fear of Miscarriage. They affront the *antient* and *inseparable Friends* of the Crown, and frown upon the *natural* and *well known Enemies* of their Country. If it be

[a] *Phaethon*'s] *Phaetons A, B.*   [b] steeled] sear'd *B.*

their fortune to rule in *Spain*, they are for granting *Liberty of Conscience*, if in *France*, they are for introducing the *Inquisition*. The *Frontiers* lie open to insults and defenceless; whilst they are hurrying themselves in fortifying the *Mid-land* Towns. They are for giving up the Citadel of AMIENS and building one at ORLEANS.

"And as their own Greatness is owing to meer *Fortune*, so the same blind Goddess (or perhaps *more detestable Motives*)[a] sways them in the choice of their *Sulbalterns*. For an *Embassy* to *Rome* they recommend a *Captain of Light Horse*, one that hath perhaps signalized himself in several Battles. At the Head of the *Finances* they place some OLD SPENDTHRIFT, who squandered away his Estate in *in his Youth*, but *talks well of OEconomy*. They recommend to an Abbey or —— a Man of the *Gown* indeed, but of the same Reach of Capacity and Depth of Learning with him, whom our Ancestors saw at *Paris*, when the *Polish Ambassadors* arrived there. These Ambassadors made their Compliments to him in *Latin*; upon which he desired[b] to be excused from answering in the *same Language*, for that he never had the Curiosity to learn the *Polish* Tongue.

"The same venerable Sage took *Seneca* for a Doctor of *Canon Law*, and thought that he had written his Book *de Beneficiis*, professedly on the subject of *Ecclesiastical Benefices*. A shrewd Wag of those Times made him believe that the *Morea* was the Country of the *Moors*; and it is certain that he spent a whole Day in looking for *Aristocracy* and *Democracy* in the Map, and at last thought his Labour fully answered, when he accidentally fell upon *Croatia* and *Dalmatia*.

"It is, no doubt, a great Advantage to be *knowing* and *learned* under *such Reigns*; and the *Muses* have a great deal to expect from the Protection of *such Ministers*. But we shall pass over this particular, and trouble ourselves no farther with the Interest of the *Muses*, whose Destiny it is to be *poor*, *neglected*, and *ill-treated* under all sorts of Reigns, and all kinds of Administrations.

"These men, you see, are perfect *Connoissieurs* in men and business. After having squandered away the Revenues of the Publick in the most *ridiculous* or *corrupt* manner, they take upon themselves the character of *prudent Managers* and *just Stewards* and to give them the last Touch of Refinement, a certain *Politick Doctor*

---

[a] (or perhaps *more detestable Motives*)] (unless some *detestable Motive* interferes) *A*, *B*.
[b] desired] *B*; is desired *fol*.

assists at their Consultations; and repeating every Day some incoherent scraps out of a translated *Tacitus*, recommends to them, above all things, *Secrecy* and *Dissimulation!* This Doctrine being inculcated into them, they become all *mystery*, and never express themselves but by a wink of the Eye, or a nod of the Head. At most, they do but whisper, not even when they compliment their *Master*, and tell him that he is the *greatest Prince* upon Earth.

"They are so much wrapt up in this *religious silence*, that they make a scruple of giving out the necessary orders to those, who are to execute them, for fear of discovering some secret of State. They devour with greedy Ears the *wild Schemes of Political Alchymists* and *Projectors*, who promise them *Mountains of Gold*. They receive with open arms, any fugitive, abandoned Traytor, who discovers[a] to them the secrets of his Prince, and points[b] out to them the method of distressing him in some tender point; and, depending on the Attachment of such a Villain, they embark themselves in some *grand Enterprize*, and begin a *big War*, which in two Days after they grow sick of, and endeavour, by all the *lowest arts*, to disengage themselves from. A thousand other Instances might be given of the *Wisdom* and *Integrity* of such Ministers; which, if they do not happen in this age, have certainly happen'd in former times; and if there are none of these *presumptuous Blunderers* and *ridiculous Atalls*[3] in *France* and *Germany*, there certainly have been such in *Italy* and *Spain*.

"By these exquisite Maxims, and this *Anti-politique*, of which I have given you a short sketch, do these men govern their deluded Country. They overturn what they would maintain. They wound where they would heal. They ruin what they would establish, and destroy every thing that comes within the Grasp of their management. The Dishonour of their Prince, and some dangerous shock to the Constitution of their Country, justly excite the Resentment of both; so that Death, Banishment or Disgrace, and a forced Restitution of their wicked plunder, are commonly the End and Result of their Administration. Being arrived by the favour of meer *Fortune*, and some *lucky Distress* of their Country, at a kind of KINGSHIP, they make the same use of it, which Children do of *Knives*, who cut their *own Fingers*, not knowing how to use them, and make their Mothers and Nurses angry with them, which commonly ends in a *sound Whipping*."

[a] discovers] will discover *A, B*.   [b] points] point *A, B*.

No. 54.   Saturday, 15 July 1727.

To CALEB D'ANVERS, *Esq*;

SIR,

BY your Paper of this Day, I apprehend that, among other Letters, you have received mine on the Death of that NOBLE LORD, to whom you pay so handsome a Compliment.[1] After your saying that you have not room to insert them, what can I offer on that head? but forgive me, if I trespass on you at this time, and impute the Fault to the over-flowings of an Heart, whose love and reverence for that NOBLE NAME will be more easy for you to conceive, than for me to express. Believe me, Sir, I set little by[a] the Piece which I sent you; but Virtue like his demands those Honours; and it is the business of so great a Lover of *Patriotism*, as Mr. *D'Anvers*, to do him Justice. If therefore you have any regard to that *Virtue*, which made him the *Great Man* we have lost, dedicate one paper to his memory and fill it with the best Essay on that subject, in your hands; for unless you do this, it can never be said that you have answer'd your own or treated his Character according to the dignity of either, on this occasion; and I dare say farther, that the Publick will think the *Glorious Patriot* before-mention'd as illustrious a Subject in *Politicks*, as any which you can at this time present them with. When the *Freeholder* spoke to the immortal Memory of the Great Lord SOMMERS, and the *True Briton* did the same Justice to that of the late Earl COWPER, Mankind thought they acted a noble Part.[2] What then would be said, should the CRAFTSMAN neglect the Theme of so sublime a Character as that of Lord LECHMERE? pardon me if I have said any thing improper herein, and be assured that I am, Sir,

Middle-Temple,	Your very humble Servant
Saturday *July* 1*st.*	*A. B.*

Ducit Amor Patriæ.[3]

PATRIOTISM has, in all Ages, and among all Nations, been acknowledged a glorious virtue; and the more generous the Genius

---

[a] I set little by] I am not vain of *A, B*.

of a People is, the more exalted Honours do they pay to those Fathers of Mankind, who, being actuated by the noble Principles of universal and unconfin'd Benevolence, have made the welfare of their Country, their great and early Care, and dedicated all their Abilities to the service of their fellow Creatures, promoting their valuable Interests, with the most hearty and disinterested Zeal, and sacrificing their own particular ease and enjoyments of Pleasure and Plenty to the more general concerns of the Publick, and the Peace and Prosperity of Mankind.

If we carry our Enquiries farther into this Quality, which has so remarkably distinguish'd some of the most shining Names in History, we shall find that none but great Souls are capable of so sublime a virtue, not any but[a] men of the most elevated understanding, who[b] soar so high. A little Genius has narrow Laws prescribed to it and acts within such Limits as are suitable to itself; it may study its own Interests, or make the Concerns of a few its principal Care, but is never susceptible of that laudable Ambition, which rouzes the latent Powers of the Soul, influenced by[c] which it exerts itself for the sake of Society, and endeavours to bless Multitudes and improve the welfare of Thousands.

Great and noble resolutions result from a sedate and manly way of thinking, from wise and careful enquiries, and are never form'd on sudden and hasty reflections; they indicate a great and masterly mind, which apprehends things with all their Relations, and leaves no intricate part of the Question unsearched, but industriously follows Truth thro' every Meander, as far as human faculties can pursue it.

Such was the Character of that Great Man, who chose for his *Motto* that noble Sentiment, which stands at the Head of this Paper, whose uncommon Abilities had enabled him to trace the most intricate Labyrinths of Knowledge, whose inquisitive Genius had led him thro' the most abstruse Enquiries, and who, when he sat down to reflect on things, form'd that remarkable resolution, which actuated every step of his Conduct, and acquired him the glorious Name of a *true Patriot*, and will transmit his memory with the most illustrious honours to all succeeding Ages.

No Man, who knew the great Lord LECHMERE can mistake the Person I mean, or be at a loss to find him out. All Lovers of Truth

[a] not any but] and that only *A*, *B*.   [b] who] can *A*, *B*.
[c] influenced by] by the Influence of *B*

and their Country are undoubtedly well acquainted with his distinguished Character, and will readily own the Merit of the *mighty Dead*, whose generous Labours now cease from amongst us, and whose fame is the glorious Charge, which he has left to our Care, which in gratitude to a long Series of zealous Endeavours to improve the happiness of our Country and in justice to Excellencies which struck the most Envious dumb, we are obliged to preserve with all possible reverence and regard.

The *Noble Lord*, to whom we now pay deserved honours, was born a Gentleman, and of a Family which had given many of its Sons to the *Law*; one of whom, in our time, wore the *Scarlet Robe*. He acquired, in his early Years, by the means of a liberal and ingenuous Education, a vast fund of curious and polite Learning, and apply'd all his great Abilities in that useful and difficult Study. He master'd so abstruse a Science with uncommon expedition, and an ease peculiar to himself, and honoured the *Gown*, even in his Youth, by the great reputation which he gain'd at the Bar, for his masculine Eloquence and uncommon Judgment.

In thinking, in speaking, and acting, he was happily superiour to most of his Cotemporaries; was blest with such a quick apprehension, and had so comprehensive a way of Reasoning, that Nature had evidently acted her noblest Part to form in him as great a Genius as ever pass'd from her Hands.

A Lawyer of his Distinction was soon elected by his Country to sit in a *Senate*, which, by its wise and publick-spirited Councils, had raised the glory of the Nation to as great a heighth as former Ages never knew, and Times to come will hardly equal.

In this station the *Great Man* was seen in every Transaction, distinguished by his unwearied Diligence in all Parliamentary Affairs. In his attendance on the House, and application to its weightiest Concerns, he was never wanting to his Country or Character; but, with indefatigable Labour, in the most solemn Deliberations, and by the finest Arts of Elocution, served the Nation, and powerfully supported its Interests on all Occasions.

Thus in the *Senate* and at the *Bar* did this prodigious[a] Man pursue the Publick Good, and acquire such vast Applause, as regularly procured him all the Honours of the *Long Robe*, till but *one* remained equal to his illustrious Merits, and worthy his Acceptance; and tho' he never enjoy'd it, yet such was the regard

[a] prodigious] excellent *B*.

paid to his Abilities, Virtue and Integrity, which had been so long experienced, and so greatly honoured, that the Wise, the Learned and Unbyass'd Patriot was, with the universal Applause of his Country, created a *Peer* of *Great Britain*, and summon'd to sit in that August Assembly, which is the standing Council of the Nation, and the *Dernier* Resort of Justice.

Here his Toils among the lower Order of the People were determined, but not his generous Benevolence to all Men: He now devoted himself altogether to an universal Interest, and it became his chief Care to secure those Laws and Liberties, which he had so long studied, to his Country, and to unborn Posterity.

By his extensive Learning in our Laws he had gained so great an Insight into the nicest parts of our Constitution, that none understood it better than himself. He was well acquainted with its invaluable Excellencies, always held it very dear to him, continually consulting its preservation, and never suffering its Welfare to be absent from his Thoughts. To his Honour, to his eternal Honour, be it remember'd, that, tho' he was a *Minister of the Crown*, and had an immediate *Dependance on the Court*, yet, notwithstanding all the Temptations, which the favours and frowns of some powerful Men could suggest, he firmly adhered to what he thought his Country's Interest in that great and never-to-be-forgotten Struggle to save the Law for TRIENNIAL Parliaments; which was at last repealed against the learned Arguments and Vote of that *Great Man*, who exerted his utmost Power to maintain it. I do not mention this with any Design to reflect on the *Septennial Act*[4] (for the Continuance of which several *irrefragable Arguments* might be produced) but only as an Instance of the Lord LECHMERE'S inflexible virtue, and to shew that no *Ministry*, or any set of Men whatsoever could awe him in his Conduct, or induce him to alter it; for he was obstinately just, and as to[a] ill-designing Persons, of what Power soever, as he never feared them[b] so he scorn'd to seek their good Graces by unworthy Methods, but honourably and immoveably bent to serve a nobler and more extended Interest, he spoke with undaunted Courage the wise and generous sentiments of his Heart, whenever National Affairs were under Deliberation, and thought it his greatest Glory to act the part of a *Briton*, wherever he was concerned, and by whomsoever opposed.

[a] as to] as He never feared *A, B.*   [b] as he never feared them] *omitted A, B.*

Amidst these uncommon Virtues, which I have mentioned, we might also observe the manly Morals which adorned this *noble Lord*'s private Life, the great *Sobriety*, *Temperance*, *OEconomy* and *Justice*, which all must acknowledge, who knew him, or had dealings with him in any part of his Life.

In short, his masterly Acquaintance with our Laws; his quickness of Apprehension; his Strength, and Fire, and Clearness of Expression; and, above all, his exact Knowledge of our Constitution and of all Parliamentary Proceedings, made him the delight of good Men, and a Terror to all wicked Ministers. He was, perhaps, apt to be a little too warm, and too much transported upon some occasions; but this proceeded from the upright Zeal of his Heart, and his sincere Detestation of *Knaves*, *Tools*, and *Hypocrites* of all kinds. We must also do him the justice to own, that he was of *no Party*, nor attached to any Interest, but that of his Country, which he constantly made the Rule and Measure of all his Actions.

The natural Concern, and just Grief, in which the Nation was involved by the Death of our late most gracious Sovereign, made the Loss of this Great Man to be less observed than it otherwise wou'd have been; but that noble, that Godlike Spirit of *Patriotism*, which inspired every Action, and shone thro' the whole series of his Life; that generous disinterested Love of Mankind, and hearty Desire to do Good to his Country, his Friends, and to Merit in any Condition; his great Benevolence, which rose superior to all the low Arts, that are made use of to gain *Popularity*, and unworthy of his great Soul, will make him the Honour of the Age and Nation in which he lived, and the Wonder and Envy of Times to come.

No. 60. Saturday, 26 August 1727.[a]

To CALEB D'ANVERS, *Esq*;

SIR,

I AM a Proprietor in some of the publick Funds; particularly, in the two great *Trading Companys*; but not being allowed the liberty of inspecting the Accounts and Transaction, of *Those*, who are in

---

[a] The substance of Bolingbroke's contributions to Nos. 60, 61, and 62 was reprinted in No. 66, 7 October 1727, where the order of his queries was rearranged. That text (here as referred to as *C*) was the basis for *A* and *B*, where the three contributions are printed as a single contribution to No. 61. The rearranged order, in *A*, *B*, and *C*, is: X, XI, XII, V, I, II, III, IV, VII, VIII, XIII, XIV, XVI, XVII, XVIII, XIX, XX, XXI, XXIII, XXII, XV, IX, XXIV, and the numerals are arabic.

the *Direction*, I shall be glad to have the following Queries resolved.[a]

I. Whether it be not incumbent on the *Directors* of the *S.S. Company* to satisfy the World, or[b] at least the *Proprietors* of the Stock, how, and by what means the *Royal George* came to be CONDEMNED?

II. What steps have been taken to do Justice to the *Company*, the two *Insurance Offices* &c. who may be very great Sufferers by her *Condemnation?*

III. If a *certain Person* be as culpable, as it is reported He is, whether the intimacy, that is, at this time, carried on between *Him* and some of the *principal Managers* (who are, in a manner, his Judges, and ought to scrutinize into his Conduct) does not justify the Umbrage, which is taken, of *male practice*[c] and of their being in the *Secret?*

IV. For *whose Account* those vast sums were *insured* on the *Royal George* outward, as well as homeward bound, which amounted to as much in value, if not more, than what the *Company* had on Board?

V. Whether it be not a breach of Trust in a *Director* to be concern'd, directly or indirectly, in any *Trade* or *Shipping*, which interferes with the Interest of the Company?

VI. Whether the large Presents, made to the *Spanish Officers* in *America*, to connive at the *Measurement* of the Annual Ships (which are almost double the *Tonage*, stipulated by the Contract with the *Court* of *Spain*) are charged to the *Company's* Account? And if they are, whether such a Charge is not a breach of Trust, and the highest injustice to the *Proprietors*, since the *extraordinary Measurement* of Ships[d] is supposed to be apply'd to the Interest of *private Persons*, and not to that of the *Company?*

VII. Whether 130,000 *Pieces of Eight*, or a *larger* sum, were not given at *one time* and for *one Ship only?*[e]

VIII. Whether some of the principal *misunderstandings*, at present subsisting between the *Courts* of *Great Britain* and *Spain*, are not owing to the misconduct of the *Directors*, their *Agents* or *Servants?*

---

[a] *To* CALEB . . . Queries resolved] From my own CHAMBERS. *A, B, It having been thought proper to promote the strictest Enquiry into the* Characters *and* Conduct *of the* Candidates *for this honourable City; I hope the Publication of the underwritten Queries [Letter* C] *will not be judged unseasonable. A, B, C.*   [b] World, or] World, *A, B, C.*
   [c] *practice] A, B; practise fol.*   [d] of Ships] of the Ships *B.*
   [e] *only?] B; only! fol.*

IX. Whether any Person, who is *known* to be *principally* concern'd in any *Frauds* or *Collusions* of this nature, can be thought a proper Person to be intrusted with the *Rights* and *Privileges* of one of the greatest *trading Cities* in the Universe?

I am Sir,

Your constant Reader,

And humble Servant,

CIVICUS.[a]

No. 61. Saturday, 2 September 1727.

Sir,

NO Answer having been yet given to those *Queries,* which you published in your last, from whence the truth of the Facts seem to be tacitly acknowledged, I have sent you some others, to be inserted in your next Paper, if you have Room.[b]

Quer. X. Whether it is consistent with the Rules or Interest of any Company for a Person to be *Governour, Sub-Governour,* or a *Director* above *Six Years?* And what Regulation is the *South Sea*[c] *Company,* in particular, under in these Respects?

XI. Whether a Person is qualified to be a *Director* of the greatest Company in the Universe, who is unacquainted with *Trade,* and consequently incapable of promoting its true Interest? And what were the Recommendations of *some Persons* to so considerable a Trust?

XII. Whether it is worth while for a *Merchant* of any eminency who may employ his Time to much greater Advantage, to be a *Director* of a Company, only for the Salary of 150 *l. per Annum?* If not, what are the *views,* which occasion such a struggle to get into the *Direction,* since they cannot acquire more, with *Justice to the Company?*

XIII. Whether the *Spotswood,* Captain *Bradly,* (which was *chartered* in 1725) went out on account of the *South Sea Company;* or what was the Design of sending a Ship of 300 Tons to accompany the *Prince Frederick,* Captain *Williams,* to the *West-Indies?*[d]

---

[a] I am . . . CIVICUS.] *omitted A, B, C.*
[b] *Sir,* NO . . . have Room.] *omitted A, B, C.*   [c] *South Sea*] S.S. *A, B, C.*
[d] *West-Indies?*] *A, F· West-Indies. fol.*

24

N.B. The *Prince Frederick* is said to measure, at least,

	— — — 900 *Tons*
The *Spotswood*	— — — 300
	1200 *Tons*.

XIV. Whether the Detention of the *Prince Frederick* at *La vera Cruz* be really occasion'd by the misunderstanding between the Courts of *Great Britain* and *Spain*, or on account of the *extraordinary Measurement* of the Ship and Goods, above the Stipulation of the *Assiento* Contract?[1]

XV. Whether all over-grown *Companies* are not prejudicial to and, in some measure, inconsistent with the *Liberties* of a free People, as well as the true Interest of a *Trading Nation*, with regard to the Influence which they have in the *Elections* of Members of Parliament, particularly for this *great* and *honourable City*; and whether it is not become the Interest and Duty of every Man, who is a Lover of his Country, to oppose such *unwarrantable* and *dangerous Practices?*

You may expect some farther *Queries* on this subject, from, *Sir,*
Mincing-Lane, Aug.   *Your humble Servant,*
30th 1727   CIVICUS.[a]

No. 62. Saturday, 9 September 1727.

To CALEB D'ANVERS, *Esq*;

I Send you some farther *Queries*, which I desire may be inserted in your next; since, I am persuaded in my self, that they are as unanswerable as the former; but being proposed only for the sake of Information, I shall be heartily glad to find my self mistaken.[b]

Quer. XVI. What is the Design of sending *Supercargoes*[c] in the Annual Ships, the *S. Sea*[d] *Company* having Factories settled at the *Spanish Ports* in *America*, where they are allowed to Trade: If the *Factors* have misbehaved, they ought to have been removed; if not,

a You may . . . CIVICUS.] *omitted A, B, C.*
b *To* CALEB . . . mistaken] *omitted A, B, C.*
c *Supercargoes] A, B, C and corrigendum in No. 63; Factors fol.*
d *S. Sea] S.S. A, B, C.*

what other Reasons can be assign'd for putting the Company to a *double* and *unnecessary Expence*, those *Factors* being sufficient to negotiate all their Affairs?

XVII. Whether it is worth the Company's while to continue or maintain the Factory at *La vera Cruz* at a very considerable Expence, since *Supercargoes*[a] are sent in the Annual Ships, and the whole Produce of the *Negro Trade* to that Place is not sufficient to defray such an Expence; or whether it be not done with some *private Views*, as well as supporting other Factories which cannot possibly answer the Charge the Company is at?

XVIII. Whether the large Quantities of Goods, which are frequently shipp'd off, for the *West-Indies*, under *borrow'd Names*, and re-exported in the *S.S.*[b] *Company's* Vessels, as well as what are sent in their Annual Ships on private Accounts, are not only prejudicial to the *Company's Trade*, but, may probably be a further[c] and much greater injury to them; such *clandestine Practices* being contrary to the express Tenour and Condition of the 42d *Article* of the *Assiento Contract*; whereby his *Catholick Majesty* allows the *Assiento Company* to send a Ship of 500 Tons Yearly, to trade in the *West-Indies*, during the continuance of the Contract, *in consideration of the Loss, which former* Assientists *have sustained; and that they shall not*, directly *or* indirectly, *attempt any* Unlawful Trade *under any* Pretence whatsoever.

XIX. Whether such unwarrantable practices (if any such there are)[d] are not only a Violation of the *Assiento Contract*, and, in many respects, very injurious to the *Company's Affairs*, but also destructive of the general good of *Trade*; since, the *fair Spanish Merchant* cannot possibly carry on his Commerce to any Advantage, while others, by Permission or Connivances,[e] stock the Markets in *America*, with Goods, that neither pay *Freight, Wages*, &c. which are born by the *Company*, and consequently can *under-sell* them very considerably, and *Engross* the Trade to themselves?

XX. Whether the *Difficulties* and *Delays* which the *S.S. Company* have met with, in obtaining from the Court of *Spain*, the *Schedulas* for their Annual Ships, were not owing to these, or such like Practices?

XXI. Whether the *S.S. Company* have not *lost* very con-

[a] *Supercargoes*] *A, B, C* and corrigendum in No. 63; Factors *fol.*
[b] *S.S.*] *S. Sea A, B, C.*   [c] further] farther *B.*
[d] are)] have been) *A, B, C.*   [e] Connivances,] Connivance, *C.*

siderably by their *Trade* in general? And whether the Exports of our *Woollen Manufacture*[a] are not greatly diminished, since they attempted it? And whether the carrying it on, in the manner it is said to have hitherto been, can be with any other View, than to serve *private Ends?*

XXII. Whether it is not incumbent on every honest Member of the *General Court*, to detect such Frauds, by enquiring more strictly than they have done,[b] into the *Conduct* and *Behaviour* of their *Managers*; more particularly with relation to *Foreign Affairs?*

XXIII. Whether such Practices (if any such there be)[c] may not have contributed to obstruct the so-much desired[d] Tranquility of *Europe*; whether they have not furnished the *Spanish* Court with plausible Pretences for taking our *Merchant Ships*, as well as for not *signing* or *ratifying* the *Preliminary Articles* for opening the *Congress* proposed; and whether we are not highly obliged to these[e] Gentlemen, who, for the sake of *unjust, private Lucre*, at the expence of the *Proprietors*, run the Risque of setting *Europe* in a new Flame, and involving this Nation in a farther, immense profusion of *Blood* and *Treasure?*

XXIV. Whether a *Parlimentary Enquiry* may not once more be[f] absolutely necessary, in order to prevent the fatal Consequences, which may justly be apprehended[g] to the Nation in general, by the Damage which our *Trade*, *Navigation* and *Woollen Manufacture* may sustain by such *Practices*, as well as by *Monopolies?*

No. 65. Saturday, 30 September 1727.

To CALEB D'ANVERS, *Esq*;

SIR,

I Flatter myself with being admitted one of your Correspondents, in regard to the Character and Memory of my *Father*, as well as the *Subject* I propose to treat of; which has a Right to claim the Countenance and Encouragement of every honest *Briton*.

---

[a] Manufacture] Manufactures *A, B.*   [b] have done] have hitherto done *A, B.*
[c] be)] have been) *A, B, C.*   [d] so-much desired] *A, B, C*; so-much-desired *fol.*
[e] these] *those A, B, C.*   [f] be] become *A, B.*
[g] apprehended] *A, B, C*; aprehended *fol.*

You must know, *Sir*, that I am the second Son of *Sir Andrew Freeport*, who had the Happiness of being one of the *Spectator's* Club, and the Honour to be often mentioned, in those celebrated Writings, in a Manner very much to his Advantage. The good old Man, notwithstanding some Particularities, which are related of him, was above the narrow Views of common Traders, and did not think that *Letters* and *Business* were incompatible: It was also his Opinion, that it was absolutely necessary for young Merchants to visit other Countries, which would give them a better Knowledge of Mankind, as well as of Commerce, and qualify them for any future Undertakings, in which they would otherwise be more liable to Mistakes and Miscarriages. I lived with him between four and five Years, in order to be instructed in *Trade*; and my twentieth Year, I went to *Holland*; from thence to *Lisbon*; and, at my Return, to several Parts of the *British Dominions in America*.

While I was at *Lisbon*, I was entertain'd by *Don Francisco Sayaò*, who was one of the most considerable Merchants of that City, and an old Friend and Correspondent of my Father's.[a] There was nothing of that *Stiffness* and *Reserve* in him, which is so natural to the Generality of the People of that Country, and even to many *Tráders* of other Nations; but an uncommon Frankness, Generosity and Affability flow'd in all his Actions; in short he was a Man of sound Understanding, strict Morals, and every way a *Gentleman* as well as a *Merchant*; I could wish my Pen were able to describe this excellent Man, that you, *Sir*, might recommend him, as an Example for *Mercantile Persons* to follow, which wou'd render them more acceptable, and more useful to the Nation.

From that Gentleman I received many valuable Hints, in relation to *Trade*, and the Conduct of Life; by him I was also made acquainted with the Rise, Progress, and Fall of the *Portugueze Assiento Company*; and though it may not seem pertinent to be acquainted with their *Transactions*, yet some useful Inferences may be drawn from thence, which may give the *Proprietors* of a certain *Great Company* a just Idea of the Ability and Integrity of their *Directors*, who have indeed hitherto avoided those Blots and Mistakes, which precipitated the Fall of the *other*. As the principal, if not the only View of the *Portuguese*, was to *amass great Riches for their Families*, a Detail of their Proceedings, like so many Foiles, will illustrate the Candour, and Virtue of our *British Directors*.

[a] Father's.] *A*, *B*; Father's: *fol.*

My good old Friend has often lamented to me, the *pernicious Consequences* of that Company to his Country, by introducing several *chimerical Schemes*, which in a Manner stopped up the former Channel of *Trade*, from whence flow'd an *uninterrupted* and *beneficial Commerce*.

He told me that the *first Managers*, instead of pursuing the pretended Design of *Trade*, with the Connivance of some *Persons*, who were then *in Power*, formed a *horrid and villainous Plan*, which intirely ruined many *antient* and *worthy Families*, involved their Country in the *utmost Perplexity*, and had like to have overset the *whole Constitution*.

That the *Projectors* and *Executors* of that Plan, who deserved the severest Sentence which the Law prescribes for the most notorious Offenders, were only render'd *incapable* of any Place of Trust, and their *Estates forfeited*, saving such a *Reserve* for their Subsistance, that many of them made a *Figure*, at the time I was at *Lisbon*, equal to the most *eminent Merchants*, who bore the clearest Character.

That *his Country* groan'd under those Afflictions, which were not then worn off; nor was there scarcely a Possibility of eracing the indelible Stains which those Proceedings had fixed upon it.

That their *Successors* in the *Direction* put a better Gloss and Colour on their Conduct, by launching out more considerably into *Trade*, which they flatter'd their *Proprietors* would yield vast Profit; though they must have been conscious that those Adventures cou'd not possibly be to their Advantage.

That this was obvious, as well as their own *sinister Views*, by the Choice they made of *Those*, whom they employed in their Service, who were generally their *Relations* or *Creatures*, without any Regard to *Merit*, or the *Capacity* of the Person.

That the furnishing the *Spaniards* with *Negroes*, on Account of the *Assiento Contract*, was chiefly to cover and carry on their own *private Trade*, the *Vessels* employed in that Service being generally half loaded with their *own Effects*, which cou'd not fail of yielding great Profit, when they were not attended with any *Expences*, which were born[a] by the *Company*.

That these and many other Practices, of the like nature, were demonstrable from the *Insurances* made in *England* and *Holland*, as well as at *Lisbon*, which generally amounted to *as much* in value as the *Company* had on Board the same Vessels; though it was

---

[a] born] borne *A, B.*

29

Notorious that no part of those *Insurances* was[a] for the *Company*'s Account; nor did they ever make any.

That the *Company* being under the Necessity of contracting considerable Debts among the *Spaniards*, and seldom having less than to the value of a *Million* or a *Million* and *half* of Money in their Territories, obliged the *Ministers of State*, who were always in their Interest, to bear with many *Insults* to the Nation, fearing a *seizure* or *reprisal* of those Effects.

That some of the *Colonies*, belonging to *Portugal*, which were equal in value to so many *Mines* to their Mother *Country* by *Trade* as well as by their Annual Produce, were in a manner ruined by that *Company*, which was of no other use, than to enrich the *Managers*, their *Relations* and *Dependants*.

That, for some Years, they made *punctual Dividends*, and amused the World with *great Advantages* to the Nation, as well as to the *Company*, by their Trade; altho' they lost very considerably thereby, those *Dividends* being made out of their *Capital*.

That, by such *fraudulent Practices* as these, they all acquired *vast Estates*, in a few Years, though they were not all let into the *grand Secret*, many of them being little more than *Tools* and *Instruments* only; nor did they blush, when their Conduct came to be disclosed to the World, being, in some measure, supported and borne up by the *Corruption* of the Times, which was so general, that like a Torrent, it over-flow'd the whole Nation, the *Court*, the *Camp*, the *City*, and even the sacred Orders of *Priests* and *Fryars*; nay, they were, at length, so far hardned, and shewed so little shame and remorse at their Conviction, that the *Grand Superintendent* being, one Day, told how freely their *Characters* were treated, even *in Print*, he made no other reply, than that, *he was not inclined to enter into a* PAPER-WAR; well knowing that their Actions would not bear being discuss'd, and that any Disputations, on that Subject, must unavoidably open more and more their *corrupt Practices* to the World.

At length, some *Publick-spirited Men* appeared, who were not to be led, by specious Pretences, or artful insinuations, and demanded a *Scrutiny* into their Books and Papers; which was for some time denied; but being more loudly and strenuously insisted upon, they were compel'd to a Compliance by the *Government:* then, and not till then, their *Chicane* and *Sophistry* manifestly appeared in a true

[a] was] *A, B*; were *fol.*

light to all the World! The *deluded Proprietors* were amazed and confounded, to find great part of their Wealth *imaginary*, and that the *real value* of their Stock, when it was ascertain'd, was not *intrinsically* worth more than 80 per Cent. or thereabouts; which was before daily transfer'd and sold, from 110 to 120; at the Discretion of the *Directors* and their *Friends in Power*, who could, at any time, *raise* or *sink* it as they pleased, according as their *own Interest* and *private Designs* required.

Upon this Discovery, the Resentment of the *Proprietors* would have carried them even farther than they proceeded with the *former Directors*, had not most of them fled to *Spain*, some to *England* and others to *Holland*; Two or Three, who were intercepted and arraigned, made away with themselves, to avoid the ignominious, tho' just Sentence of the Law.

What noble *Reflections* may be drawn from hence, to animate our Countrymen, in a steady pursuit of *Moral* and *Political Virtue*; to warn them of such *fatal Delusions*, as *Portugal* was once under; and to incite them to persevere in encouraging *Men of Probity* and *Lovers of their Country*, that we may never be wanting in such *publick Spirits*, who dare[a] attack their Enemies in any Shape or Disguise, however formidable they may appear to the *mercenary* part of the World!

I design, in a short time, to communicate some other observations, which will more particularly lay open the *unfair* and *corrupt Practices* of the *Portugueze*, in the *Assiento Trade*; and I hope will intirely prevent such *Frauds*, should they ever be attempted *amongst us*.

I am, SIR,

Bedford-Row,   *Your humble Servant,*
Sept. 20th.   CHARLES FREE-PORT.

No. 68.   Saturday, 21 October 1727.

TO CALEB D'ANVERS, Esq;

SIR,

THE Clamour which has been raised against you, by some mercenary Wretches, who will sacrifice every thing to their private

---

[a] who dare] as dare to *A, B*.

Interest, seems to have so little foundation on[a] Reason or Justice, that one would think they could not make any Impression on impartial and disinterested Persons: But, such is the malignancy[b] of the Times, that few can withstand the reigning infection, or have Virtue enough to make use of the necessary means of preventing its spreading still farther.

One of your *Antagonists*, who seems to know something of the matter, and to touch very tenderly and feelingly on the *Queries* relating to the *S.S. Company*, does not pretend to disprove any one Article, but tacitly acknowledges the Facts, and only observes, "That the *publishing* of those *Queries is not calculated to promote the general Good of this Kingdom, it being apparently the Interest of* Great Britain, *that our* Exportations *should be as* large *and* considerable *as it is possible in our Power to make them, without regarding* who *are the* Exporters, *whether the* Company *or* Private Persons." Every true Englishman will readily allow this last assertion, when the Writer has made it appear that our *Exportations* are any ways *encreased*, since the *Company* have enter'd into *Trade*; but however that may be, it is certain, that if any *private Trade* is carried on under the *Company*'s Umbrage,[1] which he artfully evades taking notice of, such Practices are hurtful to the *fair Trader*, and a manifest abuse to the *Company*; for what Merchant can pretend to carry on a Trade, which must necessarily be attended with great Expences, when others, by Permission or Connivance, deal in the same way, at the Expence of the *Company*, and by that[c] means can afford to sell at much *less Prices*, and *engross* the Trade to themselves?

Nor can it be denied, that the *Company*, in such Case, is greatly injured, not only in defraying the *whole Expence* of a Voyage, when *private Persons* are considerably interested, who bear no Part of it, but also in the *Sale* of their Goods; for it cannot be supposed, that a *Thousand Tons* of Merchandize will come to as *good a Market* or Sell for *as much*, in any Country in the World, as 5 or 600.

On the other Hand, it cannot be doubted, that those Persons, who have the management of their Affairs, will dispose of their own Goods and those of their Friends, preferably to the Company's, who must consequently be Sufferers thereby, in having their Goods the *last*, which are exposed to Sale.

I am therefore so far from thinking such hints, as you have given,

---

[a] on] in *A, B*.   [b] malignancy] Malignity *B*.   [c] that] those *B*.

to be either *base* or *wicked*, as a *certain Gentleman* is pleased to call them, that I entirely agree with you, and I believe every honest Man will be of the same Opinion, that amongst a *free* and *virtuous People*, they are *Questions* which *ought to be asked* and *ought to be answered*; but, when a Man throws *Dirt*, tis[a] because he wants *other Weapons*.

Another ingenious Writer observes, "That a *Trade to the Spanish West-Indies, is what no Englishmen have any right to; and that the Foundation of the S.S. Company, was upon an Agreement with the Spaniards, which no British Subject could pretend to be a loser by.*" That the *S.S. Company* are the first Englishmen who ever obtain'd a License from the *King of Spain*, for importing Goods into the *Spanish Ports* in the West-Indies, I agree with him; but I never yet heard that the Trade thither was ever prohibited by the *King of Great Britain*, or that any *Englishman* was punishable, by the *Laws of England*, for trading in any Part of the *Spanish West-Indies*, as many private Merchants continued to do (till the Establishment of this *Company*) with great Profit to themselves and at least equal advantage to the Nation.

Whatever right the *Company* may have by *Stipulation*, sure I am, that none of their Servants, of any rank or denomination, have any; much less ought they to carry it on under the *Company*'s *Umbrage* or *Expence*; for such Practices would not only be a *Breach of Trust* in them, but a violation of the *Contract*, it being expresly declared, that the *Annual Ship* is granted in consideration of the loss which former *Assientists* of other Nations have sustained, and that the *Company* shall not, *directly* or *indirectly*, carry on any *clandestine Trade* under any pretence whatever.

But what does this Writer mean, by saying, that the foundation of the *S.S. Company* was upon an agreement with the *Spaniard*, which no *British* Subject could pretend to be a *loser by?* He is the only Man who is not of Opinion, that if an Account was fairly stated and balanced, neither the *Nation* nor the *Company* would appear to have been any *Gainers* by it; but on the contrary very great *Losers*. The Liberty which was allowed us, of sending a Ship of 500 Tons yearly to the *Spanish West-Indies*, was never thought, by any Persons, who understand the *Trade*, or considered the *Country* where they were to be sent to, and the nature of the *People* they were to deal with, to be any advantage to the *Company*, but on the contrary, a certain loss to them, and yet, it is remarkable, that this liberty was granted them

[a] tis] it is *B*.

in consideration that the furnishing the *Spaniards* with *Negroes*, would be a *loss* to the *Company*, as it had been to former *Assientists*.

As to his Argument that the *S.S. Company* is not a *Monopoly*, because *no other Englishmen have a Right* to trade to the *Spanish West-Indies*, it is so ridiculous that it hardly deserves any Answer; for his assertion that *no other Englishmen have a Right*, &c. is so far from proving it *no Monopoly*, that it directly proves the contrary; a *Monopoly* being (as he defines it himself) when any *one Man* or *Body of Men* ENGROSSES to himself or themselves any *Art, Mystery* or *Branch of Trade*; and therefore all *Trading Companies*, which have a Power to *exclude others*, are *Monopolies*. Had you said, indeed, that the *S.S. Company* was an illegal *Monopoly*, his Argument would have been something to the purpose; but certainly it is not the less a *Monopoly*, because *that Company* have a *Right* to exercise it, *exclusive* of all other *Englishmen*.

I am, Sir,

Your humble Servant,

R. FREEMAN.

No. 71. Saturday, 11 November 1727.

TO CALEB D'ANVERS, Esq;

SIR,

EXperience (the best Instructor of human Life) hath shewn, that the mighty *Project* of the *S.S. Company* is so far from answering the wise Designs of Parliament, or being carried on according to the *original Plan*, that it hath manifestly been perverted to very different purposes; from whence have flowed numberless Evils to the *Proprietors of the Stock*, as well as to the *Nation*: Yet, for this, *Arts* and *Sciences* seem to have been discouraged; *Trade* and *Navigation* neglected; and consequently, the *Exports* of our *Manufactures* are greatly diminished; and what have we got substituted in their room? *Stock Jobbing* (the bane of *Trade*, and the fatal Rock, on which our happy Constitution had like to have been lost) together with *Chimerical Schemes*, calculated only to cover and promote, as hath sufficiently appeared, the *sinister*[a] *Designs* of a set of Men, who, like

---

[a] *sinister*] selfish *B*.

Cankers, preyed on the Vitals of their Country, till they had reduced it to the lowest and most declining Condition.

But, to set this matter in a true light, I shall consider it as fully and freely, as the narrow confines[a] of a Letter will allow, and trace it through all its Mazes, with all the[b] Temper and Seriousness, which[c] so important a subject requires.

When the[d] *Plan* was first projected, most of us may remember, what great advantages were promised to the Nation, by opening a new Scene of *Trade*, more extensive and beneficial, than any which we were then acquainted with; this was not only industriously spread among the People, in the *usual manner*, when any point is to be propagated; but the very Preamble of the *Act*, for *Incorporating the S.S. Company* sets forth, "That whereas it is of the greatest consequence to the *honour* and *welfare* of this Kingdom, and for the encrease of the *Strength* and *Riches* thereof, and for vending the *Product* and *Manufactures*, *Goods* and *Merchandize* of, or brought into this Kingdom, and *employment of the Poor*, that a *Trade* should be carried into the SOUTH SEAS, &c."

One would have thought that, after these pompous Declarations, some attempts[e] should have been made to accomplish so great and laudable a Design; but so far from it, that soon after, and without the least *Tryal*, they gave up their Pretensions of trading to the *South Seas* or, in any other manner, than is stipulated by the *Assiento Contract*. Thus, by accepting of the *Assiento*, they have excluded themselves from trading to the *South Seas*; and by the *Act* for incorporating the *S.S. Company*, all the rest of the Subjects of *Great Britain* are forbid trading within their Limits; this is the more remarkable, since neither the *Dutch* nor *French*, nor any other Nation have restrained their Subjects from trading to *those Parts*; nor have they neglected to carry on a Trade thither, with great Profit to *themselves*; whilst those of *Great Britain* only are denied that Liberty.

Had the *S.S. Company* put their *original Plan* in Execution, it would, indeed, have been a Benefit to the Kingdom, if not to the *Proprietors* of the *Stock*, by the Encrease of our *Exports* and *Navigation*; but the sending of[f] an *Annual Ship* into *New Spain*, though a new Method of Trade, yet hath it been[g] said to be so far

[a] confines] Compass *B*.   [b] all the] such *B*.   [c] which] as *B*.
[d] the] that *B*.   [e] attempts] Attempt *A, B*.   [f] sending of] sending *B*.
[g] hath it been] it is *A*, is *B*.

from being a Benefit, in point of *Trade*, that it has certainly *lessen'd* our *Exports*, and consequently the *Trade* of this Kingdom, on a general Ballance with the *Spanish Nation. Cadiz, Sevill, Port St. Mary*'s &c. were formerly the Marts for the *Manufactures*, and the Places where the Merchants, trading to the *Indies*, informed themselves what Species, and Quantities of Goods were shipped off from time to time; but since the sending of the *Annual Ships*, they are under such *uncertainties*, that they have declined dealing in our *Manufactures*, as they formerly did, and chosen rather to lay out their Money in such Commodities, as were imported from *France, Holland, Flanders* and *Hamburgh*.

The great Sums of Money, imported in one of those *Annual Ships*, makes such a Noise, that People in general imagine considerable advantages must arise from thence to the *Nation*, as well as to the *Company*, not knowing or considering the vast *Expences* they are at, nor what *great sums* were brought in, formerly, by the *private Merchants*, (who employed treble the Number of Ships and Seamen) without raising the Envy and Jealousy of our *Neighbours*, upon *imaginary Acquisitions* in *Trade*.

Thus we find, that the manner of the *South Sea Company*'s exercising their Trade is so far from being a Benefit to the Nation, in case this be[a] a *true State*, by an encrease of our *Exports* and *Navigation*, that it has manifestly lessen'd them, and has only turned *Trade* out of its *former Channel*, which was very beneficial to great numbers of *Merchants* and *Tradesmen*, as well as to the *Nation*.

If the *Annual Ship*, all things considered, be of no advantage to *Great Britain*, the *Company*'s Trade, in general, must certainly be a Damage to it, and a very considerable loss to the *Proprietors*. This is not my Opinion only, but the sense of most People, who understand *Trade* and indeed a natural consequence; for the *Assiento* was allowed, even by the *Spaniards*, to be a *losing Contract*, and it was on that express Consideration, that the *King* of *Spain* granted the *S.S. Company* the Liberty of sending an *Annual Ship*, of 500 Tons, to the *West Indies*.[b] Now if *one* be a *certain loss*, the[c] *other* of *no advantage*, at least not an *Equivalent*, or *preferable* to the Trade which we had before, they are nothing more than *Amusements*, and

---

[a] be] is *B*.   [b] *Indies.*] *A, B; Indies: fol.*
[c] *one . . . the*] the one *. . .* and the *A, B*.

ought to be thrown up, as tending to the prejudice of the *Proprietors* and the *Nation in general.*

We ought also to consider the damage, which accrues to the *British Colonies* in *America*, by being scantily furnished with *Negroes*, without which they cannot be improved, or supported; especially, since they are likewise obliged to pay *higher Rates* for them, than they did formerly; the *S.S. Company*, by sending Ships to *Guinea*, having so far advanced the price of *Negroes*, that no *private Merchant* can pretend to trade thither, while *They* carry it on; and of course the *Plantations* must in a little time be entirely dependant on *Them*; which will encrease the *Discouragements* they are already under and, supposing these Facts to be true, inevitably compleat their Destruction. I appeal to the *Merchants*, trading to *Guinea* and the *West Indies*, for a Confirmation of what I have asserted, and whether they have not, for some Years past, and by means of *that Company*, paid *double* the Price for *Negroes*, which they used to do, on the Coast of *Guinea*; and that this was done with a Design to beat them out of the *Trade*, and to *Engross* it to themselves, is evident, not only from the Behaviour of *Those*, whom they employ'd, but by sending *double the Cargoes*, which the *private Merchants* did for the same Number of *Negroes*.

The Judicious Mr. *Lock* observes, that, "When *Trade* is once lost, it will be too late, by a mis-tim'd Care, easily to retrieve it again; for the Currents of *Trade*, like those of Waters, make themselves *Channels*, out of which they are afterwards as hard to be *diverted*, as Rivers that have worn themselves deep within their Banks."[1]

It therefore deserves the Notice and Consideration of our *Representatives* in *Parliament*, what *advantages* or *disadvantages* have accrued to the Nation, by the *S.S. Company*'s acceptance of the *Assiento*, and the *Trade* they have carried on, by virtue of it; as well as it does of the *Proprietors of the Stock*, what footing they are upon; lest they should be plunged into *new Difficulties*, before they are entirely extricated out of those *Dilemmas*,[a] which they were so lately under; and it certainly becomes every one of us, to take the same Care, that our Ancestors did, to preserve *Trade*, by discouraging, as much as is in our Power, any one Branch of it continuing under a *Monopoly*. It is *freedom* of *Trade*, which is the Spring of Riches, and the Animal Spirits of any Nation; and as we

---

[a] those *Dilemmas*,] those, *A, B.*

have happily experienced this undoubted Truth, by the Figure which we have seen our Country make in the World, so we may be assured, while we pursue contrary Measures, that we shall decline in *Strength* and *Power*, the natural Consequences of *Riches*. It was *Trade* that enabled us to spend so many *Millions* in defence of our *Rights* and *Liberties*; and therefore, while we are desirous of preserving those inestimable Blessings, we cannot be too vigilant nor tender of it.

How much *publick Credit* is affected by *Monopolies* of this Nature, and how far even our *Liberties* may be, some time or other, endangered by them, if they should be tolerated or encouraged, shall be the Subject of another Letter, whenever you will please to give it a Place in your *Journal*.

I am, SIR,

Bedford Row   *Your humble Servant,*
Nov. 6. 1727   CHARLES FREEPORT.

No. 91.   Saturday, 30 March 1728.

To CALEB D'ANVERS, *Esq;*

GARRAWAY'S Coffee-House.[1]

SIR,

AS you profess a great regard for the publick Welfare and the Interest of *Trade*, I cannot help reminding you of a pretty remarkable Fact mentioned lately in one of the Daily Papers, relating to a gross and infamous *Fraud* in a *Custom-house Officer*, who put some *Prohibited Goods* aboard Ship homeward bound, with a Design to make a *Discovery* and intitle Himself to a forfeiture of the *Ship* and *Cargo*. I find this Fact has alarmed a great many considerable Merchants, and put them upon enquiring how the *Law* stands in this Case; whether an Importation, by any Trader, of *Goods prohibited*, without the Knowledge of the *Owner* of the Ship, shall forfeit the Ship and Cargo; or, in other Words, whether the Fault, or Offence of one Man, in no wise dependant on another, shall affect him, tho' innocent, and bring him to Ruin and Poverty. This, upon the stating, seems a strange Proposition, and contrary to the first Principles of *Natural Justice*. But I am informed that this

Construction may be made upon the Letter of the *Navigation Act.* You will excuse me if I trouble you with a Recital of the *fourth Section* of this Act, on which it is said the Officer would have founded his Pretensions.

No Goods or Commodities, that are of Foreign *Growth, Production or Manufacture and which are to be brought into* England, Ireland, Wales, *&c. shall be shipp'd or brought from any other Places or Countries, but only those of the said Growth,*[a] *Production, or Manufacture, or from those Parts, where the said Goods and Commodities can only, or are, or usually have been first shipp'd for Transportation, and from no other Places or Countries, under the Penalty of the forfeiture of all such the aforesaid Goods, as shall be imported from any other Place or Country* (contrary to the true intent and meaning thereof) *as also of the Ship in which they were imported, with all her Guns, Tackle, &c. a Moiety to the King, and the other Moiety to the Seizer or Informer.*

The Words in this Clause, *no Goods shall be imported but from the Place of their Growth, under the forfeiture of them, as also of the Ship,* at first sight seem to be very strong, and by a rigid Construction may be carried, not only to the *whole Cargo,* but to any *minute Parcels,* imported and may relate not only to the *Owner,* or *Principal Freighter,* but to *any Person* whatsoever, who shall bring such Goods into the Kingdom, let him be *Passenger* or *Sailor,* in whose power it may be to make a Forfeiture; for the bringing of Goods into the Kingdom, by way of [b] Merchandize, is in general an *Importation* in Law. The Gentlemen of that Profession best know the legal Construction of an Act of Parliament; but, under favour to better judgments, such a Construction must entirely destroy all *Trade*; for what Merchant, with common Prudence or safety, could trade, where no *Care, Caution,* or *Integrity* of his own could prevent Frauds in *other Men* that would be fatal to him? If there are *several Freighters,* each may bring in something *prohibited.* If *They* don't, the *Captain* may. If he should not, yet his *Sailors* may; either thro' the Hopes of a little Profit; or, which is perhaps more probable, from not knowing *what* is prohibited, there being so many things prohibited, that it is difficult even for the most sensible and experienced Merchants to distinguish what may, and what may not be imported. But supposing a Merchant may escape from all these,

---

[a] *Growth,*] *B; Growth fol.*   [b] way of] *B;* way *fol.*

what Security and Defence has he against *Design* and *Fraud*, and where this Fraud may be so easily practised, and be so well rewarded; the *Informer*, according to this strict Interpretation, being intitled to the *Moiety of the Ship* and *Goods*. And I must observe that the more valuable the Cargo, and the better the Ship, the greater would be the danger; tho' the Publick are under the greatest Obligations to Gentlemen, who deal largely, and who risque their Fortunes in *Trade*.

The *Act of Navigation* was made merely for the Interest and Advancement of *Trade*, to make us a great and flourishing People. It has hitherto had a very good Effect; but if the *Importation of Goods prohibited* (though such Importation be *impossible* to be prevented, and though the *Quantity* of such Goods be never so *small*) shall be construed to give a *forfeiture of the Ship*, &c. such a Construction must destroy all *Trade*, and make an Act designed for the benefit of Commerce destructive of it.

The first Point in this Act relates to the *Owners* of Shipping, that Ships, which trade *Hither* or to the *Colonies*, shall be *English*, and be duly Navigated; otherwise they are to be forfeited. This is but reasonable; because the whole is in the Knowledge and Power of the *Owner* of the Ship; he can tell whether his Ship be *English*, and take care that it be duly navigated.

The other Point relates to the *Cargoes* and *Effects* with which these Ships are laded by the *Owners*; for the *Owners* are the proper and immediate Subjects of *this Provision* as they are of the *former*, they having the Interest, and being the Persons principally concern'd in *Trade*, especially *at the Time* when this Act was made: Tho' of late Years Merchants have built Ships, and put them up for *Free Traders* to take Freight where they can get it. This Clause, with this Construction, is likewise very reasonable, to compel the *Owners* of Ships to bring Home immediately, and at the first hand, the Product of each respective Country. Where the whole Cargo is the Merchant's, to whom the Ship belongs, it must be supposed that he can judge what is or is not within the Prohibition; 'tis[a] all his *own Act*; and he must answer for the Consequences[b] of his Rashness or Ignorance, if he breaks the Law. But where the Act is *not his own*, there the Reason of the Law ceases, and one would think there should not and could not be a Forfeiture of an *innocent Man's*

---

[a] 'tis] It is *B*   [b] Consequences] Consequence *B*.

Interest. The *Goods* indeed prohibited shall be forfeited; but not the *Ship*, unless the *Ship* and *Cargo* belong to the *same Person*. This Distinction reconciles all, and makes the Act reasonable, regular, and consistent. For can it be supposed, when the Act says, *No Goods shall be imported but from the Place of their Growth*, &c. *under the Forfeiture of the Goods, as also of the Ship*, that this general Proposition has no Limitations? None in Favour of *Trade*, and an *innocent Merchant?* can it be thought to mean that the Ship shall be forfeited for a Trifle of *Contreband Goods* put aboard *without the Owner's Consent* or *Privity?* Is it not strongly implied, that the Goods imported, to make a Forfeiture of the Ship, must be a *voluntary* Act in him, who is to forfeit his Interest? or rather, Does it not seem to imply, that the *Ship* and *all the Cargo* are entirely under the Influence, Power, and Direction of the *Owner?* Can the Act be supposed to mean (I speak with great Deference, not being versed in the Principles and Resolutions of the Law) that an *Importation*, however made, by whomsoever, and let the Quantity imported be never so *trifling* and *insignificant*, that this shall create a Forfeiture of a Ship of *great Value*, and leave the *Owner* to take his Remedy against the *Offender*, who occasioned this Damage? Shall a *Common Sailor*, (in Confederacy, perhaps, with an *Officer*, who will be entitled to a *Moiety*) subject Men to the Loss of 20 or 30,000 *l.* and they[a] have no other Method of *Reparation*, but to sue and recover their Damage against this *Sailor?* Is this a Satisfaction, an adequate, reasonable and legal Satisfaction? 'Tis indeed a *Nominal Remedy*; but not the least real service and advantage to the injured Party. I have heard it laid down as a Rule by some Gentlemen of the *long Robe*, that all Penal Laws are to be construed *strictly*, and that Laws that[b] favour *Trade*, shall be *liberally* construed. Why should this forfeiture be extended farther than the *Goods Prohibited?* As they made the Offence, they should make reparation for that Offence. The forfeiture of them is given in the first Place, as the Act directs, for being imported *contrary to the true Intent and Meaning* of it; then follows the forfeiture of the *Ship*, if the *Owner* be guilty of acting contrary to the *intent* of this Law; for I must contend that he ought to be punished only upon a supposition that the Offence was committed by *Him*, either *actually*, by an importation of such Goods; or *virtually*, by a Permission and Connivance. If the *Owner*

---

[a] they] the *Owner B.*   [b] that] which *B.*

of the Ship be either way guilty, let him suffer the utmost Extremity and Rigour of the Law; but don't let him suffer for what he cannot help, and where he may be so easily undone and ruined. But if this were not the natural and true Meaning of these Words, as they seem plainly to me to be, yet I am informed that we have an old Law in *Edward* the *Third's* time, which is founded on the Nature and Reason of *Trade*, and expresly determines this Point as to Goods, that have *not paid*, tho' it does not extend literally to *Goods Prohibited*.

The Words are, as I find them among the old Statutes, *Whereas the* Ships *of diverse People of the Realm be* arrested *and* holden forfeit *because of a* little thing *put in their Ship* not custom'd; *whereof the* Owners *of the same Ships be* ignorant; *It is Accorded and Assented, that no* Owner *shall lose his Ship for such a* small Thing *put within the* Ship not custom'd, *without his* Knowledge.

This, I take it, is only a Declaration of one of the Principles of *Natural* Equity, and Part of the *Law-Merchant* between the Prince and the Subject, and is indeed no more than is and must be necessarily implied in all general Laws relating to *Trade*. 'Tis the Foundation of *Commerce*; 'tis[a] the Faith we pledge to *Foreigners*, who deal with us, and our own Security to have that full Benefit and Extent in TRADE, *on which all our Wealth and Grandeur entirely depend.*

I am, Yours,
A. B.

To CALEB D'ANVERS *Esq*;
SIR,

I Have, with a good deal of Attention, read a Piece just published, intitled, *A* Defence *of the* Observations *on the* Assiento Trade, *as it hath been exercised by the* S.S. Company, *&c.* wherein I expected that the Author would have taken more notice, than he has done, of the severe *Reflection*, which his Antagonist has thrown on all his *Brother Factors* and *Agents* abroad, his *Partner* only excepted. But since he has not been so full on that head, as I could wish, I must entreat you to give this a Place in your Journal, in Vindication of *those Gentlemen*; several of whom I know to be honest men and I believe have served the Company with great Fidelity.

[a] 'Tis . . . 'tis] It is . . . it is *B.*

The *Factor*, as he calls himself, (to shew how much he exceeds all others, who are employed by the *Company*, and to raise a Monument of Praise and Grandeur to his *beloved Self*) thrusts in Mr. *Pratter*, as a Man of Fortune, and says that *there lives not an honester Man, nor a more faithful Servant*. Whether Mr. *P.* will thank him for making Use of his Name, I am not able to determine; especially when he considers that this Author's principal Intention therein, is to magnify his own Name and Character. For we find, by his Account, that Mr. *P.* always *concurred* with him in Opinion. *Ergo*, If there lives not an *abler Servant* than Mr. *P.* how happy are the *Company* in the Man, who pretends to be his *Director*.

The *Factor*, it seems, could not raise himself but on the Ruin of his *Brethren*, whom he insinuates to be *faithless* and *unskilful* People; for in *Page* 63 he says, *If the* Company *had all such Servants as Mr.* Pratter, *he would take upon him to say, that the* Negroe Trade *alone would be a* profitable *one to the* Company *as well as to the Nation:* perhaps he may reply, that he has not expresly excluded all the rest of the Factors; true; but that Non-Exclusion might certainly have been supplyed by mentioning several more honest Men amongst them.

But, if the Trade would be *more beneficial*, with all such faithful and able Men as Mr. *P———r*,[a] and it is now acknowledged to be the Reverse; then it must be owing to the Want of Fidelity or Unskilfulness of the *Factors*; at least of the Majority of them. If he thus arraigns all the *Factors*, to shew that if they were all his *Homagers*, like Mr. *P.* they might be *honest Fellows*, and he has only them to account with; yet, if there be Truth in this Assertion, and the Contract is a *National* Contract, as he insinuates, then this Writer is not only the *Company's* but the *Nation's* Servant, and it would have discovered Sentiments of *Fidelity* in him, to have shewn by what Means the *Nation*, as well as the *Company*, have been such great *Losers*. But perhaps he has given this *Hint*, in order to have such foul Practices detected; and therefore it is to be hoped that a *seasonable Enquiry* will be made into such *Mismanagement*, and *Corruption*, as are pointed at by *this Author*.

I am, Your constant Reader,
And humble Servant,
R. FRIENDLY.

[a] *P———r*] *Pratter B.*

No. 93. Saturday, 13 April 1728.

To CALEB D'ANVERS, *Esq*;

BATSON's Coffee-house.
SIR,

THE Letter you were pleased to oblige the World with last Saturday, upon the *Navigation Act*, has given us great satisfaction; and if the Law be *doubtful* in that Point, it is probable that the Legislature will *declare and fix the Sense of it*, that an *Innocent, Honest Merchant* may not be ruined by Frauds impossible to be prevented by him. If prohibited Goods put aboard a Ship, without the *Owner's* [a] *Knowledge*, shall be construed to make a forfeiture of the Ship, and if the *Owner* can have no other Remedy but suing the Person, who brought them aboard, what Merchant will ever be concerned in Shipping? Where then will be your Sailors? And what will become *of your Navy, the present Terror of the World?*

If therefore the Law be *doubtful*, the Legislature, in so important a Point, will certainly *declare* the meaning of the Act, and prevent Merchants from being *harrassed* with *Prosecutions*. I am afraid that the Fraud, complained of, as lately practised by a *Custom-House Officer*, is a *growing Evil*, and that the Precedent is catching; for[b] I have heard it exceedingly well attested, that when a Ship, but the other Day, was just ready to sail from *Holland*, four Packs of brown Paper were sent aboard; but by some Accident, and great good fortune to the Owner of the Ship, the Strings of one of the Packs broke, and out dropt a Canister full of *Tea*. If this Discovery had not been made, the Ship, in all probability, had been seized and prosecuted for a forfeiture, *Tea* being prohibited to be imported from *Holland*. At this rate no Merchant, whose Fortune and Estate lies in Shipping, can pretend to take in Goods.[c] Frauds cannot be prevented; for an *India Handkerchief*, or an Ounce of *Tea* from *Holland* or any part of *Europe* will make a forfeiture. The Merchant, upon this Account, *at the best*, is liable to be *prosecuted*, and so put in fear and made *dependant*, by which means *Trade* is fetter'd, which ought, by all possible Methods, to be encouraged.

I am yours, C. D.

[a] *Owner's*] *B*; *Owners fol.*   [b] catching; for] *B*; catching For *fol.*
[c] Goods.] *B*; Goods; *fol.*

No. 96. Saturday, 4 May 1728.

To CALEB D'ANVERS, *Esq*;

SIR,

'IT is confessedly allowed by the *Factor* to the *S.S. Company*, (as one of your late Correspondents* has made appear by his own Words) that a very considerable *Contraband Trade* has been carried on in the *Company's Vessels. Contraband* it must be; because it is expresly stipulated in the *Contract*, that *no other Trade* shall be carried on in the *Assiento Vessels*, than for *Negroes*; whereas the *Factor* has not scrupled owning that their *Agents* at *Jamaica* have dealt in *European dry Goods*, and even seem to glory in it.

This is a Circumstance which the *D------rs* cannot pretend to be ignorant of, since they have in a publick Manner returned him *Thanks* for that Piece, which it cannot be supposed they would have done without *reading* it. How then will they reconcile their Conduct with that of their *Predecessors*, who, in 1714, suspended *one* of their *Members*, and render'd him incapable of ever serving the *Company*, only for *attempting* a thing of that Kind? for it did not appear upon the *Examination* of Capt. *Johnson*, before the House of Lords, that *That Gentleman* ever spoke to him on any such Affair; but, that Mr. *Da Costa*, who treated with him, intimated that the said Director was in the *Secret*:[1] Whereas there has not been the least Enquiry into the *Frauds* pointed at by this *Author*, by any Information I have been able to get; nay, so far from it, that the *very* Person *who blabbed out this Story* (and who must be supposed to be concerned, since he says he was *One* of the *Company's Agents*) is not only *applauded* by them, but has all the *Favours* and *Honours* they can bestow upon him. Undoubtedly he is qualified to represent them at *Sois---s*;[a] since he is thought to be well acquainted with all their *Transactions*.[2]

I have only a few *specious* Objections to remove, in order to set this Matter in a GLARING LIGHT; and then I shall leave it to the Inspection and Consideration of the *Proprietors* of the *Company* and *many Thousands* of other People, who are *manifestly injured*.

    1. It is said, that, *if any such Trade has been carried on, it is no detriment to the* Company.

---

    [a] *Sois---s;*] *Soissons*; B.

This is certainly a *fallacious* Way of arguing; especially if it be not made appear, that the *Company* have received *some Benefit* by it; because they are at the *sole Charge* of *Shipping, Wages,* &c. and it cannot be supposed but that, as Goods take up Room, so every Vessel must carry a proportionably[a] less Number of *Negroes.*

But this is not all: The *Company* are undoubtedly prejudiced in the *Sale* of their Cargo, which is imported in their *Annual Ship,* by the Market's being stocked with Goods. The *Spaniards* in general, who have not a fellow-feeling, are uneasy at this Trade; *Schedulas* are delay'd from Time to Time; *Rigoldos*[†] must be made, and they[b] *considerably more* than are customarily given: And if this be the Case, is not the *Company* notoriously injured? What Compensation can be made them for the *Detainment* and *Delays* of their Vessels; by which their *Charges* must be *encreased,* and their Goods receive considerable Damage, not to place *Seizures* and *other Losses* to those Accounts? And, after all, *who* receives the Benefit? why, a few *private Persons*; and, is the *Interest* of the *Company,* or the *Nation* to be thus exposed for any *private, unjust Gain* whatever?

2. It is said, That *it is a Service to the* Nation, *if not to the* Company.

This indeed must have been allowed, if the Trade with the *Spaniards* was entirely new, or that the *Exports* of our *Manufactures,* and the *Importation* of *Bullion* were in any wise encreased by it. But this is so far from being the Case, that it might be made appear that the Chanels which that Branch of our *Commerce* was formerly in, were considerably *more beneficial* in all respects; especially since it was carried on (as formerly observed[‡]) *without raising the* Envy *and* Jealousy *of our* Neighbours *upon* imaginary Acquisitions *in Trade.*

But, if the *Seizure* of the Ship *Prince Frederick,* and the Misunderstandings between the Courts of *Great Britain* and *Spain* (which had like to have set all *Europe* in a flame, and which are not yet perfectly reconciled) were in any degree owing to such *Contraband Trade* as the *Spaniards* alledge; what Atonement can the Persons concerned ever make to the *Company,* or to the *Nation?* When will full Restitution and Satisfaction be obtained for the *Seizures* which were made of the *Company*'s Effects in 1719, and 1726? What Trade can bear such *vast Losses* and *Disappointments* as

---

[a] proportionably] proportionable *B.* [b] they] Those *B.*

they have met with? Is it not high Time to promote an *Enquiry* into all such Measures as have proved injurious to them, or to the Nation? Will it be prudent in the *Company* to put it in the Power of the *Spaniards*, or any other Set of Men to treat them in the same Manner? Are they not hourly at the Mercy of the former, and liable to innumerable *Frauds* and *Corruptions* in[a] the other? In fine, can they reasonably hope for Success in *Trade*, or any *better Management* than they have hitherto met with, unless some prudent *Regulations* be speedily made?[b]

MEMENTO 1720, the *Royal George, Prince Frederick,* Cum multis aliis,

I am, SIR, *Your humble Servant,*

CHARLES FREEPORT.

---

* *Vide* the *Craftsman*, Numb.[c] 93.

† *Presents,*[d] alias ------*Q*.[e] *to* whose Account are they placed?

‡ *Vide* the[f] *Craftsman*, Numb.[g] 71.

No. 105. Saturday, 6 July 1728.

To CALEB D'ANVERS, *Esq*;

SIR,

YOU have already shewn an honourable Zeal for the Good of your Country in examining into the *State of the publick Debts*, which is certainly as necessary in order to *lessen* them, as it is for *private Persons* to use a good Oeconomy by looking into their *Accounts* and *Expences*. Riches and Power are always inseperable, and the Histories of States and Kingdoms inform us, that as their *Revenues* have been *lessen'd* or their *Debts increas'd*, their Power has been so much diminish'd that they could not make a considerable Figure in the World; nay sometimes not have been able to defend themselves from Ruin. The *same Causes* will always produce the *same Effects*.

These Considerations induce me to think that it will be of Service to inform you of a Pamphlet lately publish'd, entituled, *The Report of the Commissioners sent into* SPAIN, *relating to* GIBRALTAR, *and some other Places, never publish'd before, with authentick Vouchers*

---

a in] of *B.*   b made?] *B*; made. *fol.*   c Numb.] Nº *B.*
d *Presents,*] *B*; *Presents fol.*   e *Q.*] *B*; *Q fol.*   f the] *B*; and *fol.*
g Numb.] Nº *B.*

produc'd by the said Commissioners to prove that there had been great Discouragements to Trade, *many extravagant and unnecessary* Expences, *and great* Misapplications *of the publick Money in the said Places, and consequently that some* Debts *of the Nation have been* increas'd *thereby, or at least have not been* lessen'd so much *as they might have been, which may be of Service to the* present *Times.*

If the *Vouchers*, referr'd to by this Pamphlet, were never publish'd before, nor ever taken notice of publickly, (the Reason of which appears by the said Pamphlet) and if *those Vouchers are authentick*, and do answer[a] the *Title*, as they will effectually do upon Examination, it is of no small Importance to *Great Britain*, to prevent the *Abuses* and *extravagant Expences*, that have been formerly complain'd of in the said Places, in order to make them more useful and profitable to the Nation.

It may be justly suspected when no Notice is taken of *Abuses* complain'd of, that they wou'd[b] continue; but if any Regard is to be had to *publick Fame*, or to some *public Prints*, mentioned in the Preface to the aforesaid Pamphlet, some of the *Abuses* specified in the Report have continued. It has appeared from time to time, that those Places were not *Free Ports*, (at least, *not so free as they ought to have been*) that great sums of the *publick Money* have been put into *private Pockets*; and if[c] it be true, what is said, that a *Dollar* is paid generally, if not always, at *five Shillings per Dollar or more*; and if it has been paid at the same Rate at *Port Mahon*, which is 8 *d.* or 9 *d.* more than the Value of a *Dollar*, this will appear, by the Report of the Commissioners sent into *Spain* from *Lisbon*, No. 12. to be one of the same great *Abuses* complain'd of by them, *viz.* that there had been a Profit made of 15 *per Cent or more* during the whole Course of the War in *Spain*, from March 1704 to March 1713, by computing the Value of the Coin received at a Medium all that time, which ought to have been accounted for to the *Publick*. This *Profit*, which was made, was a vast Loss to the Service of the War, and a great Increase of the *Expence* of the Garrisons. Some of the Abuses at *Gibraltar* had been formerly complain'd of by the *Engineer* there, but without Redress, which occasioned the Expression in one of the *Vouchers, that it seem'd as if the place was then under no Body's Care.* It is hop'd that the *present Ministry*, by their Care and Zeal for the publick Good, will use the greatest *Frugality* and *good Management*

---

[a] do answer] answer *B.*   [b] wou'd] will *B.*   [c] *Pockets*; and if] *Pockets*. If *B.*

in preserving Places of such Importance to *Great Britain*, which by their happy Situation (especially that of *Gibraltar*) might not only be of great Advantage and Profit to *our Trade*, but might give *Laws* to great part of the Trade of *Europe*.

I am, Sir, &c.

No. 111.   Saturday, 17 August 1728.

—Fixit Leges pretio *atque refixit.*   VIRGIL.[1]

To CALEB D'ANVERS, *Esq*;

MONTGOMERY.

SIR,

A Late Transaction in the House of *Commons*, concerning the Right of Election for *this Borough* has caused no small Contention here among the Burgesses, and some of them have even taken the Liberty to complain of the *just* and *most righteous* Determination of that Affair.[2]

I[a] have done as much as lies in my Power to discountenance and extinguish such unreasonable Apprehensions; but finding their Resentments rather encrease than abate by *Argument*, I should be glad to have the whole Affair put in a just[b] Light, which would effectually expose all their groundless Cavils, and justify the Proceedings of that august Assembly.

For my Part, as I live entirely in the Country, at so great a Distance from *London*, and did not attend the Examination of our Case in the House, I will not pretend to give any Account of it; but leave it to others more particularly concerned. In the mean time, I will beg leave to trouble you with some general Observations on so important a Subject.

The *Privileges* and *Authority* of that House, (which is no less than the Legislative Power of *all the Commons of* England) is so considerable to every Member of the Community, that the least *Infringement* of them is a common Concern to all.

There have been Times indeed of less Virtue and Integrity than the present, when the *Freedom* or *Independence* of the Members

---

[a] *No new paragraph B.*   [b] just] true *B.*

49

(which is the essential Constitution of that House) has been fatally attempted; but we have this peculiar Happiness, that we can never expect to see it injured or impaired by any Power or Artifice of *evil Ministers*, unless we ourselves should either concur in or connive at them. The *evil Minister* may be the *Tempter*, but the Contagion must become *epidemical*, and the *Corruption universal*, before his Wiles can effectually operate.

There is mention made, by my Lord *Coke*, of a Person, who for 4 *l.* given to the *Mayor*, procured himself to be *returned* a Member of that House, contrary to the *Suffrages of the Burgesses*; but the Patriots of those Times so much resented that dangerous Practice, that the House thought fit to send the *Mayor* close Prisoner to the *Tower*, and *expelled* the Member with great Indignation; a glorious Example to *future Parliaments*, and which we have seen pursued in so many *modern Instances*, no doubt with the same *Justice*, as well as the same Zeal and Regard for the *Constitution of Parliaments!*

A *County* or *Borough* thus represented, *without their own Consent in a free Election*, cannot be properly said to be *represented at all*, and is thereby excluded its Right in the Legislative OEconomy; so that in respect to *other Parts* of the Nation, it may be said to be in a State of *Slavery*, inasmuch as it has no Share in the *Government*, but is absolutely under the Dominion of *others*; for what is *Slavery* but to be *violently* or *fraudulently* divested of that Share of Power to which a Man is legally entitled; or, which is the same thing, to be *subject to the absolute Power of another?*

Could we suppose, that, at the time mentioned by my Lord *Coke*, there had been a *Majority of such Persons* return'd to Parliament, by the general Corruption of the *Returning Officers*, there can be no doubt that whoever had apply'd for Redress to it would have met with the greatest Discouragement, and *such Members*, by countenancing one another, would have established their Seats there; and then, where would have been the *Commons of England?*—it is plain they could not have been presumed to be duly represented by such an *usurped Authority*.

A *Corruption*, of this Nature, would not have ended there; I mean in merely establishing themselves; for if they had any *Views* of their own to carry on, they would have had it likewise in their Power (being now, by their *Majority*, become sole Judges *of Elections*) to remove any *Person*, who They might imagine would oppose their *destructive Scheme* and introduce *others*, who they knew would cooperate with them. Indeed many wholesome Laws have been since made to support the *Freedom of Elections*, and a constant Adherence to them gives us no Prospect of such a Violation of our Constitution.

And yet such a *general Corruption*, as I have above supposed, is not merely so fantastical as one would at first imagine, by looking into the present Frame and Composition of that House, and observing the universal Abhorrence of any *indirect Means* to obtain a Seat there, as well as the inevitable Expulsion of those, who make such an Attempt; for you was pleased, in one of your Papers, to mention a *great Man* in that House, who formerly boasted, that he was just come from voting *the minor Number to be the Majority*; than which one would imagine there could not be a greater Instance of *Corruption*, as it tends to efface the first Rudiments of common Honesty and common Sense. Such an Abuse to[a] the Understandings of Mankind could not easily be believed, did not History too well attest the Possibility; and indeed, what else can be expected from such a *venal, sordid Majority*; for such they must be who willingly are led blindfold, to pursue the irregular Temper and Passions of *some great Minister*? but our own happy Times are not only free from such Abuses, but they have been discountenanced and exploded in so vigorous a Manner, that we hope they will never revive.

Sir *William Temple*, in his *Essay upon the Original and Nature of Government*, observes that[3]

"The Safety and Firmness of any Frame of Government may be best judged by the Rules of *Architecture*, which teaches us, that the *Pyramid*, of all Figures, is the *firmest*, and least subject to be shaken or over-thrown, by any Concussions or Accidents from the Earth or Air; and it grows still the *firmer*, by how much *broader the Bottom*, and *sharper the Top*.

"On the contrary, (*says he*) a Government which by alienating the *Affections*, losing the *Opinions*, and crossing the *Interests* of the People, leaves out of its Compass the *greatest Part of their Consent*, may justly be said in the same Degree it thus loses Ground, to *narrow its Bottom*; and if this be done to serve the *Ambition*, humour the *Passion*, satisfy the *Appetites* or advance the *Power* and *Interest* not only of *one Man*, but of *two* or *more*, or *many* that come to share in the Government, by this[b] Means the *Top* may justly be said to grow *broader*, as the *Bottom narrower by the other*. Now by the same

---

         [a] to] on *B*.   [b] this] these *B*.

Degrees, that either of these happen, the Stability of the Figure is by the same lessen'd and impaired, so as at certain Degrees, it begins to grow subject to Accidents of Wind and Weather, and at certain others, it is sure to fall of itself, or by the least Shake that happens to the Ground."

So that the larger the *Base*, the more easily the Equilibrium will be preserved; but the *Basis* of our Government (by our Representatives in Parliament, sent from all Parts, at the free Election of the People) is as great as the Kingdom itself; and therefore if, by the *Corruption* and *Contrivances* of *evil Ministers*, Persons are deterred and influenced from a *free Choice*, and Members should sit in that *Assembly* rather at the Appointment, or Election of *such a Minister*, than by the *People themselves*, so much of the *Basis* must be supposed to be taken away, or impaired as the Members, *who sit* for such *Counties* or *Boroughs*, are not *freely elected by them*, but being placed there by *such a Minister*, all that Part of the *Basis* is, as it were, removed and incorporated into himself, which would render him *big* and *unwieldy* and consequently the Building unsteady; by which Means the Frame would become an *inverted Pyramid*, with the *Point on the Ground* and the *Basis uppermost*. How dangerous such a preposterous Alteration would be to the whole Building is easily perceived. But this is only the Result of Sir *William Temple*'s Observations, and is impossible, as our *Laws* and *Inclinations* now stand, to happen in this Nation; for how can we *Englishmen* suppose, that Men qualify'd by their *Fortunes* as well as *Abilities*, should be ever influenc'd by *Bribery*, *Gain* or *Pensions*, to throw down the Inclosures of their Constitution, and draw upon themselves an *universal Odium*, by acting in Opposition to the *Persons*, whom they pretend to represent; and, what is more mean and inglorious, divest themselves of their Reason, Understanding and all Regard to Posterity, and condescend to be led, by a *great wicked Minister*, thro' all the *intricate Mazes* and *dirty Passages*, which *private Interests*, *insatiable Lusts* and *unruly Ambition* shall suggest to him, to the Destruction of their Country in the End.

A Parliament, thus packed, would be far more dangerous than *no Parliament at all*; for it would be much better to rely on the Justice, Wisdom and Lenity of the *Prince*, whose Interests are interwoven with their own, than on *one*, whose private Views, inconsistent with the Good of his Country, naturally lead to its Destruction; much better would it be that *such a Minister* should stand alone under the

Eye and *Controul* of his *Prince*, as well as of *others in Power*, who might restrain his exorbitant Designs, than to be thus prop't by the *seeming Consent* and *Suffrage of the People*, which might at last divert, if not close the Eyes of the *Prince*, from viewing his Conduct, and put him out of the Power of others to contend with him; it is supporting, abetting, strengthening and confirming his *Iniquities*, and putting a great Part of the Load upon *our own Shoulders.*—God forbid that this should ever be the Fate of *England!*

We now see a *Parliament* composed of Persons, elected by our *free Choice*, without the least *Corruption, Bribery* or *Influence*; all Contentions about *Elections* are now fairly adjusted, and *such*[a] *only* removed, who, by *unfair* and *wicked Means*, have had the Assurance to obtrude themselves.

From such a *Parliament*, what Fruit may we not expect, when every Individual has, by his *just Representative*, a proper Share in the Legislature, and when all Laws imposed are by and from ourselves; at least with our own Consent and Approbation? What *Peace*, what *Quiet*, what *Unanimity* must ensue? What *Submission*, what *Deference*, ought we not to shew to all the Debates and Results of it?

As we can fear no Danger but from *ourselves* in this Part of our Constitution (for in no other Part of it can we admit of the least Apprehension) so we have much less to dread from the Practices or Designs of *any evil* or *corrupt Minister*, since all Persons at this time in Power vye with one another in their Duty to their Prince, and Regard for the Prosperity of the Commonwealth.

Sir, I have been, perhaps, too tedious in this Epistle; but I was willing to set these Mischiefs in the strongest View, that my *Townsmen* may not suspect me of the least Design to countenance any *indirect Means*, which can possibly be used to the procuring a *British Parliament*; and, at the same time, to let them see that nothing of this Nature can be now dreaded, leaving the Particulars of their *Case* to be represented to them by *You* or some *other Gentleman*, who resides in a *Place* proper to enquire into the *Facts*, and able to pacify their Discontents.

I am, your humble Servant, &c.

---

[a] *such*] *Those* B.

No. 114. Saturday, 7 September 1728.ᵃ

To CALEB D'ANVERS, *Esq*;

SIR,

WHEN I consider the State of the *British Commerce*, and view the several *Monopolies*, which are established amongst us, in various Shapes, I am under all the Anxiety, which naturally fills the Breast of every Man, who hath a true Regard for the Interest and Prosperity of his Country.

Our illustrious Ancestors were equally jealous of their *Trade* and of their *Liberties*; they justly esteemed them *dependant* on each other, and therefore were always upon the watch, and ready to oppose any *Innovations* or *Encroachments* upon either of them; they considered that their *Religious* and *Civil Rights* could not be safe without *Strength*; that *Power* was to be procured and preserved by *Wealth*, and that no Nation can become rich, but by a *well managed* and *extensive Commerce*; for the Soil of few Countries is rich enough to attain any great Share of Wealth, meerly by the Exportation and Exchange of its own Product; and whoever will enquire into the Affairs of this Kingdom, will find sufficient Matter to convince him, that the Wealth and Figure of *Great Britain* is chiefly owing to its extensive *Trade* and *Plantations*, and that not one fourth Part of our Riches hath arisen from the Vent of our *native* Commodities and Manufactures.

It was therefore the Wisdom and Care of our Ancestors to preserve and encourage *Trade* in all its Branches, by making it free to all the Subjects of *England*; and we find that when some of our Princes had granted Charters to select Bodies of Men to carry on an *exclusive Trade* to any particular Place or Country, *Acts* of *Parliament* were made for restraining *Monopolies*, and giving the Subjects of *England* an *equal Freedom* of Trade to all Countries, and declaring, that *Charters* of *Incorporation* disabled all other Subjects of the Realm, and debarred them from enlarging the Traffick of it,

---

ᵃ *Fol.* begins: 'THE following Letter came from the same excellent Hand, which hath so often obliged the Publick, in this Paper, with Discourses on TRADE; and They were all so well received by every sincere Well-wisher to the Prosperity of his Country, which depends almost solely upon a *free* and *beneficial* Commerce, that this will, I doubt not, meet with the same Reception, especially from the *Mercantile* Part of my Readers, as it is written with the same laudable Design, on a Subject of the utmost Importance to *Great Britain*.' *omitted, B.*

to the manifest impoverishing of all *Owners* of *Ships*, *Masters*, *Mariners*, *Fishermen*, *Clothiers*, *Tuckers*, *Spinsters*, and many Thousands of *Handicraft Men*, besides the Decrease of the *Subsidies*, *Customs*, and other Impositions, and the *Decay* of *Navigation*, as well as that it abated the Price of our *own Commodities*, and enhanced those from Abroad.

It is evident, that the more Traders there are to any Country, the greater will be the *Exports* of their *Product* and *Manufactures*; and consequently all *exclusive Companies* are generally allowed to be *prejudicial* to the Nation, as they *lessen* our *Exports* and *Navigation*, and enable Men to set their *own Price* upon such *Commodities* as they *import*; which must give our *Rivals* in *Trade* a very great Advantage over us in those particular Branches.

Whether those *wholesome Laws*, which were provided to suppress all *Monopolies*, are abrogated or suspended, will not here be a material Enquiry; since it is sufficient to shew the *Inconveniences* and *Mischiefs* which have attended them to the Nation, and even to those *select Bodies themselves*.

The *Whale Fishery*, which was once very advantagious to *Great Britain*, and a considerable *Nursery* for *Seamen*, was lost by its being *monopolized* by the *Greenland Company*, while the *Dutch* and *Hamburghers* have since employed therein[a] above 400 Sail of Ships yearly.

We once shared the Trade to *India* for *Nutmegs*, *Cloves* and *Spice*, with the *Portugueze*; but by their Negligence, and the *Mismanagement* of the *old East India Company*, the *Dutch* supplanted us both, and have engrossed those *valuable Commodities* to themselves.

The *Trade* to *Africa* might have been made much more beneficial, had it never been vested in a *Company*, but left free and open to all the Subjects of *England*, without any *Imposition* or *Restraint* whatever; for by the *Avarice*, *Negligence*, and ill *Conduct* of the *former Managers*, their Stock fell from 480, as every Share of 100 *l.* in that *Company* was once sold for, to *Forty Shillings*; and the *Portugueze*, *Dutch*, *French*, and *Danes*, by those Means, became Sharers with us in that Trade which we might have engrossed to our selves, and would thereby have been more valuable to *England* than the *Mines* of *Mexico* and *Peru*; which would likewise have been

---

[a] therein] in it *B*.

dependant and in effect our own: Nor were these the only Mischiefs which happened to the Nation; the *Sugar Colonies*, being then in their Infancy, were stinted in their Growth, by being scantily supplied with Negroes, which were absolutely necessary in them, and laboured under many other *Hardships* and *Oppressions* from that *Company*. If we now consider the vast *Encrease* of our *Exports* and *Navigation* in that particular Branch of Commerce, since it was laid open; and the Duty to the *Company* (which was for some Years paid by *separate Traders*) taken off; and the great *Improvements*, which have been made in our *Plantations*, by being furnished with a sufficient Number of *Negroes*; there can be no need of any other Arguments to convince every disinterested and impartial Person of the Truth of the Position which I have here laid down.

The South Sea Company may not improperly be said to be in their *Meridian*; yet the most sanguine of their *Friends* are doubtful, how their Account stands with relation to *Trade*; while their *Opponents* give very plausible Reasons, without bringing into the Estimate any *Frauds* or *Seizures* which have been made by the *Spaniards*; of their having lost very considerably thereby; and that they have only diverted the Channels of Trade, without making any new Acquisitions to the Nation; and though their Charter is not *exclusive*, excepting in the *South Seas*, (which they have given up by their Acceptance of the *Assiento Contract*) and the *Whale Fishery*; yet it is worth considering, says a late Author, how far it is consistent with their *Charter* to trade either on the *Coast* of *Guinea*, or in our own *Plantations*; and that whenever any Company attempts to trade beyond their *Limits*, it ought to alarm every Man, who has any Regard for Trade, or the true Interest of his Country. This is indeed a very just Observation, and worthy the Notice and Consideration of our *Representatives* in *Parliament*; for if that *Company* be not restrained by their Charter, or any Law in being, and they are left at Liberty to carry on a Trade to *Africa* and other Parts, which are not expresly mentioned or intended to be granted them, they are enabled to drive so considerable a Trade, as must consequently diminish the Number of *British Merchants*, and make *all other Traders* and *Manufacturers*, and almost *every Corporation* in *England* dependent on them; and how mischievous may such an Influence be, some time or other, to our Constitution? we may then perhaps bid farewel to our *Trade* and *Liberties*: we shall no longer hold the *Ballance of Power* in *Europe*, nor ride *Masters* of the *Seas*.

It is undoubtedly a very great Grievance to the Nation, among others which have crept in, by means of those *Companies*, that a *Charter* is no sooner granted to a *Select* Number of People, but immediately arises a Sett of Men called *Governours, Sub-Governours, Directors, Stock-Jobbers*, &c. who divide their Stock into *Shares*, and then negotiate them in the *Alley*, before it is known whether they have any *intrinsick Value* or not; and if there be any *true Value*, which few of them ever had, instead of carrying on the Design by *fair and industrious Means*, some wicked *Artifice* is contrived to raise it to an *imaginary Heighth*, and thereby delude and ruin many Thousands of innocent and unwary Persons.

Such *delusive Arts* were unknown to our virtuous Ancestors; and therefore our *antient Laws* are either *defective*, or so far doubtful as not to restrain, or sufficiently discourage those *infamous Practices*. But it is, methinks, a melancholy Consideration, that unhappy Persons shall suffer the Law for Crimes which they committed through *Necessity* and not Inclination (as without doubt many have done) even for small Sums, whilst Villains of the deepest Dye who, in effect, rob the Fatherless and Widows, in common with thousands of others, usually escape with Impunity.

It would, in some Measure, prevent such *artful* and *designing Men* from enriching themselves, at the Expence and Ruin of others, by raising and falling of Stocks at their pleasure, if all *Companies* were obliged, once a Year, to state an *Account of Trade*, and lay it before their *general Court*; and if they were tied down from *dividing* more than their *Profits*, as the *Dutch East-India Company* are said to have done, with great honour to that Society. Nor indeed can the *Trade* of this Kingdom be *improved* or *preserved*, unless some *such Rules* are *established*; for how few have Virtue enough to encourage *fair Trade* and withstand the Temptations of *Dividends*, and the Advantages which are made by the rise and fall of *Stocks?*[a]

Hath not this easy Way of getting Money engross'd the Time and Attention of many wealthy Persons and others, who might be usefully employ'd in the Service of their Country as well as themselves, if they would bend their Thoughts to *Trade*, and other Professions, which *really* improve our National Stock? Hath not *Trade* decay'd ever since *Stock-jobbing* flourished and met with encouragement? have not our *Manufacturies* diminished, our

[a] *Stocks?*] *B*; *Stocks. fol.*

Imports and *Exports* in general declined, and our *Poor* become more numerous for want of Employ? are not his Majesty's *Customs* impaired, and will they not waste still more and more proportionably with our *Trade*?

In fine, to what dangerous uses may these *Companies* be made subservient, by *corrupt* and *enterprizing Ministers*? Is it not in their Power to conceal any *Advices* from Abroad, which may affect our *Stocks*, till they have *bought* or *sold out*; and may they not, at any other time, raise or fall them at their Pleasure? Is not the *Common-Seal* of all *Companies*, by which they may at any time raise what *Sums of Money* they please, equal to a Power of *Coining*, or *taxing* their Fellow Subjects; which even the *King* himself cannot do, without consent of Parliament? Have not all *Ministries* an influence over those *Companies*, and may they not by their means be able to *influence* the *Elections* of every City, and *Trading Town* in *England*? and what may we not justly apprehend from such a formidable, complicated Power, which may, one time or other, destroy our happy Constitution?

We are indeed secure under the *present Administration*, who have given such demonstrations of their virtue and disinterested love of their Country, that they can never be suspected of any *corrupt or dangerous Practices*; but though the Prospect is distant, and perhaps may never be nearer, yet it is certainly incumbent on us to imitate the great Examples of our Ancestors, in the care of *Trade* and of *Posterity*. What will all other Cares avail, if we cannot secure to our Children the Fruits of our Labour, and those invaluable Blessings which we enjoy?[a]—However *remote* or *imaginary* these apprehensions may seem to be, my Pen shakes in my Hand, at the very Thoughts of them. I tremble for *Posterity* and for my *Country*.

I am Sir,
Your humble Servant,
CHARLES FREEPORT.

[a] enjoy?] *B*; enjoy *fol.*

No. 123. Saturday, 9 November 1728.

To CALEB D'ANVERS, *Esq*;

MONTGOMERY

SIR,

SInce my last from hence, which you were[a] pleased to insert in your Paper of the 17th of August, I have thought fit to review that Subject, which I think deserves a little further[b] Enlargement, by considering what may be the *Motives* that induce an *evil Minister* to corrupt and influence *Parliaments* by any indirect Means, and the *Consequences* of such a Practice; which as they would be most odious to our Constitution and Liberties, I think a just Observance of our Laws in this Point cannot more properly be urged and inculcated, than at a Time, when the Breach of them is least to be apprehended; for in a different Season, an[c] Animadversion upon them might be very fatal, by drawing down the Resentment of *Those*, for whose Security such extraordinary Methods should be set on Foot and encouraged; but at present those Thoughts can only tend, as they are designed, to encourage a *Perseverance*[d] and confirm in my Country-men an unbyassed and disinterested Conduct in their *Elections*.

I say then such a Practice will never be set on Foot but when *Blunders* and *Miscarriages* have happen'd in the Government, either thro' the Ignorance and Incapacity, or to promote the private Interests or Avarice of some *wicked Minister*; extraordinary Arts must then be made use of to *screen* the Authors from the general Resentment and Odium of the People; Votes, Resolutions and Laws must be made, however otherways unnecessary, to raise a Cloud over such a mischievous Administration; and. thus, by casting a Mist over the Eyes of the People, prevent that Vengeance which would naturally fall on the Contrivers and Abettors of such destructive Schemes.

All Governments are then only stable and lasting when they closely pursue the Laws and Constitution upon which they were founded. This appears from the Duration of all States, that have ever appeared in the World; for Laws were first made and instituted, in every Country, by some prudent Law-Giver or competent Number of People, who best understood the Nature and

---

[a] were] was *B.*   [b] further] farther *B.*   [c] an] *B*; and *fol.*
[d] *Perseverance*] *B*; *Perseverence fol.*

Genius of the People and the Interest to which they were nearest attached; and such Laws having had the Sanction of Time, and by Experience found to be the best that could conduce to make the People happy, they then became sacred, and the Violation of them was justly esteemed the greatest Injury to the Commonwealth; for it is as preposterous to conceive that a Government can be dissolved, while the Laws are observed, as that it can long subsist when its Foundation is undermined and subverted.

If therefore all Governments ought to have a careful Eye over the Constitution, and never to deviate from it, how ought Englishmen to be jealous of the Rights and Freedom of *Parliaments*, the Basis of their Constitution, the Mediator between King and People, the just Scale and Ballance of his Prerogative and their Liberties, the safe Repository of their Properties? This surely ought always to be sound, free, unbyass'd, unrestrain'd, disinterested, and to have no other Principle to inspire it but Loyalty to the King and true Patriotism, a tender Care of the People's Privileges.

Machiavel observes that "there cannot be a more profitable or necessary Power given to those, who in a City are appointed as *Guardians of Liberty* than in[a] that of *accusing* the Citizens before some Magistrate or Council, whensoever they offend in any thing against a Free State."[1]

This *profitable, necessary Power* no Constitution enjoys so eminently as the Guardians of *England, the Commons in Parliament*, who are the grand Inquest of the Nation, to detect the Corruptions and Errors,[b] and to curb *despotic, evil Ministers*; this restrains their Ambition and directs their Counsels to the Advancement of the Honour, Splendour and Glory of the Crown, and to the Preservation of the People's just Rights and Privileges; but if Parliaments should therefore, at any time, come under the Influence and arbitrary Controul of an *evil Minister*, how might he not proceed from one Iniquity to another, with Impunity? And that Part of the Constitution, which is a Curb to restrain and punish him, will become his *Prostitute* and be made his *Protector* and *Defender*. If it were only to preserve this one great Privilege of the Commons, the Right of *Impeachment*, all honest *Britons* would tremble at an Attempt made on the *Freedom of Parliaments* and ought inviolably to maintain the Right of *Elections*.

[a] than in] than *B*.   [b] Errors,] Errors of Government, *B*.

It is somewhere justly observed, that Magistrates made by *themselves*, not those chosen by the People, endamage their[a] Liberty; this will hold in the Choice of a *Member in*[b] *Parliament*; which ought always to be at the *free* Election of the People, and not at the Appointment of *Great Men*; the People always know their own Interests best, and what more[c] promotes their Trade, Traffick and Merchandize, and likewise what it is that injures or oppresses them; because they more intimately feel and are affected with it; they will therefore, as long as they are *free*, neither tempted with Bribes nor awed by *Power*, chuse such Representatives as will give the best Counsel to the Prince, and be most careful of their freedom, or which is the same, the Constitution; such as will best promote the Good of the Commonwealth and redress its Injuries; and therefore if a *base*[d] *Minister* has, by a foul and wicked Administration, drawn upon him the Odium and Resentment of the People, how dare he trust, nay how ought he to fear Power? He knows he will[e] be made a Sacrifice to their just Rage, if not prevented; then will it be high time for him to cast about some Way or other to infringe this sacred Branch of the Constitution, a *free Election*, and by any Means gain a Return of *Those*, who if they will not assist him, in the carrying on his Schemes, yet will not molest or obstruct them; this would perhaps engage the Treasure of the Nation (especially if such a Minister should happen to be *Treasurer*) laid aside to support and *defend* it, to *corrupt* and *destroy* it; some People's Voices must at any Rate be *bought*, *others* afrighted[f] into a Complyance, and *Pensions* make up what before was not effected; *Pensions*, which would make the Partakers generous and free of their *Election Money*, and with a grateful Alacrity, vote any Sum demanded for *Secret Services*, by so *honourable* and *bountiful* a Distributer of it, and so[g] circulate from the *Treasury* to the *Electors*, and at last to the Treasury again; but whether the *Ebb* from it would be as great as the *Tide* to it, would deserve some Consideration; such an Abuse, I say, would be the natural Effort of a *guilty, hated, Minister*; and if we should complain of our *Representatives*, they might then lay it all on the *uncontrouled, irresistable Power of such a Minister*, but he would, no doubt, as properly retort it, with a *Sneer*, on *ourselves*, and tell us, we had sold

---

[a] endamage their] endanger publick *B*.   [b] *in*] *of B*.   [c] more] most *B*.
[d] *a base*] a *B*.   [e] he will] that he shall *B*.   [f] afrighted] menac'd *B*.
[g] and so] by which Means it would *B*.

our *Freedom*; if[a] we take Money, we must expect it is for something; and if we feel a Burthen on our Shoulders, we have the Wages in our Pockets, tho' never so small a Pittance; what should we say to ourselves? what indeed to our Posterity, who for a Shadow have disinherited them of so fair a Patrimony?

Again: Suppose *such a Minister*, thro' *Incapacity* or *Ignorance*, *Pride*, or *Insolence*, should offend some *foreign Power*, incroach on his just Rights, and invade his Possessions, and seeing Vengeance pouring upon him by just Reprisals, should want *Courage* or *Means* to avert the Storm; what Hopes, what Redress could we expect from an *adulterated Parliament*; who, instead of punishing the *Minister*, would support and avow the Fact, and so justify him in the Eye of his Prince? but when the gathering Cloud is ready to burst over his Head, and all other Methods unreguarded, because not so well understood, he will then fly to his experienced Traffick, and from the *obsequious Pensioners*, lavish all the People's Treasure,[b] who would enable him to buy his Quiet with large Sums *without Account*, the only modest Part of the Transaction; for with what Face could *such a Minister* make up or expose such an Account fairly to the Eye of a plundered People? or, how could they receive so ungrateful a Reproach, so glaring a Mark of their own ill-placed Confidence and venal Complyance? This then would be a natural Consequence of a *corrupted Parliament*; the Treasure of the Nation would be squandered, and the People must groan under burthensome Taxes to support and gild over the Iniquities of a *corrupt Minister*; this would be the *Case*, instead of those reasonable and just Supplies, which are now from Time to Time chearfully granted, and without which no Government could possibly subsist, especially under a Ministry so sparing in *secret Services*.

From such Measures, would naturally result a Necessity for a *standing Army*; for the Hatred of the People at Home against such an *over grown Minister*, wanting an Opportunity to awake the Prince, and apprize him of such foul Measures, and to demand from his gracious Hand so ripe a Sacrifice, their proper and natural Approach to his sacred Person by Parliament being now stopt, a *standing Army* might then be a proper Expedient to silence their Murmurings, and choak up their just Complaints; for tho' a

[a] if] that if *B*.
[b] and from the . . . Treasure,] and lavish the People's Treasure for his own Support, with the Concurrence of his *obsequious Pensioners*, *B*.

standing Army, under a good and gracious King, and under an upright Administration, may deter our Enemies from any Insults at Home, and would effectually preserve our Liberty, yet how dangerous such a Weapon might be in the Hands of a *wicked Minister*, every *Englishman* can judge.

I must now congratulate my Country, that this is not our Case at present, nor ever can be, as long as they hold fast their Integrity, and pursue their own plain Reason and Understanding both in *Elections* and in *Parliament*.

I am, SIR,

Your most humble Servant,

CAMBRO-BRITANNUS.

No. 130. Saturday, 28 December 1728.

To CALEB D'ANVERS, *Esq*;

SIR,

TRADE is of that general Use and Importance to every Country, that whatever relates to it, can never be unseasonable, nor too often discussed; especially in this Nation, which has so great a Dependance on it. I am the more encouraged to enter into this Subject at present, when the Tranquility of *Europe* is under Negotiation, and we may reasonably hope, that our *Ministers* and *Politicians* will be at leisure to attend more heartily to Matters of *Trade*, and the Improvement of our *own Manufactures* and *Plantations*, which ought not to be esteemed beneath their Care and Study. They will then be convinced, that there is something more in the main Springs and Principles of *Commerce*, than to manage a *narrow, selfish Intrigue*, or to procure and promote a *Monopoly* of any kind; to encourage the Exportation of *Corn*, when cheap, and to discourage it when dear; to raise or fall the Value, Name, or Interest of *Money*; to restrain or prohibit not only the Industry of his Majesty's Subjects with *other Nations*, but even with *one another*. They will find that these and many more pretended *Encouragements* are so far from being what they are called, that they are generally calculated to promote some *sinister Design*; or arise from mistaken Notions of *unskilful Men*, in Matters of this Nature and who will not allow themselves Time or Opportunity of being better informed, but take them upon trust from *Others*, who confound Effects with

Causes, and Causes with Effects, and measure the *Trade* and *Interest* of *Great Britain*, and even of all *Europe*, according to their own fond Conceptions or imaginary Notions.

Whoever will look into the present State of the *British Commerce* will find that the *Ballance* runs against us in many Branches; and that the *most valuable* (if not the *only Remains*, which are intrinsically so) are to our *own Plantations*; for, upon enquiry, it will appear that They employ above one half of our *Navigation*, and consequently are a very considerable Part of the *Trade* and *Riches* of this Kingdom. They are likewise to be consider'd, as entirely *our own*; and therefore it is highly our Interest to *encourage* and *improve* them, since they may be useful to us, and be a considerable Support to the Nation, when *other Branches* may possibly fail us, through the Designs and Contrivances of our *Rivals in Trade*, who have in a Manner worked us out of several Parts, which we formerly enjoyed.

Those Plantations, which have already contributed so much to the Wealth and Figure of *Great Britain*, look as if they were intended by Providence for some *greater Ends*; to which undoubtedly they may be made subservient, if we are not neglectful of the Opportunities which are put into our Hands; for They have not (as some vainly imagine) sprung from the deep Contrivances of any *one Man*, or *party of Men*, but from various Causes, at several Times, and indeed, in a great Measure, from our *own* and *other Peoples Weakness*.

Our *Northern Colonies* have chiefly had their rise from our *intestine Broils*, on account of *Religious* and *State Affairs*; which obliged great Numbers of People to remove to those distant Countries: "Such therefore, says Dr. *Davenant*, as found themselves disturbed and uneasy at Home, if they could have found no other Retreat, must have gone to the *Hans Towns*,[1] *Switzerland*, *Denmark*, &c. (as many did, before the *Plantations* flourished, to our great detriment) and they who had thus retired to *European* Countries, must have been for ever lost to *England*. But, Providence, which[a] contrives better for us, than we can do for our selves, has offered in the *new World* a Place of Refuge for those People, where their Labour and Industry is more useful to their *Mother Kingdom* than if they had continued among us."

The *Southern Colonies* sprung from the same, or such like Causes, and owe their Success, principally to the *Netherlander's*[b]

Loss of *Brazil* to the *Portugueze*; after which, the Product of that noble Country, for want of Industry, and by the Mismanagement of those People, gave our Countrymen the Opportunity of settling the *Caribee Islands*, and to raise *Sugar, Indigo* and such like Commodities, sufficient for our *own Consumption*, and also for the Supply of *other Nations*; which, as *America* is constituted, could never have otherwise happen'd.

Jamaica, it is true, became ours by *Conquest*, and beside being really a better Soil, and containing a far larger Extent of Ground, than all the *British Islands* in *America*, has also such a Conveniency, by its Situation, for *Trade* or *War*, as cannot be exceeded, if it is to be parallell'd by any Country in the World. But, I need not enlarge upon this, or shew the Importance of this Island to *Great Britain*, since it hath been so fully set forth in a little Piece, which was lately published, entitled* *Some Observations on the* Assiento Trade, *as it hath been exercis'd by the* South Sea *Company*, &c.

To form a more perfect Idea of our *Trade* and *Plantations*, it is necessary to observe that *England*, as an Island, hath no Way of conveying its *Product* and *Manufactures* abroad, but by *Navigation*; nor any Way of being considerable but by its *Fleets*; and of supporting them but by our *Trade* and *Plantations*, which breeds *Seamen* and brings in *Wealth* to maintain them.

The *Plantations* likewise consume vast Quantities of the *British Product* and *Manufactures*; furnishes us with many *useful Commodities*, which we formerly bought of *other Nations*, and employs great Numbers of People *at Home*, as well as *Abroad. They* therefore, who are thus useful to the Nation, ought certainly to be *cherish'd* and *encourag'd*; for on *Them*, in a great Measure, depends our *Navigation* and *Seamen*; and on our *Navigation* and *Seamen* depends our *Strength*, which is our *Security*.

If we had nothing more than our *own Product*, and a little *foreign Traffick, with other Nations*, could we be able to maintain those *mighty Fleets*, which render the *British* Name formidable in all Parts of the known World? Would one Man's consuming what another raised, add to our Wealth? *No Commodity* is truly an Increase of the *National Stock*, but that which is *exported*, and *all Trades* receive their Life and Vigour from the *Merchant*. By him the *Mariner* is subsisted; the *Planter* supplied, who mutually assist each other in promoting the general Interest of the Nation. Why then are not these several *industrious Societies* more valued and encouraged;

since it is so very obvious, that the Wealth and Grandeur of *Great Britain* are principally owing to them? Her Prosperity and Safety in a great Measure depend on *Trade*, and *Trade* on the *Plantations*; it is therefore highly her Interest to cherish and protect them, not only as they are subject to her; but as she draws, from thence, by a kind of magnetick Force, all that is *good* and *valuable*. She is the *Center*, to which all things tend.

Nothing can be of greater Importance to every *English man*, than a true Knowledge of the *Manufactures, Trade, Wealth* and *Strength* of his Country; and it were to be wished that our *Nobility* and *Gentry* would make them their Care and Study; which, however they may be *neglected* or *slighted*, are notwithstanding the only Foundation of a *solid* and *lasting Greatness*.

The present Grandeur of the *French*, as Dr. *Davenant* observes, is chiefly derived from a Succession of *four very active* and *able Men*, in Matters of State, *viz. Richlieu, Mazarine, Colbert* and *Louvoy*; but *Richlieu* was eminent above the rest. He neglected *no Part of Government*; *raising Money* was not his *only Care*; for it is well known that He inspected the *Lives* and *Manners* of the *Church*, the *Discipline* of the *Army* and the *Corruption of the Law*. He fortified the *Frontier Places* of his Country. He provided *Military Stores*. He put *France* into the Way of having a *Naval Strength*; and, at the same time, encouraged *Manufactures* and promoted *Trade*, as if his Thoughts had been taken up with *no other Business*.

Such a *Genius* would go a great Way towards securing the *Trade of England*, against the *Power* of *France* and the *Wealth* of *Holland*—But, an Understanding so sublime is hardly to be found in any Country.

I am, SIR,
Your humble Servant,
CHARLES FREE-PORT.

* *Printed for* H. Whitridge *at the Corner of* Castle-Alley *in* Cornhill.

No. 131. Saturday, 4 January 1729.

From my own Chambers.

I Presume and am pretty well[a] assured, that the foregoing, excellent Piece[1] will, by all unprejudiced Readers, be thought sufficient to clear up the Dispute between me and my Adversaries, concerning the *present State of Affairs*; but as I have lately received another very *seasonable Letter*, on a Point of great Importance, from a *worthy Citizen and Merchant of London* (to whom I shall always pay the utmost Regard) I hope it will be esteemed no improper Sequel to what hath been already advanced.

To CALEB D'ANVERS, *Esq*;

Mr. *D'anvers*,

THE ill Usage our *Merchants* have met with from the *Spaniards*, hath long been the Subject of complaint; and I am afraid will continue to be so as long as they know that our *Fleets* come into their Seas, *only to be seen*, as *Publicola* informs us[b] hath been their Business hitherto.[2] But there is a Circumstance of another Nature, which tho' not of equal Consequence, must secretly weaken us; and which I believe hath escaped the Observation of most Men out of *Trade*. I mean the *Course of Exchange* between us and other Nations; which, for *two Years past*, has been declining, and now runs very greatly in our disfavour.

I am no *Remitter*, and therefore don't pretend to be Master of this Affair; nor would I take Notice of every trifling Variation; but what I send you arises from a Comparison in my own little Business which I do with *Holland*.

It will be needless to observe here, that Bills are drawn some at a *Short*, and some at a *longer* Time of Payment; so that no Judgment can be form'd upon one and the same; Or that the Measure of *Exchange* is made by *their Coin* and not by *Ours*; namely, by *Skellings* and *Grotes*, twelve of the *Latter* being equal to one of the *Former*. What I have to say is this.

About two Years ago, I find myself drawn upon at 35 *Skellings* and 2 *Grotes* for a *pound Sterling*, (which I believe is not an

---

[a] I Presume and am pretty well] I am well *B*.   [b] us hath] *B*; us; hath *fol*.

Equivalent in *real Value* neither) but now it is come down so low as
33 *S.* 8 *G.* at which I have been also drawn upon within a Fortnight
past. Moreover my Correspondent tells me, that *plenty of Bills* offer
there still, and but *little Money*.

	s.	*g.*
Now if from what it was, *viz.* ————	35	: 2
You deduct what it now is, *viz.* ————	33	: 8

There will remain a *Skelling* and a *half* ———— 1 : 6

and if 1 in 33 be 3 in Cent. by the same Rule 1 and an half will be 4
and an half in Cent. from whence it will follow that

———— lb. 100 Sterling.

is at this Time in *Holland* worth but ———— 95 : 10 : 0

and I am inform'd this is not the Case between *Us* and *Holland
alone,*[a] but that the same Proportion holds generally in *other
Nations.*

Indeed, it must be confess'd, that the Times have been when it
hath been worse; but then the Reasons have been obvious. As in the
memorable Years 1720 and 1721; or when there have been *Armies* in
the Field, and we have had *our own*, and *Foreign Troops* in Pay; but
little of this can be pleaded now. On the Contrary, very lately, we
have[b] had an *East India Sale* here, the largest that hath been known,
and in which the *Dutch* are supposed to have been Purchasers, to
the Value of not less than lb. 400,000. But neither hath this any
Effect upon the *Exchange*, which is a Proof that they are in no want
of Money here.

Of late Years *England* hath boasted much of the Extent of her
Trade; but be that as it will, from the Instance before us, one would
be tempted to believe[c] that the *Ballance* was against her, did not our
gravest Merchants here assure us to the contrary; who, tho' they are
not able to determine *What is*, yet all agree in *What is not the Cause*;
namely, that the present Demand for Money abroad is not to pay
for Goods and Merchandize *Imported.*

I don't know, Mr. *D'anvers*, whether an Affair of this Nature may
come within your Province; but as Standers by are said to see most,

[a] *alone,* | *only*, *B.*   [b] very lately, we have | we have very lately *B.*
[c] from the Instance . . . to believe | one would be tempted to believe from the Instance
before us, *B.*

and as Sedentary Men have sometimes had better (general) Notions of *Commerce*, than those engaged in it; so, I should be glad to see this Mystery unriddled, and for that End I send it you.

> *I am, your humble Servant,*
> CIVICUS.

P.S. I have Reason to believe 35 *S.* 2 *G.* to be but a *low Exchange*; for, upon looking further[a] back, I find I have been drawn upon at 35 *S.* 6. 8 and 10[b] and sometimes as high as 36 *Skellings* for a *Pound Sterling*.

No. 133. Saturday, 18 January 1729.

To CALEB D'ANVERS, *Esq;*

SIR,

HAVING shewn, in a *former Letter*,[1] the Importance of our *Colonies*, especially in *America*, and how much the *Trade* and *Navigation* of this Kingdom depend on them; I shall now enquire into the State and Condition of our Neighbours, in those Respects; particularly of the *Dutch* and the *French*, who are our most dangerous *Rivals* in Trade; though *one* of your Adversaries was pleased very lately to assert (out of *Ignorance* indeed I believe) *that neither the* Dutch *nor the* French *have any* Settlements *or* Trade *in those Parts like US*.

This therefore is a Subject, which seems highly seasonable at present and deserves the Consideration of every *Englishman*; since it is notorious that the *former* have deprived us of some valuable Possessions both in the *East* and *West-Indies*, which we once enjoy'd; and that the *latter* have made so great a Progress in their Settlements in the *western World*, within thirty Years past, as must give *England*, and even all *Europe*, but a melancholy Prospect.

It is certain that *Spain* and *Portugal* are in Possession of the richest Countries in the Universe; notwithstanding which, the Liberties of *Europe* can be in little Danger from either of those Nations, considering their Constitutions and Policy, which are the Security of Christendom; but we cannot be too vigilant and jealous of *another Nation*, which hath always had more extensive Views and

---

a further] farther *B.*   b 10] 10 *G. B.*

69

hath not only encroached upon some of her Neighbours, but hath almost incredibly improved and strengthen'd her Colonies and Plantations in the *West Indies*.

The *Dutch* are, at this Time, in Possession of no considerable Places in *South America*; for *Curasoe*, *Eustatia* and *Saba* are small barren Islands, or rather Rocks; but in *North America* They have *Surinam*, which is Part of *Guiana* on the main Continent; where, after great Labour and Difficulty, They have cultivated a low, boggy Soil, almost as bad as their own Country once was, and have extended their Settlements above an *hundred Leagues* up the Country; by which Means They have not only the Conveniency of several navigable Rivers, but have very much improved those Parts, which now produce great Quantities of *Sugar* and several other valuable Commodities.

They have likewise a Settlement at the Cape of *Good Hope* and several others on the West Coast of *Africa*.

But the principal Acquisitions of the *Dutch* are in the *East Indies*, where They have outstript all other *European* Nations; for by their wise Institutions, for the Increase of *Trade* and Dominion, They have been enabled to settle *potent Colonies*, to make many and great *Conquests*, and to erect a *mighty Empire* in those remote Parts; where They are able to equip a *considerable Fleet* and to raise an Army, capable almost of controuling and giving Laws to the *Eastern World*.

Though the *French* were none of the first in Undertakings of this Kind, yet They are not far behind Hand with other Nations: especially in the *West Indies*.

In *North America* They have *Canada* and the Isle of *Cape Briton*; and by their Settlements on the River *Misisippi*, even as far as the Borders of *Mexico* (which our News Papers have lately informed us are in a flourishing Condition) They have the Opportunity of erecting Forts along the several Lakes between That and *Canada*; which may in Time become very troublesome to our *Northern Plantations*. We have the more Reason to be jealous of their Proceedings in those Parts, since we have had repeated Informations and just Grounds to believe that the *Indian Nations*, who have given so much Disturbance to our People in *New England* and *Carolina*, have been spirited up by them, notwithstanding the *Harmony* and *good Agreement*, which at present subsists between the two Crowns in *Europe*.

In *South America* They have *Martinico*, *Guadalupe*, and some other Islands of less Consequence; as also near two Thirds of the great Island of *Hispaniola*, which is in a very thriving Condition and gives just Apprehensions to the neighbouring Islands and even to the Continent of *New Spain*.

In *Africa* They have some Settlements on the River *Senegall*, *Gambia* and other Parts of the *West Coast*; as likewise some places in the *East Indies*, though of no great Consequence.

It would undoubtedly be a very seasonable and useful Employment to make some Enquiry into the different *Methods* and *Policies* of those Nations, with Respect to their *Colonies*, and to compare them with our *own*. This will be the most probable Method of finding out the true Causes of the present Declension of our *Plantations*, and enable us to rectify any Mistakes, which have been committed and may have given our Neighbours an Advantage over us in *those Parts*.

The *French* are so intent on the Improvement of their *Colonies*, that They omit nothing, which may contribute to their Prosperity. *Lands* are not only assigned to such Persons as will go over and manure them, but They have Credit given by the Publick for *Negroes* and *other Materials* necessary for *Planting*. The *Salaries* of their Governours are paid by the *King*. Care is taken not to send over *necessitous* or *ignorant Persons* to preside over Them; and They are restrained, under severe Penalties, from accepting *Donatives*, of any kind, from the People. *Justice* is duly and impartially administer'd. In short, They are supported and encouraged in their *Manufactures* and *Commerce*, instead of being *pillag'd* and *oppressed*; for though They are *Slaves* at home, They are *Freemen* abroad; whereas some of their Neighbours may be truly said to be the Reverse, and however They may boast of *Liberty* at home, too often find themselves in a State of *Slavery* abroad.

I need not mention the Depredations of the *Spaniards*, for several Years past, on the *British Trade*, both in the Ocean and the *West Indies*. They are too severely felt, and have been too often complained of, though without Redress, to need any Repetition. But I think it very surprizing, that the *French*, who are cordially engaged in the *same Allyance* with us, and have besides made such *formidable Encroachments* on the Dominions of *Spain* in *America*, should be allowed to carry on their Trade without any Interruption or Annoyance, whilst the *British Subjects* have been forced to submit to such provoking Indignities and almost irretrievable Injuries.

It is likewise Matter of no less Wonder, that a *Nation*, so unequal in *Naval Power* to that of *Great Britain*, should be suffered to repeat their Insults upon us so long together, under an Administration, which is so watchful over the Rights and Properties of their Countrymen.

We are told indeed, by a * *late Writer* (who seems to speak with the Confidence of a *Plenipo*,[2] though He blunders in the *Dates* of almost every Particular) *that these hostile Measures of the* Spaniards, *after the* Præliminaries *were ratified, were greatly owing to the* Indifference *of our Merchants, who might have check'd their Insolence, had They sued out Letters of* Marque *and* Reprisal;[3] and, if I am not mistaken, you too, Mr. *D'Anvers*, imputed these Insults and Depredations to the *same Cause*; but if I could suspect *two such grave Writers* of *Irony* and *Banter*, I confess it would be on this Occasion; for surely you cannot be ignorant (at least we *Citizens* are very well convinced) that our late *Inactivity* is not oweing to the *Tameness* or *Indifference* of the *British Merchants*.

The *profound Politician*, before-mentioned, observes very justly, *that our Trade is a very* tender *and* popular *Concern*. He might have added, that it is an *essential Concern*; for, what could *England* do, under her present great Burthen of *Debt*, without *Trade*, which *only* can support our *Credit*, by enabling us to pay the *Interest* of it? and, what must become of that *Trade* without *due Protection*? Hath it not been a Point chiefly regarded by the best and greatest of our *Princes*? Hath it not employ'd the Attention of our *Legislature* in all Times past, and been the principal Object of our *ablest Ministers*?

From whomsoever therefore this *Indifference* or *Neglect* hath proceeded, I believe there is no Instance in our History, nor in that of any other Nation, where for so many Years past, the Subjects of *one Prince* have been suffered to commit Depredations on those of *another*, of much *superiour Strength*, without any Attempt to prevent them by *Ships of War*, or *Letters of Reprisal*.—I hope the *Spaniards* are not to be always thus in a State of Hostility with *Us*, in *America*, and We always at Peace with *Them*, though at the same Time under all the *Inconveniencies* and at all the Expences of a *War*.—I am glad at least to hear, from *this Writer, that the Court of* Madrid *hath not only formally recalled their* Privateers, *but that They are now actually returned to their Ports and their Commissions cancelled.*

The chief Design of this Letter was to compare the present Condition of our *Colonies* and *Trade* in the *West Indies* with that of our Neighbours, and to shew the Advantages, which They have over us. There is another Circumstance, which seems to affect *Them*, as well as *us*; and that is the *Settlements* and *Manufacturies*, which are springing up in all Parts of *Europe*, and seem to have taken their Rise chiefly from some *late unaccountable Measures*, which occasioned the Disturbance of *Europe*.—But this, perhaps, may be the Subject of another Letter.

Bedford Row   *I am, SIR*, &c.
Jan. 10. 1728–9.   CHARLES FREEPORT.

* See the *British Journal* of *Saturday January* 4.

No. 134. Saturday, 25 January 1729.

AN ANSWER to a Letter *in the* Daily Journal *of the 8th Instant, relating to our* Exports, Coinage, Paper Credit, *&c.*.

To CALEB D'ANVERS, *Esq;*
SIR,

AS nothing can be more grievous to an honest Man, who has any Regard and Concern for the Welfare and Happiness of his Country, than to find it from a rich and flourishing Condition, daily declining in its *Wealth*, *Power* and *Reputation:* So next to this, scarce any Thing can be more provoking than to see *those Persons*, who have had the chief Hand in bringing these Misfortunes upon the Publick, insulting them, under their *Distresses*, with false and fallacious Reasonings to prove their *present Prosperity*, in Contradiction to the general *Sense* and *Feeling* of the whole Kingdom; and this is the more mischievous, when bold and positive Assertions come from *those Persons*, who are presumed to be perfectly apprised of the Truth and Certainty of Facts they alledge, upon these Occasions; but there are some Cases, in which no *Assertions*, no *supposed Authority* can have any Weight; which I take to be the Case of the *Daily Journal* of the 8th Instant. I shall therefore trouble you with some few Observations upon it, and if in doing this, any Thing should be mentioned, which *these Gentlemen* express so great a

Desire to conceal from the Publick, they must blame themselves as the *Authors* of them; since if they did not think it their Interest and make it their Endeavour to spread these Delusions over the Kingdom, and, if possible, to put out the Eyes of the People, I should not have engaged in so irksome a Task, which cannot be more displeasing to *them*, than it is disagreeable to *me*.

This Writer, in order to prove his Assertion, that we are at this Time in a *thriving* and *flourishing Condition*, has heaped together, and reckoned up all the Benefits and Advantages, which the Nation has reaped from a successful and improving Trade of almost two hundred Years past, by which Our Wealth and Riches have been greatly encreased; as well as *Luxury*; from whence chiefly proceeds the great Quantity of *Plate, Jewels*, &c. and we have been enabled to make great *Improvements of Land*, &c. mentioned[a] by this Author, and the Yeomanry and Farmers of *England* have lived better than they did formerly; but is this any Contradiction to what is too well known and felt, that Our *Trade* and *Manufactures* are *now*, and have some *few Years past*, been in[b] a *declining Condition*, and that we are gradually falling from that Prosperity we have injoyed; which it is not to be imagined is to be so totally lost and destroyed at once, that we shall have no remaining Marks of it left?[c]

The great Stress he lays upon the *advanced Price of Land*, and the present *low Interest of Money*, is as little a Proof of the Truth of his Assertion; For both these have, in a great Measure, arisen from quite *other Causes* than the Increase of Our *National Riches*.

The sudden great Rise of the *Price of Land*, it is well known, was occasioned by an unequal Distribution of the Money of the Kingdom into few Hands, by the *South-Sea Scheme*; and this, together with the *Reduction of the Interest of the publick Debt*, continues it at present. The Collection of above *Thirty Three Millions* into one Capital by the *South-Sea Scheme*; and the *Reducing the Interest* at once of this Great Sum, which so much exceeds all the Cash of the Kingdom, is the true Reason of the present *Low Interest of Money*, which has by Degrees been diverted out of the useful Channels, in which it was formerly employed, before the *National Debt* was contracted; and this, like the collecting together many Rivulets, may give an Appearance of *Plenty*, even in the midst of *Scarcity*; but, it is to be feared, will, in

[a] mentioned] as mentioned *B*.
[b] have some . . . been in] have been some . . . in *B*.　　　[c] left?] *B*; left. *fol.*

Time, waste and destroy, instead of increasing our real Riches.

The Proprietors of the Funds having now no other Way of gaining a Subsistance by the Improvement of their Money, but by lending it to the Government, they must take what Interest they are pleased to give them: And the *Great Corporations*,[a] as long as their *Credit* subsists, are enabled to carry this Diminution of Interest, and the Value of Money still farther, since they are at no other Charge but a little *Paper* to effect it; and by these Means they may facilitate the encreasing *our Debts*, instead of promoting our *Wealth* and *Riches*; and I believe every considering Man dreads the Consequences of it.

I readily agree with this Writer, that a *Paper Credit* cannot long subsist, without a *sufficient Fund of Riches* to support it: And I believe he will not deny, that the *Lands* and *Revenues* of *Great-Britain* are an ample Security for the Payment of the *Publick Debt*, for which they stand engaged; and therefore whilst we continue in a State of Tranquillity and Safety, and keep a reasonable Proportion of *Specie* to carry on the Circulation, this *Paper Credit* will, and does answer all the Uses of *Money*, and give us the Appearance of the *real Wealth* we enjoyed before the Community spent *Fifty odd Millions*, and contracted the *National Debt*: And it is well known, that the *Mississippi* and *South-Sea Schemes*, whilst they lasted, gave the same Proof of Riches in *raising of Land*, &c.[1] But was a greater Absurdity ever endeavoured to be imposed upon Mankind, than to argue from hence that our *Paper Credit* (whose Rise and Foundation is[b] our *Debts*) can be the Effect of our *Wealth*, when nothing but Necessity created them, and still continues this heavy Burthen upon the Kingdom?

It must be allowed that our *Paper Credit* has been, and is, in our present Circumstances, of great Service and Conveniency to us; but the Example of the *South Sea* and *Mississippi* ought to be sufficient Warnings not to fancy that we may stretch it to any Lengths we please; for tho' the Extravagance, to which *these Schemes* were carried, made their Fall as sudden and surprizing as their Rise, yet it is manifest, that a Mischief of this Kind may come by *slower Degrees*, and a Man may be as certainly ruined by the continual Loss of *small Sums*, as he who is undone by *one Chance of the Dye*.

As long as we continue to make use of our *Credit* in the

---

[a] *Corporations,*] *monied Corporations, B.*
[b] whose . . . is] which owes its . . . to *B.*

Improvement of our *Trade* and *Commerce*, and in Services which visibly tend to the Benefit and Advantage of the Kingdom, so long we may depend upon its Continuance with us; but if it is employed in *Luxury* and *unnecessary Expences*, *Credit* from that Moment decreases, and destroys what it was design'd to support.

I shall, for Argument sake, allow that all the *Extracts*, published from the *Custom-House* Books, tho' supported by no *Authority*, are genuine; which is a very large Concession, considering the many *Accounts* that have been found to be *otherwise*, which had the Appearance of much *better Vouchers*; yet notwithstanding this, I shall proceed to shew, that they are a very *chimerical* Foundation to support what they are brought to prove.

To begin with the *Entries* of the *Exports*; It is well known that the Merchants, to save themselves the Trouble and small Fee of taking out *another Cockett*,[2] always enter *much larger Quantities* of Goods than they actually *Export*; and other *fictitious Entries* are frequently made of these Commodities, in order to raise the *Value* of them, from the Appearance of the great Quantities *exported*, and the less remaining to be sold: And these[a] *fictitious Entries* are often encreased, by the Practice of the Owners, and Masters of Ships, to incourage the Merchants to load Goods on board a Ship, put up on a general Freight, with the Hopes that she will be very soon dispatched. And I believe it is not unusual for Merchants themselves to put this in practice sometimes, to support their *declining Credit*, and at others,[b] to give them the Reputation of being *greater Dealers* than they really are. So that the *largest Entries* may be made when the *fewest Goods are exported*; and it is not impossible that the same Arts may be used to support the Assertion of our *present Prosperity*.

To these Uncertainties of making any Judgment of the *Quantities* of Goods *Exported*, from the *Entries*, we must add the Impossibility of making any reasonable Estimate of the *Value* of the Goods so exported, because[c] of the great Variety, different Kinds and Prices of them; for Instance, will any Man pretend to make an Estimate of the Value of *Perpetts*,[3] *Stuffs*, *Long* and *Short Cloths*, from the *Quantity* only, when they differ in their *Price* more or less as one is to four or five; so that he may very easily be mistaken some hundred thousand Pounds in every Year?

---

[a] sold: And these] sold. These *B*.   [b] and at others,] or *B*.
[c] because] by Reason *B*.

He has indeed very artfully compared two Periods of *Six Years* each; from 1715 to 1721; and from 1721 to 1727; but *two Years* of the first Period were during the Time of the *Sicilian* or *Spanish War*, when our *Trade* was prohibited in *Spain*, and greatly interrupted in *other Parts*; and in 1720 and 1721, two other Years of the same Period, the Mischiefs of the *South-Sea* Scheme put almost an entire Stop to all *Trade*; and yet these Accounts, uncertain as they are, shew the contrary of what they are brought to prove; for the *Exports* of 1716 and 1717 are above a *Million* and *forty thousand Pounds* more than the *Exports* of 1726 and 1727; and in this *last Year* they are *less* than they have been at any Time within this *Twelve Years*, except 1718 and 1719, for the Reasons before-mentioned; and I am inclined to believe, that the Year 1728 is still less favourable to his purpose, since he has not thought fit to give any Account of it.

But as I do not think *these Accounts* can enable us to make any certain Judgment, either of the *Decay* or *Encrease* of Our *Trade*, I only mention this to shew, that if they prove any thing, it is that Our *Manufactures* are in a *declining Way*, which is all that I ever heard lamented or complained of; for I suppose no body is so foolish as to think or say, that the *weakest* or *wickedest Ministry* that ever was in any Nation can, in the Compass of a few Years, wholly deprive them of a *Trade* that[a] has been acquired by the Labour and Industry of almost *Two Centuries*.

If we would be fully instructed in the Truth, which is contended for, we must have recourse to other Means for our Information than the *Entries* of the *Custom-House*: and these I take to be what follows.[b] *First*, The *Prices* of the *Woollen Manufactures* in all Parts of the Kingdom; and these I may venture to assert, have gradually decreased some few Years past, and are now from 20 to 25 *per Cent.* less than they were formerly; except the *Superfine Cloths* chiefly consumed at home, and the Price of *Wooll* is fallen in proportion.

In the next Place, the *Quantity* of *Woollen Goods* made is much less than it was a few Years since. Many of the Traders in these Commodities are broke, and Numbers of Workmen unemployed; by which Means the heavy Rates paid to the *Poor* in all the *Clothing Towns* of the Kingdom are severely felt from *Exeter* to *Norwich*; and no *Entries* from the *Custom-House* Books will, I believe,[c] be thought

---

[a] that] which *B.*   [b] follows.] follow. *B.*   [c] will, I believe,] will *B.*

of any Weight in Contradiction to these too well known Truths. And it is[a] very much to be feared, that if the *Fleet*, which is now going from *Spain* to the *West Indies*, should be wholly laden with the *Manufactures* of *France*, as I am assured it will, the *English Merchants* not being suffered to put any on Board, the People in those Parts may be reconciled to the[b] wearing the *French Commodities*, and we shall find the utmost difficulty to retrieve this valuable Branch of our Commerce.

As to what *This Writer* mentions upon the Articles of the Exportation of *Coals, Lead, Tin*, &c. we have, by the Profits of our *former Trade*, as I before took Notice, been Enabled to open and work more *Mines* than in the preceding Age. And as these Commodities can be had no where but from us, they will be sent Abroad, more or less, as there is a Demand for them: But this is no more a Proof of Our *flourishing Trade* at present, than the *Gold* and *Silver* the[c] *Spaniards* bring from *Mexico* and *Peru* is of the *Trade* of that Nation.

The Increase of the *Tonnage* of *Shipping*, employed in *Trade* these twelve Years past, is likewise no certain Proof of a *flourishing* and *beneficial Trade*: for the *Imports* and *Exports* being in this Account blended together, there is no Judgment to be made from them; for great Part of this *Shipping* may be employed to our Prejudice, in *importing* greater Quantities of Goods than formerly from Abroad, to supply our *Luxuries* at Home. We see every Year many Ships, at the Time of the *Vintage*, sent out empty for the Wines of *France, Spain* and *Portugal*, and an Increase of *Tonnage* on this Account is, I believe, no Increase of *Riches* to Us.

There is a considerable Number of Ships now employed more than formerly in the *Norway Trade*, to bring *Deals* and other *Timber* to supply the great Increase and Luxury of Our *Buildings*, and the Decay of Our *Own Timber*, to the no small Loss of the Kingdom, these *Imports* being purchased by our *Specie*.

The late great Addition to Our *Capital* has likewise very much increased the Shipping employed in bringing *Coals* to this Town, and they are[d] more used in most Parts of *England* than in former Times. And this Trade, tho' a very desirable Nursery of Our Seamen, yet brings no *New Wealth*.

---

[a] And it is] It is, besides *B*.   [b] to the] to *B*.   [c] the] which the *B*.
[d] and they are] which are also *B*.

There is Another Reason to be given for this Increase of *Shipping* likewise, that,[a] I am afraid, is, on many Accounts, very detrimental to Us; and that is the late Fabrick of Ships in *New England*, which are sent here to be sold to all Nations.

These, with many other accidental Causes, as the Transport of Our *Land Forces*, sending Provisions to Our *Fleets Abroad*, &c. may very well account for the Increase of *Tonnage* on the *Custom-House Register*; but are far from being any Proofs of the Improvement and Increase of a *beneficial Trade*, that[b] brings any new Acquisition of Riches into the Kingdom; for in some of the Instances before-mentioned, it appears they are constant and certain Drains of Wealth from Us. And this[c] is so far confirmed by this Account; That there appears to be 17160 Tons more entred in 1726 and 1727, when the Exportation of our *Woollen Manufactures* was so much less; than there is[d] entred in 1716 and 1717, when that[e] Exportation was greater.

This Writer was well aware of one Argument, that may be brought against him of more Force than all those he has produced to prove our present *prosperous Circumstances*; and that is the *Exchange* being against us; He therefore attempts, as well as he is able, to give some Sort of Reason for it; but let us now examine the Strength of it. He allows that *Amsterdam*, by its Wealth and Situation, is the *Centre of all Commercial Correspondence* between the several Parts of *Europe*, and that the Rate of *Exchange* between *us* and *Holland* must, in some Degree, affect that between us and all other Countries; and does it not follow from hence, that if the *Exchange* to *Holland* is not in our Favour, the whole *Ballance* of *Trade* is against us? He endeavours indeed to amuse and divert us from the Subject, by saying this was commonly the Case, during the two last Wars; but what is this to the present Purpose? For whatever Sums we may send abroad for *Troops*, *Subsidies* and *other Services*, which, by what he insinuates, must be very considerable, and perhaps more than is known; yet I hope they bear no Proportion to the many *Millions* which were necessarily remitted for the Maintenance of near 200,000 Men, and the other Expences of these[f] *Wars*.

The Interest that we pay to *Foreigners* for their great Capital in our *Funds*, which I am heartily sorry for, will as little account for the

---

[a] that] which *B.*   [b] that] which *B.*   [c] Us. And this] us; which *B.*
[d] is] were *B.*   [e] that] the *B.*   [f] *these*] *those B.*

present Difference of *Exchange*; for this must certainly have affected it much more, when our Interest was at 5 or 6 *per Cent.* or higher than at this Time, when we pay but 4 *per Cent.* only.

And his other Argument is as little convincing, since I believe the Fact is not true; but suppose, as he affirms, that *Foreigners* are drawing away their *Principal* from us; yet he owns, and the Nature of the Thing will satisfy us that this must be done by *Degrees.* If therefore the Profits of our whole *Trade* do not enable us to pay these *Debts*, and supply the *Specie* taken from us; is any Thing more evident than that we must become *poorer*? and this[a] is one further[b] Proof that all our *Paper Money* is not *real Wealth.* And in case *Foreigners* have so large a Sum, as he mentions in our *Funds*, He and his Patrons will do well to consider what further[c] Mischiefs may arise to us, in case they draw away this Money, and do not leave us a necessary Proportion to circulate our *vast Credit* under the Circumstances of a *declining Trade.* But instead of *Foreigners* having sold great Sums out of our *Stocks*, and taken away the Money, the Truth I believe is, that their Transactions this Way have been rather with a View to *buy in again* with Advantage, and knowing the Secret of Affairs, as well as *some People* at Home, they have joined with them in preying on the Needy and the Ignorant; and consequently this has had little or no Influence in turning the *Exchange* to our Prejudice.

Nor will the large *Importation of Corn* the last Year account for[d] it; for an Accident in our Favour fully repaired if not over ballanced this Calamity. And that was, a much larger *Exportation of Sugar* than usual, occasioned by the entire Failure of the *Martinico* Crop by a violent Earthquake, which affected the whole Island; and there was but a very small Crop in the *Braziles.*

The *Gentleman* has thought fit to decline his Comparison of *Six Years* and *Six Years* upon the Article of *Coinage*, and has luckily picked out the Year 1726, for coining a greater Quantity of *Gold* than in some Years before, except 1714, 1715, 1716, and 1720; but as the same Time, I believe without intending it, he gives the Reason for it; and this was, the Apprehensions of an immediate War with *Spain*, upon Admiral *Hosier's* Expedition to the *West-Indies*, which made many of our Merchants bring home their Effects as fast as they could from *Spain.* But is it not certain that the *Coinage*

<hr>

[a] and this] This *B.*　　[b] further] farther *B.*　　[c] further] farther *B.*
[d] account for] *B*; account, for *fol.*

has gradually lessen'd, as I have proved that our *Manufactures* have declined these few Years past? and if the *Coinage* of the *last Year* would have contradicted it, I doubt not but[a] we should have seen an Account of it.

We may add, upon this Head, that as *Moidores* were very plenty in all Payments not long since, we scarce see any of them now;[4] which shews, that there has lately been no small *Export of Gold*; and there being more Profit on *Guineas* than *Moidores*, it is to be feared that some of our *Guineas* are gone along with them; and common Experience daily convinces us of the Want of *Silver*.

It is estimated, that the yearly Import of *Gold* into *Europe* from the *Braziles* has for some time past been *three Millions* or more; and as this is not exported into the *East-Indies*, as the *Silver* is, but remains in *Europe*; if we have not annually a Share of this Increase, we must become *poorer* in respect to our Neighbours, tho' we retain the same Quantity of *Specie* we had formerly; but if our Riches decrease on this Head, our Circumstances must be allowed to be much worse, and will be daily more felt.

The Reader will observe that I have taken no Notice of the *daily Bankruptcies* that we find in all our News Papers; though I presume even this Author will not pretend that they are the Effects of *Wealth* or *Prosperity*; and the World, I believe, will allow they are stronger Proofs of a *declining Condition* than any which he hath brought to support the contrary Position.

Having now thrown together such Particulars as occurred to me upon Reading this Paper, I shall leave it to others, who have more Leisure, and greater Knowledge in the Affairs of *Trade*, to enlarge upon them; but I believe these Hints will shew that *this Writer* has produced no one Proof of his Assertion, that we are, at this Time, in a *thriving* and *flourishing Condition*. I do, with great Pleasure, acknowledge, that many of the Particulars he has mentioned are indisputable Marks that we are yet a great and powerful People; and I hope we shall ever continue so; but we cannot expect to secure this Happiness to Posterity, but[b] by our hearty Endeavours to retrieve the Loss and Decay of our *Trade* and *Manufactures*, to rectify those Mistakes which have occasioned them, and[c] contract our *publick Expences* to the *annual Sums* we are able to raise *within the Year*, and put a Stop to that fatal and destructive Evil of *new Debts*; and it will

---

[a] but] that *B*.   [b] but] any other way than *B*.   [c] and] to *B*.

in the End be found that *They*, who honestly propose the Service of their Country, in pointing them out to the Publick, will much better deserve their Thanks and Esteem, than *Those*, who, for the Support of their Power, and the satisfying their Avarice and Ambition, endeavour to conceal these growing Evils, and deceive us into a false Opinion of our *increasing Wealth*, which must end in certain Ruin.

But, Mr. *D'Anvers, this Writer* and any others may argue as long as they please upon this Subject; the Determination of the Question must be left to the Judgment of the Publick, and it would be in vain for any Man to endeavour to perswade the People that they are *poor, distressed*, burthen'd with *Taxes*, decaying in *Trade* and *Manufactures*, when they really know and feel themselves in *Plenty*, and growing more *rich* and *happy*; and though any Person, on the other Hand, with never so great an Appearance of *Authority* from any *supposed Accounts*, should assert[a] and assure, in the strongest Manner, that they are *rich* and *happy*; will they, when they suffer these Evils, be perswaded to believe it? This would be supposing *implicite Faith* in a much greater Degree than even Lord *Peter* in the *Tale of a Tub* pretended to. *Such Writers* are like the *Physician*, who endeavour'd to convince one of his Patients, under a *Complication of Distempers*, that He was in *perfect Health*; and we may give Him the same Answer, which the poor Man did at last to the *Doctor*, upon asking how He did, that *He was* languishing *with the Lord knows how many* good Symptoms.

I am, SIR,
Yours, &c.

No. 142.   Saturday, 22 March 1729.

To CALEB D'ANVERS, *Esq*;

SIR,

I FIND that nothing gives your Adversaries more Offence or Uneasiness than those *Historical Dissertations*, which they call *Parallels*. The Reason seems to be, that *Facts* are *stubborn Things*, and cannot be so easily evaded as Discourses upon *general Subjects*, however strongly supported by *Argument* and *Reason*. The *Writers*

---

[a] and though . . . should assert] On the other hand, though any Person should, with never . . . *Accounts*, assert *B*.

against you are grown out of all Patience with the Names of *Sejanus*, and[a] *Wolsey*, and *Buckingham*;[1] and *one* of them (I think it is *Publicola*)[2] hath lately desired that you will *mention them no more*. I hope, Mr. *D'Anvers*, you will be so good as to grant Him this Request, and suffer these three great Predecessors of *Publicola*'s FRIEND to rest in their Graves, without any farther Disturbance (unless upon very extraordinary Occasions) after they have done you such eminent Service. I am however very far from advising you to leave off *this Manner of Writing*, which I take to be of the greatest Use and Service to the Publick, as it tends to forewarn all *Ages* against *evil Counsels* and *corrupt Ministers*, by setting before their Eyes, in the strongest Light, what have been the Consequences of *such Counsels*, and the terrible Fate of *such Ministers* in *former Times*; but I have the more Reason to hope, that you will oblige Mr. *Publicola* in this Point, because there are Multitudes of *other wicked Ministers*, whose Characters are as yet intirely untouch'd by you; and you need not be afraid of *exhausting* so copious a Subject.

The Fate of the famous *Pensionary*, *De Wit*, hath lately been urged against you, as an Instance of an *able* and *honest Minister*, who was sacrificed to the Rage of *popular Resentment*; and the general good Character which He hath left behind Him, both as to *Ability* and *Integrity*, makes it worth Examination, how this Opinion came to prevail; for though his *Capacities*, in other Respects, should be allowed as large as the most sanguine Partizans can desire, yet I think it demonstrable that, with Relation to *France*, they were not employed for the *Good of his Country*; but that his whole Conduct was influenced either by *selfish* and *corrupt Views*, or very *absurd Politicks*, manifestly contrary to the Interests of the *United Provinces*.

I observe that the Authority of Sir *WILLIAM TEMPLE* hath been quoted against you on this Occasion; and I am of Opinion, that it is, in a great Measure, owing to the candid Representations of this *excellent, great Man*, that so much Tenderness hath been shewn to the Memory of Monsieur *De Wit*.

I speak this with great Deference to the Judgment of Sir *William Temple*, and without any Intention of reflecting on his Character; for the *Pensionary*'s criminal Correspondence, and Intrigues with the *French* Court, were not then fully *proved*, though

---

[a] and] *omitted B.*

generally *suspected* and *believed*; whereas the Evidence, upon which I build my Argument, is taken from the *Letters* of the Count *D'Estrades*, Ambassador of *France* at that Time in *Holland*, published since the Death of Sir *William Temple*.

This *great Minister* had the sole Management of Affairs in *Holland*, when the Power of *France* was becoming justly formidable to all *Europe*, and when it was the true Interest of the *United Provinces* to have given a seasonable Check to the growing Greatness of so terrible a Neighbour, by a Conjunction with *Spain*; but He suffer'd *Himself* and his *Country* to be deluded by *false* and *repeated Professions of Friendship*, without *one visible Proof* of it, 'till the Designs of *France* were ripe for Execution, and their Arms broke in, like an Inundation, upon the *Low Countries*; and (what ought *never to be forgotten*) this notorious Violation of *Faith*, *Alliances*, and the most *solemn Declarations*, was perpetrated without any other *Provocation* or *Pretence*, than that *His most Christian Majesty was not pleased with some Part of their Conduct.*

It must be confessed, that many considerable Persons in the State had early Views of the mischievous Projects of the *French Court*, and endeavoured, not without Success, to apprise their Countrymen of the impending Danger. But the *Pensionary* was so far from paying any Regard to the *Voice of the People* (whom He always *despised*, knowing *where his great Strength lay*) that He AVAIL'D HIMSELF of their just Apprehensions, and endeavoured to rivet his Interest with *that Court*, by his easy and complaisant Conviction of *their Sincerity*, and the *unreasonable Jealousy* of their Neighbours; for we find the *French King* expressing Himself to his *Ambassador* in these Terms.

"I am very glad the *Sieur DE WIT* is sensible, and sees so plainly (by your discovering to Him my most secret Thoughts and Intentions, on the Proposals which have been made Him) that I am not so *dangerous a Neighbour*, nor a Prince so *immoderately ambitious*, nor so covetous of *another's Territories*, as my Enemies have published with odious Exaggerations, to create every where a Jealousy of my Power."

The *Sieur DE WIT* was no sooner convinc'd Himself, than He made it his Business to possess his Countrymen with the same Sentiments, by diverting their Fears to *another Object*; and the *Emperor of Germany* being too weak at that Time to be made the *Bugbear*, He insinuated the Danger of being over-run by the *Turks*;

as appears from the following Passage in one of *D'Estrades* Letters, where He says that "*DE WIT* told the Deputies, He could not but be apprehensive, that in a little Time their Country would have a *barbarous Nation* for their Borderers, whose Power was so great, that their[a] State would not be able to resist it."

He therefore proposed to enter into a *Defensive League* with *France*, as the best provisional Security against all *dangerous Designs* of the *Turks*; but as these Suggestions, though very industriously propagated, were not supported by any *outward Appearances*, but only by Pretences of *undoubted, secret Intelligence*, and *strong Asseverations* of *DE WIT* and his *Party*, they gained no Credit, but were look'd on as a palpable Cheat and Pretext to cover an *odious Alliance*, which was so universally against the Bent of the People, that *this Minister* was not able, by all his Artifices, to reconcile them to it. Accordingly we find *D'Estrades* says, "We are not look'd upon here as *Friends*, but are *declaimed against* at an horrible Rate. I cannot enough describe to you how we are *rail'd* at here."

But however They were *rail'd at*, and *exclaim'd against* by the People in general, the *Pensionary* had instill'd more favourable Sentiments of them into the *Deputies*, who were ready to come into all his *Proposals*, as appears from the two following Passages in the *Ambassador's Letters*.

"The *States* would certainly have received your Majesty's * *Declaration* with more Joy than they did, but Monsieur *De Wit*, who prepares Mens Minds to take Things in a *good Sense*, and shews them to be for the *Advantage of the State*, is not now here."

In the *next Letter* it appears that the *Pensionary was present*; for *D'Estrades* tells his Master:

"I can assure your Majesty, that you are in such Consideration here, that They have resolved this Morning, to form no *important Design*, in the Affairs which may happen to them, without first consulting *your Majesty*."

This Management of *De Wit*, in bringing his Country into such an absolute Dependance on the *French Court*, was so acceptable a Service, that the *King*, in a Letter to his *Minister*, expressed his Desire *of having the Means put into his Hands, to give* Him *some effectual Marks of his* Esteem *and* Affection. Accordingly He commands his *Minister* to declare, "That He had sent positive

[a] their] the *B*.

Orders, if *De Wit* thought proper, either for his *greater Security*, or
the better and sooner to disperse the *Cabals* forming against Him,
that the *Ambassador* should do Him any good Office in *his Name*
with the *States*; to favour the *Pensionary*; to praise his *Merit* and
Services, and let them know how much his *most Christian Majesty*
thought it for their Advantage to *continue the Trust* They put in
Him; or if *his (the Pensionary's) Name* was not thought proper to be
mentioned, then the *Ambassador* was to inform them, that the *King*
had a great Esteem for the PRESENT MINISTRY, which
seemed to his Majesty to be the *best*, and the *most conducive* to the
Safety and Preservation of the State; that, as their *good Friend* and
Ally, and one so much concerned in their *good Conduct*, He
exhorted them vigorously to oppose the *Intrigues*, which were too
well known to be carried on in the *Provinces*, to change the
Administration; and his Majesty did it the rather; for, that if Things
should so happen, He could no longer have the SAME
CONFIDENCE in them, because *their Enemies* would be then
Masters, and *HE could expect no GOOD from them*."

The *Pensionary* judged this *Recommendation* to be not only
seasonable, but a *necessary Expedient* at that Time; and *expressed
Himself very sensible of his Majesty's Favour, and to desire nothing so
much as an Opportunity to shew his* Gratitude *by some Service*.

And I think it evident, that He wanted neither *Opportunity* nor
Inclination to demonstrate the Sincerity of his Professions. He was
now become perfectly *French*. Every *Advice*, every *Direction* from
that Court was received with *implicit Observance*; and the
Ambassador, in Return, put on an *outward Appearance* of the
tenderest Concern for so *valuable a Friend*. He often expresses his
Fears for his Safety. Sometimes the *Spanish* Intrigues give Him
terrible Apprehensions; for He says, "*De Wit* having advanced far
in the Business, without much *Communication*, and having had the
Boldness to do it of *Himself*, and *without Order*, He fears the *Spanish
Ambassador* will make *fine Work* of it."

Sometimes *domestick Enemies* give Him the same Uneasiness;
for, says He, "*De Wit* perceives, that if the *Treaty proposed does not
go forwards*, He is not strong enough *alone* to maintain his *Party*,
against the *Cabals* which are forming to destroy it."

At other Times He is apprehensive of the *Pensionary's Want of
Skill*, and complains that "He abounds in his *own Understanding*;
and not knowing any thing of *War*, and being fond of doing every

thing *Himself*, He too easily gives into *Proposals* that are made to Him; and by *this*, I perceive, that He *loses his Credit*."

Much more might be extracted from the *above-mentioned Letters*, to shew the absolute Prevalence of *French Counsels* over *this Minister*, and, through Him, over his *unhappy Country*; but I believe what hath been quoted will be thought sufficient. Better had it been both for *Him* and the *Commonwealth*, had He treated the *Professions* and *Artifices* of *France* with that *Penetration* and *Integrity*, for which He hath been celebrated; tho' I think it is clear, from the *Authority* which I have produced, that He must have been intirely destitute of *one*, if not of *both*; for otherwise He would never have enter'd into such Measures for nursing up a *Power*, which, at once forgetting all *Engagements* and *Obligations*, in a most *faithless* and *unprecedented Manner* attempted the total Destruction of his *Country*, and thereby work'd up the Populace to such implacable Rage, as ended in that dreadful and well-known Tragedy upon *himself* and his *Brother*.[3]

Here, Mr. *D'Anvers*, my Letter should have concluded, did I not think it necessary to obviate a Reflection, which some of your *little*, *captious Adversaries* may be ready to make. As I am very confident that They cannot falsify the Account, which I have given of *this Minister* and his *ruinous Politicks*; so I plainly foresee that, according to Custom, They will have Recourse to invidious Interpretations of *my Meaning*, and charge me with a Design of insinuating, that *all Men in Power*, who pursue the same *destructive Measures*, ought to meet with the *same Fate*; whereas I assure you, Mr. *D'Anvers*, that I am so far from having that[a] Intention, that nobody can have a greater Abhorrence of such *outragious* and *unwarrantable* Methods of Resentment. I will not dissemble my constant Opinion, that the Welfare of a *whole Community* is infinitely preferable to the Safety of any *single Minister*; and therefore no Punishment can be too severe for a *Minister*, who betrays his Country in this infamous Manner; but I think every Man, who wishes well to the Cause of *Liberty*, ought to detest all *irregular* and *tumultuary Violence*; because the Generality of Mankind are as prone to *Compassion*, as they are eager in *Resentment*; for which Reason it often happens, that when a *wicked Man* is taken off by *Assassination*, the Memory of his *ill Deeds* is obliterated by the *unjustifiable Nature of his Punishment*. This may,

[a] that] any such *B*.

perhaps, be the Case of the *Great Minister* under our present Consideration; for I cannot help thinking, that if *De Wit* had suffer'd by a *legal* and *judicial* Sentence, He would have been generally mentioned in History as a *Traytor*, not a *Friend to his Country*.

But however I may differ from *some Persons*, in my Opinion of *this Minister*, I have the Consolation to reflect, that I cannot be charged with traducing his Memory upon *Jacobite Principles*; for if it should be still maintain'd, that He was a *Friend to his Country*; I am sure it cannot be denied, that He was the *most profess'd* and *inveterate Enemy to that immortal Prince*, who was the Deliverer of his *own Country*, as well as of *this Nation*, and left us that invaluable Legacy of the *Protestant Succession*, in his Majesty's most illustrious House.

I am, SIR, &c.
W. RALEIGH.

---

* *The* French *had obliged themselves by the* Defensive Alliance, *to assist the* Hollanders, *in case their Dominions should be invaded* by any Power; *but it is remarkable that, instead of* adhering to their Engagements, *according to their* solemn *and* repeated Assurances, *they lay under violent Suspicions of secretly abetting their* Enemies *against them, and could not be prevail'd upon to make this* Declaration *in their Favour, 'till they had been* well-beaten, *and it could do them* no Service.[a]

No. 147.   Saturday, 26 April 1729.

To CALEB D'ANVERS, *Esq;*

Mr. *D'Anvers,*

You obliged your Readers some Time since with the Speech of a *worthy Senator* against *Bribery* and *Corruption.*[1] I have met with one, of a later Date, which, as it seems to have proceeded from a like honest Spirit, may not be unfit for your Consideration. I have ever thought it the most noble and useful Part of History to transmit to Posterity the Sentiments of *Great Minds*, as they have been express'd by *Themselves*, in *solemn Councils*, upon the most *important Occasions*. They naturally tend to raise the same Thoughts in noble Breasts, and frequently animate them in like

[a] *The* French . . . Service.] *omitted B.*

Exigencies; but without further[a] Preface it is submitted to your Judgment.

A Speech of Sir *CHARLES SIDLEY* in the Reign of the late King *WILLIAM*

Mr. *Speaker*,

"We have provided for the *Army*: We have provided for the *Navy*; and now at last a new Reckoning is brought upon us. We must likewise provide for the LISTS. Truly, Mr. *Speaker*, 'tis a sad Reflection, that *some Men* should wallow in *Wealth* and *Places*, whilst *others* pay away in Taxes the fourth Part of their Revenue, for the Support of the same Government.

We are not upon equal Terms for His Majesty's Service. The *Courtiers* and *great Officers* charge as it were in *Armour*, and feel not the *Taxes* by Reason of their *Places*; whilst the *Country Gentlemen* are shot through and through by them. The *King* is pleas'd to lay His *Wants* before us; and I am confident expects our Advice upon it. We ought therefore to tell Him what *Pensions* are *too great*; and what *Places* may be *extinguish'd* during the War and the *Publick Calamity*.

His Majesty sees nothing but *Coaches and Six*, and *great Tables*; and therefore cannot imagine the *Want* and *Misery* of the rest of his Subjects. He is a *Brave* and *generous Prince*; but He's[b] a *young King*, encompass'd and hemm'd in by a Company of crafty old Courtiers.[c] To say no more, some have Places of 3000 l. some of 6000 l. others of 8000 l. *per Annum* each. Certainly *Publick Pensions*, whatever they have been formerly, are much too great for the *present Want* and *Calamity* that reigns every where else; and it is a Scandal that a *Government so sick at Heart as ours is, should look so well in the Face.* We must save the King Money, wherever we can; for I am afraid the War is too great for our Purses, if Things be not managed with all imaginable Thrift: When the People of *England* see all Things are sav'd that can be sav'd; that there are no *exorbitant Pensions*, nor *unnecessary Salaries*; and all is applied to the *Use*, for which it is given; we shall give, and they shall pay whatever his Majesty can want to secure the *Protestant Religion*, and to keep out the King of *France*, and King *James* too—I conclude, Mr. *Speaker*; let us *save* the King what we *can*, and *then* let us proceed to *give* Him what we are able."

---

[a] further] farther *B*.   [b] He's] He is *B*.   [c] Courtiers.] *B*; Courtiers: *fol*.

No. 149. Saturday, 10 May 1729.

Aude aliquid, brevibus Gyaris, *&* Carcere *dignum.* JUV.[1]

To CALEB D'ANVERS, *Esq;*
SIR,

WHOEVER has read *The Report of the Committee of the* HONOURABLE HOUSE OF COMMONS, concerning the many Frauds and Corruptions, notorious Plunderings and Exactions, arbitrary and tyrannical Insolences and Oppressions, Subornations, Extortions, and inhuman Barbarities, by *Dungeons, Irons* and *Torture,* (lately committed within the *Fleet Prison*; to the Inslaving, Ruining, and finally Destroying many of the Subjects of this Kingdom;) cannot but be warmed with a just and uncommon Indignation against those Little Tyrants, the vile and mercyless Managers of this amazing Scene of Iniquity; and at the same Time, he cannot but have a Heart full of Praise and Gratitude towards those *worthy Patriots,* who have so carefully search'd out, so fully detected, and will, no doubt, as severely punish these High Crimes and Horrible Misdemeanors, for a Terror to others, and to their own immortal Honour and Reputation.

It is evident, from this single, glaring Instance, that notwithstanding the Popular Exclamations of Liberty and Property! Peace and Plenty! good and glorious Times! a great, free, and flourishing Nation! yet Tyranny and Arbitrary Power, Oppression and Male-administration, may reign in a little Society *in Covert,* and secretly skulk in the very Heart of such a Nation, and at the very Gates of its Capital; so that every Attempt to discover and expose any Incroachments or Corruptions of this kind, is by no means to be called *Libelling the State*; but, on the contrary, ought to be look'd on, as the genuine Issue of a publick Spirit; and to be encouraged as the Fruits and Produce of the Love of our Country.

Thomas Bambridge, Esq; Warden and Guardian of a little Territory and unfortunate Sett of People under his Power (*Guardianus, sive Custos Prisonæ de la Flete*; that is, *Keeper of the Liberties* of a small District in our Great City, called the *Fleet*) Solicitor of Solicitors, and Councellor of Councellors; Founder of Dungeons, and sole Inventor of the noble Manafacture of *Iron Bolts* and *Manacles,* commonly called *the King's Plate*; to the Terror of all

Debtors, and for the Support of Publick and National Credit; this
Man, I say, under all these great Names and Titles, may perhaps
insist upon Privilege, and plead an Exemption from all *Enquiries* of
one so far beneath him, in Station and Dignity. But, for the sake of
the Publick, I hope I am at Liberty to make some Reflections upon
his Conduct, and to justify the Proceedings of our *Representatives*,
against Him and his Chief Ministers, *Barnes, Pindar, King*, and
Everett.

The *Honourable Committee* do, with great Truth and Justice,
impute the Abuses in the *Fleet* to the *Venality of the* Warden's
Office. He buys of a *Lord*. His *Deputy* or *Successor* buys of Him. The
Underagents buy of the *Deputy*; and the *poor distress'd Prisoner*[a]
pays all. Here is a blessed Reformation indeed; where *Insolvent
Debtors* become in an[b] Instant the best of *Paymasters*; only they
happen to pay in the wrong Place, and to mistake their *New Keepers*
for their *Old Creditors*. The Antients had a very odd Law. They
sold *Debtors*[c] into Slavery and took Money for them; but the Wiser
and more generous Moderns suffer a Stranger to take their Slaves
gratis, and make the most of them; to the great Encouragement of
Trade and *Commerce*. This *Venality of Offices*, that Sprout and
genuine Fibre of the *Root of all Evil*, is very well observ'd to be the
Parent of many Abuses; and if it happens to spoil a *Gaol*, it cannot
fail of doing some Mischief even in *Courts* and *Palaces*.

I can imagine this *great Minister* Mr. *B*. summoning his
Creatures and demanding Contributions for *Guards* and *Jane-
zaries*—for *strong Rooms* and *Dungeons*—for *Irons* and *Manacles*—
for *Musquets* and *Bayonets*—for *Tortures, Tipstaves* and *Spunging-
Houses*—all indeed highly necessary for maintaining the Peace, and
promoting the Wellfare of his Vassals; But then closing the Whole
with an Item *for re-imbursing the Patent*; for unless this were done in
the *Current Year*, it would be full two long Years more, before he
could be worth 10000 l. and should the Industry of his Slaves or the
Charity of their Friends, be misapplied and diverted to improper
Uses (such as the Payment of their *Honest Creditors*, or their *Just
Fees*) some of them might perhaps run a madding after Liberty, and
meditate a decent escape out of his Dominions.

Tho' the *Committee* apprehend that, upon putting down the
Star-Chamber, in the Reign of King *Charles*, I.[d] no *Warden* could

[a] *poor distress'd Prisoner*] *poor Subject B.*   [b] in an] *B*; an *fol.*
[c] *Debtors*] their *Debtors B.*   [d] I.] lst *B.*

91

pretend to take Fees of *Archbishops*, *Bishops*, *Temporal Peers*, or *Baronets*; *or to put them in Irons, or exact Fees for not doing so*; Yet the Patent of K. *Charles*, II. reciting that of Q. *Elizabeth*, has a Table annex'd, of all the Fees payable by those High Orders of Quality, to the High and Mighty *Warden, for the Liberty of the House and Irons*; and no doubt Mr. *B.* insisted on this latter Authority. 'Tis plain he did so, in the Case of a *Baronet*.[2] Now with what Pleasure must our *Nobility* read and digest this memorable Passage? One would think indeed it must be somewhat grating for a Person of the first Extract and Dignity to obey the Nod, or to wear the *Manacles*, or take the *King's Plate*, at the Hands of an *insolent Commoner*.

Our *Honourable PATRIOTS* observe further,[a] that *Pikes* and *Halberts* were the only Weapons heretofore in Use, and *Watchmen* the only proper Guards, for the Preservation and Security of the *Fleet*. But Mr. *B.* has now levy'd and introduc'd a *standing Force*, instead of a *Regular Militia*, always ready to be call'd together on any emergent Occasions. He arms them with *Musquets* and *Bayonets*; keeps them in his *own Pay*; gives them the Word, *To Fire*; leads them on to the Attack of Doors and Locks, and to the stripping and plundering of Rooms, and orders them to stab, kill, insult, iron, torture, staple down, and drag into noisome Dungeons and Vaults, (the Receptacles both of the *Living* and the *Dead*) sometimes perhaps a *Baronet*, now and then only a *Squire* or *Gentleman*, and sometimes even *Captains* themselves (as in Mr. *Sinclair's* Case) provided they are *reduc'd*, or not in his own Pay. By the Help of these Mirmydons, and for the Augmentation of his Forces, besides the Troops regularly *listed* and enroll'd, he can *press* Men into the Service, upon the very Verge of his Territories (as was the Case of *Tom Hogg*) and for all these *military Preparations*, he gives the best political Reasons imaginable; *First*, by pleading his *Prerogative*, that it is done by his *own Authority*, and *secondly*, by declaring the Ends and Necessity of these wise Provisions, and their Usefulness to the Publick; that it is done *for preserving the Quiet and Safety of his People.*

The admirable *Quevedo*, in one of his *Visions*,[3] speaks of a Sett of Wretches, whom a Hard-hearted Devil would not admit into *Hell*; and of their great Concern and Uneasiness at this Disappointment. This seems to be the Case of some Prisoners, whom Mr. *B. would*

---

[a] further,] farther, *B.*

not admit into Gaol. No; They must first pass the *Purgatory* of a *Spunging-House*; and there be drain'd of their Money; Then the *Fleet* takes them, where their *Spirit*, the last Thing they have to lose, is broken by *Irons* and *Dungeons*; and *Death*, the last and only Favour, is deny'd them. At least it must not be brought on too soon (as in *Castell's* Case)[4] but with a slow lingering Pace, not with a *Twitch*, or in a *Blaze*, which is the less arbitrary Practice of *Persecuting Tyrants* and *Popish Inquisitions.* How great a *Machiavell* is Mr. *B?* He knows how to discipline and train Men to Slavery. They must first be impoverish'd; then tempted to complain; then check'd and restrain'd for Complaining; their Spirits gently tam'd, and leasurely reduc'd—*Damn him* (says *B.* of Mr. *Macpheadris*) *he is easy*—This was his Crime; and to punish him, Drive him out of his Room—Down with his Hut—Let him lie in the Cold and Rain—And still is he *easy?*—Then attack him Sword in Hand— Away with him to the *Dungeon*—Iron and torture him—Disable him of his Legs and his Sight— And if he is *easy* still, he is deliver'd over to a reprobate Spirit of Disaffection and Apostacy.

Mr. *B.* seems to be well experienc'd, and improv'd, in the Management and Disposition of *Publick Accounts* and *Revenues*; For some *Books* he conceal'd or destroy'd; and others he kept indeed, but with a decent and proper Negligence. *Smuglers* and Debtors to the *Crown* he would suffer to escape, and assist them in it. But if they went into *Trade* (of which he was a great Encourager) they must be strictly accountable for his *Share* and *Dividend*; and whilst they paid *unjust Fees* punctually and honestly, if they were deficient in their *just Debts*, he gave them the Protection of the House. For Fear of any Mistakes, he order'd Fees to be paid *six* or *seven Times over*; and to shew his Impartiality, tax'd Rooms to *Rent*, that never paid before; whereby[a] he brought all Things to an Equality. He valu'd *Liberty* by the Day, not as some Niggards do by the Hour or the Moment; and gave his *Rules* accordingly. His *Scape Warrants* were not intended to confine or injure the Person, but to bring him to a fair Account and Dividend of what he had gotten during his Elopement. How noble and extensive a Charity was it, to *discharge and exonerate* no less than 119[b] Persons in the Space of three Days only, and for Debts of no less Value than 17099 l.? *Charity hideth a Multitude of Sins*; and shall we forgive the Sins

---

[a] whereby] by which *B.*   [b] 119] one hundred and nineteen *B.*

committed against others, without any Good or Benefit to our selves? No; The *Consideration-Money* is not mention'd; and This, with all other incidental Charges of Mr. *B*'s Administration, are flung at once into the *Christmas-Box*; by which he makes and insists upon no further[a] Demands, but generously relies on the Benevolence and Free-will Offerings of his Creatures.

Swearing the Truth[b] ought, no Doubt, to be encourag'd; But Mr. *B*'s Manner of Swearing by *Proxy*, is an Improvement upon this Scheme. His Method of preparing *Affidavits*, and drawing in Persons by *Riot* or *Menaces*, to confirm them upon Oath, appears to be exactly copied from Serjeant *Kite*'s Principle, *Swearing for the Good of the Service*. Indeed, his Way of *Indicting others first*, to prevent being *Indicted himself*, and of drawing Men in to *plead Guilty*, in Hopes of Favour, and afterwards treating them as the worst of Criminals, are not without *Precedent*; But then his refusing *Sollicitors* to have Access to their *Clients*, and taking away, instead of suspending *the Writs of Habeas Corpus*, would appear to be extraordinary Steps, were they not to be accounted for, upon That High Fundamental, *The Reason and Necessity of State*.

I admire Mr. *B*'s Notion of the Use of *Women* and *Informers* in a well-regulated Government: And therefore he did wisely, in committing the Oversight of his *Spunging-Houses*, to *Mary Whitwood* and others, for the more effectual draining and dispiriting of his Vassals. Hence also it is, that the *Lyon's Den* and *the Women's Ward* are so near to one another; tho' Both are said *to be noisome and out of Repair*.

But lastly, and above all other Accomplishments, I like his Skill and Conduct in the *Disposal* and *Ingrossing* of the several Places of *Trust* and *Profit*, within his Jurisdiction. All these were *Venal*, that they might be exactly like his *own*. He assum'd the Power of changing *Sides* and *Rooms*, and turn'd many out of *Places* which they had paid for, on Purpose to be paid for them again. He took large *Premiums*; but gave his Dealers a Power, to reimburse themselves out of the Pockets of his Vasals. He excell'd in *Quartering* and *splitting* of Places, by putting Two, Three, or Four Beds in a Room, and Two or Three Lodgers in a Bed. And he was so skilful an *Engrosser*, that when he took the *Sum Total* to himself, charged in a *Bill* or *Table* delivered to the Judges, he acted both as

[a] further] farther *B*.   [b] Truth] *B*; Truth, *fol.*

Warden, Clerk, Chamberlain, Goaler, Porter and *Chaplain*; to the *last* of which Officers he gave a small *Stipend* or *Donative*, and took up all the *great Tythes* in kind, to himself. How he justifies this Incroachment upon the *Church*, I know not; but I am told that he is subtle enough to find an *Error* in the great Lord Chancellor *King*'s Opinion, who has plainly *declared*, that there ought to be *no Prison in a Prison*, by shewing clearly, that one of them is only a *strong Room* or a *Dungeon*.

The ever memorable[a] Sir *John Falstaff* dyed a Prisoner in the *Fleet*.[5] I wish he had left us some Memoirs and Account of the Place in his Time; but there his *Wit* and his *Fat* both fail'd him together. Gossip *Quickly* seems to intimate that he talk'd much of *Hell*; but were he now going to the *Fleet*, he would chuse rather to dye in the *Ditch*, than to linger in the *Prison*.—You may expect a *Panegyrick* from Mr. *B.* or Company, upon the superior Glories and Privileges of *Newgate*.

I am, SIR, Yours,
BOULEPHORUS.[6]

No. 161. Saturday, 2 August 1729.

Venimus ad Summum Fortunæ.—Hor.[1]

To CALEB D'ANVERS, *Esq*;

Mr. *D'Anvers*,

YOU have frequently inveighed against *Corruption* in general, and forewarn'd us of the Consequences,[b] which it must naturally have on our Constitution, unless speedily restrain'd. You have exerted your laudable Endeavours to alarm our Apprehensions on this Account; to raise our Indignation against *Those*, who are the Authors and Promoters of it; and to excite our Zeal in opposing Them. Every wise and honest Man, I hope, thinks Himself obliged to you for these Writings, which with Pleasure I observe have not been altogether without Effect. But as it hath been objected by your Adversaries that *Fallacies lurk under general Assertions* (which is very true in many Cases, whatever it may be in this) I wish you

---

[a] memorable] *B*; memorable, *fol.*   [b] Consequences,] Effects, *B*.

would descend a little more into *Particulars* and, by a Review of the *present Age*, shew how generally depraved it is grown; how *Corruption* hath gain'd Ground amongst Men of almost all Orders and Professions; and what a Deluge of most pernicious Vices and Enormities it hath introduced.

Here, Sir, you will find a large Field to expatiate in, and too many Proofs, particular Proofs, of what you have so often asserted.

Luxury and *Extravagance*, with their constant Attendants, *Necessity* and *Prostitution*, are too visible in all Parts of the Kingdom; especially in this great City, where a general Spirit of *Prodigality* and *Excess* is seen to prevail (I wish I could not say it was encourag'd) amongst all Degrees of Men, from one End of the Town to the other. What can this produce at a Time, when there is such a general Stagnation of all Trade, but *Distress, Bankruptcy, Dependance* and other numberless Evils to the Publick? And if *Extravagance* is of such mischievous Consequence in the Center of Trade, which draws all the Riches of the Kingdom to it; what terrible Effects must it produce in those Parts, which are constantly drain'd to support this great, over-grown *Leviathan*, and which can subsist only by *Labour, Industry* and *Frugality?*

You will find, Sir, that the abominable Crimes of *Perjury* and *Forgery* were never so frequent amongst us, as They have been of late; especially amongst Men of *Family* and *Fortune*. I need not put the Reader in Mind how many notorious Instances of this Kind the Course of a very few Years hath produced; and I am glad to decline it, out of Humanity to Those, who may unjustly suffer by a particular Enumeration.

I hope the *Bill*, which was lately pass'd to suppress this Evil, will have its Effect.

These Mr. *D'Anvers*, are heinous Crimes; and very prejudicial to human Society. But the greatest *Political* Evil is *Venality of Offices*; because I think it demonstrable that This is generally attended with *Corruption* in Office; which is the original Source, from whence all other *political Evils* may be properly said to flow.

The *Sale of Offices* is therefore to be principally avoided by a wise State; for if Places are to be sold, it is *Money*, not *Merit* that will be the Qualification; and if a Person is to give away half the Profits of his Place to the Person, from whom He receiv'd it, He will endeavour to reimburse Himself by Extortion and Oppression. In the mean Time those, who are fit to supply the Places of Trust will not accept of them and the Insufficient only will fill them; as if the *Drawback of an Office* were but a kind of Compensation for the Defect of the *Officer's Capacity*.

Nay, if Men of *Merit* should be sometimes induced, by unequal Fortune, to submit to hard Terms; yet it is certain that when Places are brought to Market, they will generally be fill'd with Persons of ordinary Capacities, and the only Criterion of their Worth will be either the[a] Weight of their Pockets to *give most*, or the Indigence[b] of their Fortunes to *take least*.

This great Abuse of buying and selling Places hath always been treated with the utmost Detestation, whenever it hath been brought to Judgment. In the *Church* it is *Simony*, attended with great Penalties; and I do not see why it ought not to be made as infamous and dangerous in the *State*. What are the Consequences of it we have lately seen in the Cases of the *Masters in Chancery* and the *Keepers of our Prisons*.[2] It was come to such a Pass, that a poor Wretch could not be admitted to die a lingering, tormenting Death in a noisome Dungeon, without paying *exorbitant Fees* for it.

The late glorious (and I hope immortal) Act against *Bribery* and *Corruption* seems to guard against all Possibility of purchasing a Seat in Parliament;[c] so that now, it is to be wish'd, nothing will be sought for but Merit in the Candidate; and Men of Capacity, Fortune and Freedom of Judgment only will be introduced into that Assembly.

If venal Abuses were to grow in the *Senate* and the *Administration*, it would be difficult to invent a Punishment severe enough for the Promoters of such an Evil, which is of so contagious a Nature, being attended with *Profit*, that if it is once countenanced amongst the *Great*, it soon spreads amongst the lower Class of Men. I remember an Instance, in low Life, of an Abuse of this Kind, which hath made the Offender justly detested by all Those, to whom his Wickedness was known, which was aggravated by the Character of the Person, who was a *Clergyman*. The Case was this.

A Gentleman being desirous, on his Death-Bed, to do a generous Act which might out-live Him, left by his Will, amongst other Charities, an handsome Allowance for a *School-master*, to instruct a Number of poor Boys in the Christian Religion, to assist them in a proper Education to get an honest Livelihood. This Part of his Will

---

[a] either the] *B*; either of the *fol*.   [b] Indigence] *B*; Indecency *fol*.
[c] guard against . . . in Parliament;] guard very well against the Venality of Parliament; *B*.

was left to Trustees; amongst whom was my *Clergyman*; a bold, troublesome, over-bearing Creature, always creating Animosities and Divisions; and a common *Barreter*[3] in his Country; which soon made it very disagreeable to the rest of the *Trustees* to act with him, so that he got the whole to himself, and accordingly made a *Political Use* of it; put in a *poor, ignorant Woman*, who was fitter to be taught herself than to instruct others; from whom he received, *in Imitation of his Betters*, a yearly Allowance of what the *Donor* directed; and because he would be more fashionable and get all he could, no Boy was permitted to receive the Benefit of this Charity, who did not first shake him handsomly by the Palm. This little mean Avarice, and sordid Wickedness, in robbing the *Poor*, hath made him justly obnoxious to the Hatred of the whole Neighbourhood. I mention this only as an Instance how some Men, for the meerest Trifle, will prostitute their Consciences and Profession, and will forfeit a good Name, for the Advantage of a little Gain. How glad would any honest Man be, to have such an Opportunity to do Good at another Man's Cost; to feed the Hungry and instruct the Ignorant, both the greatest Works of Charity, and this without Expence? A good Man would rejoice in this; but what must that Man be who rejects the Occasion, and, which is worse, perverts it; who renders the good Intention of another of[a] none or very little Effect, and this only to gratify his own Avarice? A Man of this Bent of Mind wants only the Opportunity, and he would without Remorse rob the *Exchequer*; levy[b] *heavy Taxes* on the People; bribe with 50,000 l. those who would give him 100,000 l. A Man, by this low Example,[c] gives a plain Indication what he would do in the highest Offices, could he obtain them; and if a Person, in this Instance,[d] procures the just Hatred of his Parish and Neighbourhood, by injuring a few; what Indignation must arise against *Those*, who by *publick Misapplication* should occasion *publick Miseries*, and who should pillage and rob the Subject, in order to make good the *Deficiencies of his own Mismanagement*, and to enable him the better to get more when *further Mismanagements* should cause *further*[e] *Deficiencies.*—Such a *Minister* would soon tire out the most giving People; and the Resentment of the People in their Turn from Murmurs, Discontents, and universal Clamour, would soon teach him that

---

[a] of] *B*; to *fol.*   [b] levy] raise *B*.   [c] Example,] Instance, *B*.
[d] Person, in this Instance,] Person *B*.
[e] *further . . . further*] *farther . . . farther B*.

Ministers are answerable for their Actions, and[a] that there is a King
above them that will hearken to the Cries of his People, and will[b]
punish, severely punish Him, as soon as his Crimes are ripe for
Judgment; but this can now scarce ever happen in *England*. The Act
against *Bribery* has so compleatly[c] secured the *Freedom of
Parliament*, that henceforward it will be almost impossible[d] for an
evil Minister to escape their jealous discerning Eye. His wicked
Projects will be nipt in the Bud; and the[e] Nation saved from the
pernicious Consequences which the Execution[f] of them would
draw upon it.[g] We shall see, *as we have lately done*, our *Parliament*
paying due Honour to the wise and prudent Management of our
Ministers, and our *Ministers* answering their Place and Character;
opening, without Reserve or Fear, the Springs of their Actions and
Conduct; and making the World Judges of their disinterested and
wise Measures; *Ministers*, who will *ask for Money only when it's
wanted*, and will justly and clearly *account for it when disbursed*. By
this Act a *Ministry*, being always under the Inspection of an
unbyassed Parliament, can have no Views but what are honourable,
and their greatest Honour will be to meet with publick
Approbation. Such a *Ministry*, joined with the *Prince*, will be doing
all the Good their high Stations enable them to do, in Order to
deserve the People's just Blessings and Applause.

   In short, if our *Constitution* is the best in the World, and our
Liberty the natural Result of our Constitution; if the *Parliament* is
the Guardian of Liberty, and *Freedom* the Essence of *Parliament*,
our Constitution may now be[h] said to have received from *this Act*
the greatest Security[i] that human Wisdom can contrive or add to it;
it's[j] *Excellence* will preserve it from a *Repeal*, and it's *Clearness* and
Simplicity; capable to be understood by the meanest Capacity, will
preserve it from an *Explanation*.

I am, SIR,
Yours, &c.

---

[a] and] *omitted B*.   [b] will] *omitted B*.   [c] compleatly] far *B*.
[d] almost impossible] very difficult *B*.   [e] Bud; and the] *B*; Bud. The *fol*.
[f] Execution] *B*; Executors *fol*.   [g] it.] *B*; him. *fol*.   [h] now be] be now *B*.
[i] the greatest Security] one of the greatest Securities *B*.   [j] it's] for it's *B*.

No. 167. Saturday, 13 September 1729.

The present State of Affairs in *Europe* hath obliged me to postpone several ingenious and useful Letters from my Correspondents, which deserve a Place in this Paper; but *these Affairs* being, I think, sufficiently explain'd and discuss'd for the present, I have Leisure to look over my *great Thesaurus of Intelligence*, which contains Variety of Matter upon all Subjects, and shall from Time to Time (as Opportunities offer) give[a] Those Pieces to the Publick, which will bear the Light. Amongst the rest, I find the following, which I have collected together for this Day's Entertainment, being all written on Subjects of much the same Nature; and as the Thoughts are generally *new*, I doubt not They will prove agreeable; especially to Those, who have any Compassion or Regard for the inferiour Part of thier Fellow-Creatures.

To CALEB D'ANVERS, *Esq*;

Dear CALEB,

AS I am a constant Reader of your *Journal*, I find in one of them, lately publish'd, a Description of a Piece of *Dutch Drollery*, express'd by a *Picture*; wherein[b] is pourtray'd a generous *English Bull-Dog* thrown upon his Back; unfairly held down; depriv'd of all Self-Defence; and exposed to the Insults and unmerciful Drubbings of a *sniveling Hero*, in a *short Cloak* and *sable Whiskers*. This did not a little raise my Indignation; for you must know, Mr. *D'Anvers*, that I am by Nature very compassionate to all the dumb Part of the Creation; but my Regard extends itself more particularly to *Dogs*; and I must tell you that my Respect for these *grateful, affectionate Creatures* is almost, if not altogether, as warm as that which *Gulliver* expresses for his favourite *Houyhnhnms*. It is therefore with no small Pleasure that I read of the great Esteem and Veneration, which hath been express'd by the Antients for this *sociable, good-natur'd Animal*. The *Egyptian* Sages with Reverence adored their Deity *Anubis*, under this Shape; and I am informed that the *Mahometans*, to this Day, leave them considerable Legacies; frequently declaring it to be a principal Part of their Will, that so much Bread should be charitably dol'd about to the *Dogs* of such a Street. Our Forefathers not only reposed an intire Confidence in the Fidelity of these Creatures, as *domestick Guardians*, but took them likewise as a Sort of *Companions* Abroad, to participate with them in their Sports and rural Diversions; and it is well known that a *late, noble Lord* put Himself to the Expence of erecting a *fine Monument* to the Memory of a faithful, favourite *Dog*, with an *Inscription*, which enumerated the several *Virtues* and *Accomplishments* of the Deceased.

I was very much pleased, the other Day, with an Account in one of our News-papers, of the great Encouragement which had been given to a *learned Dog* in *France*; who, it is said, can already distinguish all the *Letters in the Alphabet*, and begins to *put them together*; from whence They conceive Hopes that He will, in time, make great Improvements in *Literature* and, perhaps, make a considerable Figure in their *Royal Academy of Sciences*.

Now as it affords me the highest Satisfaction to see our *Canine* Fellow-Creatures treated with Kindness and Humanity; so, on the contrary, how am I provoked at some *Barbarians* (in Reality much more *Brutes* than *They*) who use them with Contempt and even with the most shocking Cruelties? I am often in Pain to hear a Couple of good-for-nothing Scoundrels, in a Passion, call one another *Dogs* and *Sons of B————hes* by Way of Reproach. But what hath given me the greatest Alarm is, that an Attempt hath been lately made to reduce *these Animals* from their *glorious Immunity* into a State of the most *abject Slavery. Hunger and Ease* were always allowed them as their undoubted Privileges; but *these Innovators* have discover'd an Intention of continuing to them the *former*, without the pleasing Alleviation of the *latter*. The vile Designs of these *Invaders of publick Liberty* are to make them labour like *Horses*, instead of accompanying us as *Companions*, or serving us in the Capacity of *Household Stewards*; for it is notorious that a Couple of sordid Tyrants have already made the Tour of this Kingdom, imperiously lashing a Sett of *free-born Dogs*, slavishly harness'd to their triumphal Car. It must be own'd indeed, that as there are Degrees of Perfection in the human Kind, so doubtless there is likewise a Difference in this Species, and some of them merit only to be treated as the meanest Drudges; such are your *sad Dogs*, your *Dogs in Doublets*, and *Dogs* that, *for Hire, jump over Canes, play Tricks for the K——g*, and dancing Attendance upon a Rope for a little *pensionary Bread*, are intirely subjected to the Will, and most obsequiously observant of the Nod, Call or Whistle of an haughty, *two-legg'd Monster*, who derives his own Ease and Plenty from the vile Submissions of these *abject, degenerated Brutes.*[1]

But far, very far different from *These* was that antient, genuine Race of *true-bred English Bull-Dogs*, who were not only famous at Home, but likewise acquired a glorious Reputation Abroad; excelling in Fight; victorious over their Enemies; undaunted in Death; and, in the midst of crackling Blazes and artificial Thunders, resolutely continuing *tenacious* to the last.

But much I fear that few of *that Race* are now surviving; for the *Tyrants* before-mention'd could not have chained them tamely to their servile Vehicles. When their *Freedom* was invaded, They would doubtless have shewn a generous Resentment, by their angry Snarlings; and if urged by Violence to receive the Yoke, would certainly have turned all their Rage and Strength upon those *arbitrary Men*, who endeavoured, with Bits, Reins and Whips, to Lord it over them. It must therefore be a *mungrel Race of Dogs*, who submit to this vile Servitude. But let all such *Charioteers* beware how they attempt the Liberties and endeavour to subjugate these *nobler Brutes*; for though fix'd in their Seats, and driving a full Career, they may meet with the Fate of that *antient Coachman*, the *presumptuous Phaeton.*

I am, Sir,
Your very humble Servant,
PHILOCUNOS.[2]

P.S. If this meets with a tolerable Reception, you may in a little Time expect a Dissertation on the several *foreign* Species of *these Animals*; such as your *French Harlequins; Italian Grey-hounds; Spanish Pointers; Dutch Mastiffs*, and *German Wolf-Dogs.*

No. 181. Saturday, 20 December 1729.

To CALEB D'ANVERS, *Esq;*

CORNHILL,
Dec. 13th, 1729.

SIR,

I Belong to a Club of *Merchants* in this Part of the Town, where your Health is constantly toasted, as an Advocate for *Trade*, and am desired by the whole Society to congratulate you on the late

Acquittal of Mr. *Francklin*, at whose Tryal I had the Curiosity to be present.[1] We direct our Congratulations to you, Mr. *D'anvers*, because we apprehend you to be principally concerned in this Affair; and we hope that we are at Liberty to do this without giving Offence to any Body. We should be far from wishing you Joy on this Occasion, if we thought you *guilty* of the Crimes laid to your Charge; that is, of being *disaffected to his Majesty* and an *Enemy to your Country*; no, we rejoyce because you have justified your *Innocence* in the Face of the World and proved yourself *not guilty*. We rejoice that the *Verdict* of an *honest, English Jury* hath confirmed our former, good Opinion of you; and we heartily wish that you may be able to justify yourself as fully upon all Occasions, when you shall be called upon to do it in the same Manner.

We hope, I say, that we may do this without Offence; for in Cases of a *capital* Nature the *Court*, that is the *King*, prays to God to send the Prisoner at the Bar a *good Deliverance*; and we look upon all *criminal Cases* in the same Light. The only just End of *Prosecutions* being to punish those, who are hurtful to the Publick, and to deter others, by their Example, from committing the same Crimes; it is always to be wish'd, for the Good of Society, that the *Person accused* may be able to purge Himself and prove the Charge against Him to be groundless. It is the Duty of a *good Judge* to state the Case indifferently between the *Crown* and the *Defendant*, to whom, in some Respects, He is a Kind of *Council*, and ought to assist Him, if through Inadvertency or Ignorance of the Law, He should slip any Thing material in his own *Defence*.

We can't tell, Mr. *D'anvers*, what Opinion *some People* at the other End of the Town may have of you; but We can assure you that your Writings upon *mercantile Affairs* and our *late Sufferings in Trade* are very much approved of by us in the *City*. We are fully satisfy'd of your Intentions to *serve us*; and therefore We should be very sorry to see you involved in any Difficulties on *our Account*.

For this Reason, We could wish that you would, for the Future, be very cautious of publishing any of the *insolent Bravadoes* and *Rhodomontades* of the *Spaniards*; I don't yet know whether I am to call them our *Friends* or our *Enemies*. Let Them flatter and caress Themselves as much as They please with an Opinion of their *own Wisdom* and the *Figure*, which They have lately made in *Europe*, either *with* or *without striking a Blow*. They are naturally *proud* and given to *Boasting*, which can do us no Hurt, and deserves only our

Contempt. Why therefore should you run any Hazards by publishing their *vain* and *insolent Braggadocios*, which are liable to be construed in a *criminal* Light, though you do it only with a Design of *exposing* them?—I grant indeed that the *Reflections* and even *Menaces* of our Enemies have been often published, for this Purpose, without giving Offence; particularly by the Author of the *Enquiry*, (as *one* of your Council very well observ'd) who put into the Mouth of the Duke *de Ripperda*, at that Time *Prime-Minister* of *Spain*, several insolent Expressions which reflected very grosly, and without any *Disguise*, on the *Person* of his late, excellent Majesty; even such as threat'ning to *dethrone Him* and *set up the Pretender to his Crown*; telling the World *that the People of* England *began to be weary of Him*, and calling Him, in plain Terms, PETIT MONSIEUR. Yet this Book, you say, was never call'd in Question by *Those in Authority*; and, what is more, even the Duke *de Ripperda* himself, upon whom all these flagrant and most insolent Speeches are father'd, hath judg'd *England*, which He us'd in this Manner, the only proper Place, of all the World, for his *Retreat* and *Asylum.*[2]

This is very true; but you cannot be ignorant,[a] Mr. *D'Anvers*, that the vulgar Proverb is often verify'd, which says *it is safer for* some Men *to steal an Horse than for* others *to look over the Hedge.*[3] We often consider the *Man* who speaks, as well as the *Words* which are spoken; and this *Distinction* often makes the same Things *criminal in one Man*, which are esteem'd *meritorious in another*. I would therefore advise you to leave this dangerous Province to *those Writers*, who seem to be, at present, in an higher Degree of Favour than your self. *Ictus Piscator sapit.*[4] I leave the Application to you and am, in the Name of our *Club, Sir*

Your sincere Well-wisher, and
Humble Servant,
C. T.

---

[a] ignorant,] *B*; ignorant *fol.*

No. 182. Saturday, 27 December 1729.

To the Author of the admirable COUNTRY JOURNAL
of Saturday the – – 1729.[a]

SIR,

I AM asham'd to own my Name, when I confess my self to be one of those *Criminals*, whom you so justly rebuke in your Paper above-mentioned.[1]

I am not able to keep my self from shewing this Piece of Sincerity, and confessing the Abhorrence, which you have raised in me of my self, by painting in such lively, such strong and true Colours, the Figure, which an Actor of such a Part makes, both in Town and Country; a Picture, which must infallibly reform all such Minds, as are not abandon'd, beyond the Possibility of Amendment; which,[b] I hope, will appear to be the Case of very few *Britons.*

For my own Part, I am unable to give any one Reason, that can well bear the Light, for the Conduct, which I have been publickly guilty of, for several Years past. I have frequently found my self moved, warmed, delighted with the Spirit, the[c] Honour and Eloquence, with which several great Truths have been delivered to us by *some Persons*, who have dared to exert themselves, boldly and nobly, toward[d] redressing the Grievances and Sufferings of their Country, though in Opposition to great Power, a great Majority, and notwithstanding the Odium, which they were sensible it would draw upon them from some *particular Persons* in Authority.

The Consequences, indeed, have been the most unjustifiable Slanders, spread zealously, though insignificantly. The falsest Motives, such as *Resentment* and *wrong Ambition* have been ascribed as the Cause of a *noble Behaviour*, which they, who had neither Virtue nor Courage to *imitate*, were forced to *envy.*

This I have frequently observed with inward Indignation; and I have ventured to express it very freely in *select Companies*; nay, I have resolved within my self to be one of the *illustrious Few*, on the next proper Occasion that should offer; but when it came to the Point of Performance, I do with the utmost Shame acknowledge

---

[a] 1729.] 1729, *upon Non-Attendance in Parliament. B.*
[b] which] and This *B.*   [c] Spirit, the] Spirit of *B.*   [d] toward] towards *B.*

that my Heart and Spirits have failed me, and I have either servilely followed *Numbers*, though blushing with inward Consciousness at what I was doing; or, which is almost as bad, made a mean Composition[2] between *Principle* and *Interest*, by *absenting* my self in the Day of Trial.

The Truth is, I could not hitherto bring my self to support, with proper Indifference, *angry Looks* and some *other Inconveniencies* that might ensue upon them; such as the Loss of a *Place*, or *something equivalent to a Place*, which being *more secret*, might be less liable to *Suspicion*.

I own, I have heard it said (and I think with Justice too) that receiving a *present*, *private Advantage*, whilst *publick Ones* are totally neglected, is like keeping up one's Constitution by *strong Spirits* and *Cordials* only for a Time; which Method must infallibly bring on a speedy and ruinous End; yet I have sometimes flatter'd my self, that those Things, which I secretly condemn'd, might be redress'd without my Assistance; and for that Reason have frequently endeavour'd to satisfy my Conscience and avoid the Resentment of *great Men*, by an *inglorious Neutrality*; but now, at last, I am so touch'd, so affected by your admirable Reasonings,[a] on the whole of this Subject, that I feel strong Resolutions forming in my Mind to shew myself, on all future Occasions, a new Man; that is, to throw in my Mite toward promoting the Success of whatever I shall, at any Time hereafter, think *right* and *just*.

Accept, SIR, of this Return of the *Prodigal Son*, in
  Your unknown Admirer, Respecter, and faithful Servant,
  A WHIG *in Profession.*
From my Country-House,
Dec. 2, 1729.

No. 185. Saturday, 17 January 1730.

To CALEB D'ANVERS, *Esq*;
Mr. D'ANVERS,

NO sooner did the *Articles of Peace*, lately sign'd at *Seville*,[1] arrive here, than his Majesty shew'd an early Instance of his Goodness to his People, by ordering an *immediate Reduction* of 5000

---

[a] Reasonings,] Reasons, *B.*

of the Land Forces in *Britain*, as tending to an Ease of the *Publick Expence*, which of late Years has run to so great a Height as to make every Body rejoice to see the least Prospect of a Diminution of their *Burthen*.

But what I have more particularly remark'd upon this Occasion is the general Bent of People against maintaining of *Foreign Forces* in *English Pay*; for, say they, if there is a Necessity of keeping up an Army in the *North*, notwithstanding a Peace in the *South*, why should one be kept useless at Home, and not be employed where Honour calls or the Service requires?—Why should *Foreigners* take the Bread out of the Mouths of *Englishmen?*—Why should the *Trading Part* of the Nation suffer such a Loss in vending so much of the *English Manufacture* and *other Commodities*, as such a Body of *English Troops* must necessarily every Year consume? for many Trades must be employed in equipping one *brave English Soldier* of six Foot high from Head to Foot. Such and such like are the common Topicks at this Time.

There are many more Arguments to be urg'd for maintaining this Proposition. We have seen, of late Years, many Occasions of *levying* of Troops and of *disbanding* them again. Happy would it be for the World, if there were no such Occasions at all; but that Princes might reign in the Hearts of their Subjects, and think them their *best Guards!*—However if the Fate of Affairs makes it become necessary, let us enter into the plain Merits of the Cause.

It is not only very chargeable to the Nation at first to *raise an Army* at 3 *l.* a *Man* and 15 *l. a Horse*, or more by Way of *Levy Money*; but it is likewise so in *reducing* them again by allowing *Bounty Money* and other Gifts to the Soldiers upon *disbanding*, as well as *Half-Pay* to the Officers disbanded; and when this comes to be a Case often repeated of *raising one Year* and *disbanding the next* and *raising again*, the *third*, perhaps at every Ebbing and Flowing of the Tide of Things, as we have almost seen to be the Case, the Difference of *saving* to the Publick in keeping the *English* Soldiery on Foot, till a *glorious* and *lasting Peace* is establish'd, or of disbanding them for a Time only, cannot be very great; but to disband our *own Countrymen* and maintain *Foreigners in Pay*, at the same Time, is what sticks in *English* Stomachs and may be call'd a *Saving* that tends to *Poverty*.

In this *late Reduction* it has been observable that there never was so much Heart-burning and grumbling among the *Officers*, to whose unhappy Fate it fell to be disbanded as at this Time; by seeing themselves reduced to *Half Pay*; at the same Time that[a] *Foreigners* are continued in *whole Pay* upon the *English* Establishment.

Suppose therefore (if there should be Occasion) that instead of the *Hessians*, or other *Foreign Forces*, there were the like Number of *Subject Troops* sent over Sea, where *Military People* are not such a *Terror* as in *Old England* (a Draught which the *British* and *Irish* Establishments seem to be still capable of bearing upon the *Peace* concluded with *Spain)* it would not only be carrying the Honour of the *English* Arms Abroad, and an Ease of the Charge of so many *Foreigners*, who might be dismissed from *English Pay*, but be a great Advantage to *Trading People* at Home, whose Cries are very loud at this Time, a lessening likewise of the *Half-pay*, by providing for those Gentlemen again, as fast as *Vacancies* happen[b] in such Regiments Abroad as well as at Home; and also by recruiting the said Regiments with Soldiers from Time to Time from *England*, great Numbers of *Vagrants* and *idle Persons* would be drawn off and[c] be a Means of reducing the Number of *Highwaymen* and *Street Robbers* about Town, and other *Pilferers* and *Poachers* in the Country, who now infest the Nation, and leave more room for the People remaining to get an honest Livelihood.

These, Mr. *D'Anvers*, I find to be the Sentiments of most People at this Juncture and are communicated to you by

LONDON, Jan. 5   *Your humble Servant,*
1730.   ANGLICANUS.

No. 186. Saturday, 24 January 1730.

To CALEB D'ANVERS, *Esq;*

Mr. D'ANVERS,

Having cast an Eye casually upon your *last Journal*,[1] in which there is a Letter in favour of the *British Soldiery*, and hearing at the same Time the Case between *Them* and *Foreigners* reason'd over a Dish of Coffee, amongst some of the unfortunate Gentlemen, lately

---

[a] at the same Time that] whilst *B*.   [b] happen] should happen *B*.
[c] and] which would *B*.

cashier'd, and others, I found the chief Arguments in favour of the Latter to be—That *foreign Forces*, being upon a *lower Establishment* of Pay, They were consequently *cheaper*; and that the Charge of *transporting National Troops* was thereby saved.

Now Mr. *D'anvers*, if there are no other Reasons of State for this Option, which I don't pretend to dive into, nor weightier Arguments in Behalf of the *Foreigners* than the foregoing, I take Leave to observe that though the Pay of *foreign Forces* may be in some Degree *less* than that of our *National Troops*, yet the Difference is so little that it does not seem to counter-ballance the *other Advantages* which would accrue by employing those of our *own Nation*; for as *Money* is become one of the scarcest Commodities at Home, so the sending it abroad is become a Grievance to those, who would be glad to earn it in the Service of their Country; which is one certain Consequence of hiring *foreign Troops*, whose Pay must be entirely remitted Abroad to them, without any Defalcation[2] or Abatement whatsoever; or without laying out one Shilling of it in *Britain*.

Whereas, on the other Side of the Question, not above *two Thirds* of the Money, at most, would be actually remitted Abroad to our *National Troops*; since the Remainder must necessarily be detain'd and consum'd here in their Service, *viz.* by the *Cloathing* of all such Regiments, which[a] would be made and paid for here; by the *Respits*; the Foreigners being supposed to be paid compleat; by the *Assignments* that would be made by many of the Officers on their Pay in Favour of their *Wives* or *Families* here, or for Payment of *Debts* or other Occasions; and not only so, but by the Number of *Officers*, who would from Time to Time be employ'd in *Recruiting* here; so that great Part of the Money granted in this Case, for *British Troops*, would (notwithstanding their being Abroad) circulate here at *Home*. I need only mention one Thing more; which is, That keeping up such a Body of Troops Abroad would prove a *Sinking Fund* also to that Head of Expence, *half Pay*; especially the *first Year*, by providing for so many Officers at once, and be an annual Decrease of it afterwards (if we should unhappily have any Occasion to continue them) by filling up the Vacancies from amongst the *Half-pay Officers*.

And as to the other Objection about their *Transportation*, it is

<hr>

a which] as *B*.

probable that the *British Soldiers* would rather bear the Charge of their *own Transportation* in so short a Voyage than not have the Post of Honour, so valuable to a *bold Briton*. Besides,[a] *British Bottoms* would be employ'd in their *Transport*; *British Sailors* would receive *Wages*; *British Tradesmen* be concern'd in their *Victualling*, and would otherwise profit by it; and *British Money* would by these Means circulate amongst *British Subjects*.

If you think this worthy of Notice it is submitted to your Consideration, by

Westminster, 20th Jan.
1729–30.

Your humble Servant,
BRITANNICUS.

No. 199. Saturday, 25 April 1730.

To CALEB D'ANVERS, *Esq*;

SIR,

I Have lately read a few short Reflections upon the *Seville* Treaty, in a *Letter from an Elector of the Borough of Great Yarmouth to Mr.* Horatio Walpole, *&c.* which seem to have been offered to the Town, after we had been already generally tired with Enquiries upon this particular Subject; and which, on that Account perhaps, have been less regarded than the Importance of them calls for. I doubt not however but that a Place for them in your Paper, and your Opinion of them that they deserve it, will still sufficiently recommend them to the Attention of the Publick. The Author, after taking Notice of what has already been explained as to the *Emperor*'s Danger and Apprehensions from the Introductions of *Spanish*, instead of *Neutral* Troops into the Garrisons of *Tuscany* and *Parma*, proceeds farther to observe, That *Spanish* Troops are likewise *by no Means proper for the Security of* Don Carlos. To this Point, in particular, he quotes not only the *Quadruple* Alliance, but the late Treaty of *Seville* too, to prove This to have been *the Sense of all the contracting Parties to both these Treaties*. He observes that the Sovereignty, intended to be secured to *Don Carlos* by both these Treaties, is to be independent on the Crown of *Spain*; That it is the Interest of, and must be a Favourite Point with, the present Queen

---

[a] Besides,] *B*; Besides *fol.*

of *Spain*, from a Regard to her own Family, that it should be so; That no such *Independent* Sovereignty, nor[a] any other, will be rendered secure to him by *Spanish Garrisons*, or any Troops in the *Pay* of the Crown of *Spain*, longer than she lives, or indeed than her present Power and Influence continues at the Court of *Spain*; after which the uniting these Dominions to the *Crown of Spain* will be the most probable Consequence of their being garrison'd by *Spanish* Troops, or any Troops in the Pay of that Crown.

Upon this State of the Case, the Author proposes an Enquiry what can have been intended by any of the Allies of *Seville*, besides, or farther than, securing this Succession to *Don Carlos*, in this Alteration of the *Quadruple Alliance*, in a particular, not material or proper for the Security of *Don Carlos*; and which appears, at the same Time, so much to alarm the *Emperor*. And indeed this is a Question, which I do not find myself, from the Assistance of any of the Advocates for the Treaty of *Seville*, qualified to make such an Answer to, as is at all consistent with the Advantages they have promised us from this Treaty.

They generally agree in observing that this is an Alteration in the Treaty of *London*, which cannot *materially* affect the *Emperor*. Now was it possible for us to make this particular Concession to them, They must however admit that it is an *Alteration* in the *Treaty* of *London*, which Treaty hath been since confirmed and ratified by the Treaties of *Vienna* and by the *Preliminaries*; an *Alteration* in that Part of this Treaty, that,[b] of all others, has been most *solemnly* stipulated by *all* the contracting Parties to it. This Consideration *only* will, I fear, in the Opinion of some Persons, be thought a sufficient Reason to have dissuaded us from it, unless it had appeared a *material* Alteration, with Regard to the *only openly avowed Interest* or *Designs* of the Court of *Spain*. And if it can't be now made appear to be so, it is to be hoped that, from what we have already done, and for the same Reason, we are as much at Liberty to *deviate* from the Treaty of *Seville* too, in this particular; and undoubtedly we shall do so, with still less Difficulty, rather than destroy the *Balance* and *Peace* of *Europe*.

As to the Expence, which *Great Britain* and *France* were to be at, by the Treaty of *London*, in the Pay of *Neutral* Troops, and which is now to be saved, it is to be observed that, as far as this Expence was

---

[a] nor] *B*; not *fol.*   [b] that,] which, *B*.

thought of Consequence at either Court, so far it still remains a
Proof of their Opinion, at that Time, as to the Importance of this
particular Stipulation. Nor can the Case be since so much altered
with us, that the same Expence should now appear of any Moment,
to the People of *Great Britain*, compared with the Consequences to
Them of an *approaching War*. A War, in which, I believe I am not
alone in thinking, that our *Success* is *even more* to be apprehended
than our *Disappointment*. On the other Hand it would not be
difficult to point out some Conveniencies to this Kingdom to be
expected, from keeping in our Pay a Part of these *Italian* Garrisons
for the Interest and Security of the Queen of *Spain*'s Family, which
would be thought more than an equivalent for the Expence of it.

But I cannot think that Frugality will be so much as pretended to
have been our *only Motive* to this Proceeding. From whence, Sir, I
conceive that, if you are of Opinion with me that *Spanish* Troops
are less proper than *Neutral* Troops for the *Security of Don Carlos*
as to that Provision, which it has been *alone openly proposed* to make
for him, you will likewise think it a very material Question what
Designs, *besides, or beyond this*, are to be served by this *Variation*
from a *solemn* Stipulation in the *Treaty of London*, which has been *so
lately* confirmed by the *Preliminaries*.

Undoubtedly the Queen of *Spain* may think the immediate
Possession of the Dutchy of *Milan*, or of the Kingdoms of *Naples*
and *Sicily*, as good a Provision for *Don Carlos* as a Reversion in the
Sovereignty of *Tuscany* and *Parma*. And certainly it can't be forgot
what Pretensions were formed, what Attempts were made, with
these Views by the Court of *Spain* in 1717 and 1718; and before their
Accession to *that Treaty of* London, *which they have now again
receded from.*[a] I cannot imagine that we now intend to assist them in
the same Designs upon the *Emperor*; but some such Design, from
another Quarter, is plainly to be apprehended by him, till he can be
satisfied that this Variation from the Treaty of *London*, in the
Introduction of *Spanish* Troops, has been proposed and agreed
upon, *for the Security of* Don Carlos *as to the aforesaid Succession*
only. He must otherwise, I think, expect it, as the most probable
Event of a successful War made upon him in *Italy*, whilst he
opposes it; and yet he must know that the Execution of the same
Design will become still more practicable if he consents to it. Six

[a] *from.*] B; *from?* fol.

Thousand *Spanish* Troops will pave the Way for the Introduction of as many more as may be thought necessary for this Purpose. Nor would it be, in my Opinion, absurd to suppose *Spain* assisted, in a Design of this Kind, by the Arms of the Duke of *Tuscany*; who perhaps may chuse to see *Don Carlos* provided for in *any Manner*, rather than at his own Expence, and be glad, upon *any Terms*, to recover his own Dominions, to be disposed of as he pleases, or preserved in his own Family.

These Reflections, as well as what the aforesaid Author has mentioned to the same Purpose, are what, I sincerely think, deserve still to be attended to. I shall however, no more than the same Author, be unwilling to be confuted; on the contrary I shall be glad if the Gentlemen, who inform us that this Alteration does *not materially* affect the *Emperor*, will so far convince me that it was necessary, or proper for effecting the *only avowed Designs* of the Court of *Spain*, as to cure me of my Apprehensions that something, *more than this*, must have been intended by some or other of the Allies of *Seville*; and is still intended by those of them, who still insist upon it, to the apparent Hazard of the *Balance* and *Peace* of *Europe*.

I am, SIR, &c.

No. 225. Saturday, 24 October 1730[a]

From my own Chambers

Though I find my Readers are generally agreed with me that it would be ridiculous and inconsistent with the Design of this Paper to follow the *profess'd Hirelings* through all their tedious Ambages[1] of *false Argument* and *dirty Ribaldry*; yet when any Paper appears to be written in a *different Manner*, (though it evidently comes from the *same Quarter*) it may, perhaps, be expected that I should pay some Regard to it; especially when it hath any Relation to the Subject in hand.

This must be my Excuse for taking Notice of a Paper, publish'd in the *Daily Courant* of *Wednesday October* 7,[b] intitled, *Some*

---

[a] The essay appears as No. 230, 28 November 1730, in *B*.
[b] *of Wednesday October* 7] omitted *B*.

113

Reflections upon the Reign of Henry VI. *occasion'd by the last Craftsman.*

The *Author of these Reflections* charges me with *slipping over the Reign of this King;*[2] (*which I allowed to have been a Reign of Faction;*) and therefore tells the World that *it is his Intention to supply my Defects;* after which He *insists on my dissimulating the most* seditious *Transactions of that Time from the Proceedings of Those whom He shall not stick to call* Factious *in the late and present Reigns.*

The Reason of our passing over *this Reign* in so cursory a Manner did not proceed, as the *Reflecter* suggests, from any Apprehension that the *seditious Transactions of that Reign* bore any Resemblance to the *Proceedings*, which are call'd *Factious in this*; but in Order to hasten down, as fast as We could, to *later Times*, which would furnish us with more Matter to illustrate our general Doctrine of *Liberty*. We did not think proper to enter into a minute Detail of all the Circumstances of the civil Wars between the Houses of *York* and *Lancaster*; nor to spend our Time and tire our Readers with shewing all the Examples, which We might have produced, of the Mischiefs done by *Faction*. This would be writing the *History of England*, instead of making *Remarks* upon it; and would exceed the Limits, which We are oblig'd to prescribe ourselves in *these Essays*.

We did not however intirely *slip over* this Reign. We observ'd, in general, *that it was a Reign of* Faction; *that it discloses an horrid Scene of* Iniquity, Folly, Madness; *that the scandalous Management of* publick Affairs, *which brought infinite Loss and Dishonour to the Nation, gave real Occasion, as well as Pretence, to* Commotions *and* Insurrections; *and that the* National Interest *was sunk, to the Shame of the Nation, in the particular Interest of* two Families.

Had We enter'd into more Particulars of the Reign of *Henry* VI. I confess We could not have given them the Turn, which is given in the *Daily Courant*; because it appears to us that this Turn is absolutely inconsistent with the Truth of History and framed purely to introduce the Insinuation, which runs through the whole Paper, that Those, who complain of *Mismanagements, Corruptions* and *evil Ministers,* are *Treason-mongers* and that too *curious and strict an Enquiry into the Conduct of* Governours *is dangerous to the* Government.

According to *this Writer,* all the *Discontents* under *Henry*'s Government, all the *Clamours* against it, and all the *Opposition* made to it were owing to the Intrigues of the Duke of *York* and his

Faction. He says that *the Reign of* Henry VI. was not *oppressive*, though it was *unfortunate*; that He was not a *bad King*; yet *People of all Ranks were led into Murmurs and Discontents*; that if He had been a *bad King* (as if it were possible for a *weak Man* to be a *good King*) *He would have been easily dispossess'd; but That not being the Case, his Friends struggled for Him, till the whole Kingdom was laid waste.*

Now, if we had treated this Subject in any Extent, we should have been oblig'd, by the concurrent Testimony of Historians, to shew that the *Murmurs* and *Discontents* of the People did not arise from the Intrigues of the *York Faction*, but from *real Grievances*; that the Nation bore long and much; and that the Faction of the *Queen* and her *first Minister, Suffolk*, gave those Advantages to the *other Faction*, which were so cruelly improved.

This Minister seems to have been the first Contriver, as well as the Negotiator of the Match between *Henry* VI. and *Margaret of Anjou*, with a View to his own private Interest and Ambition. *Rapin*[3] says, the Earl of Suffolk *was sensible that* Henry *was incapable of holding the Reins of Government*[a] *Himself; and consequently it could not be otherwise but that his Ministers would be liable to Envy, and bear the Blame of every Thing, that should not be relish'd by the People.* In *this Belief, he fancy'd the best Way to support Himself was to give the King a* Wife *and the Kingdom a* Governess *at the same Time.*

As much as the Conclusion of this *French Match* was contrary to the Interest and Inclinations of the whole Kingdom, *Suffolk* and his *Creatures* pretended that it would be very instrumental in procuring a Peace between *England* and *France.* He was immediately created a *Marquiss* upon this Account, and having got a *Parliament* at his Devotion, they voted him *Thanks*; addressed the King to *reward* Him; and even granted a *Subsidy* to defray the Expences of his *Embassy.*

The Fruits of this Marriage soon appeared evident to the whole Nation. The *Queen, Suffolk* and their *Creatures* govern'd with an absolute Sway. The *good Duke of Gloucester*, who had oppos'd the *Match*, and was very formidable to the *new Faction*, on Account of his popular Virtues, fell a Sacrifice to their Resentment. They found it impracticable to convict him legally of a *Sham-Plot*, which they had trumpt up against him; but being determin'd on his Ruin, they found Means to dispatch him privately. In short, he was found

[a] *Reins of Government*] B; *Reigns of the Government fol.*

dead in his Bed; and nobody doubted that he was murthered, having been either smothered, or put to the same cruel Death with *Edward* the *Second.*—Was this unfortunate Prince a *Yorkist* or a Bubble of the *Yorkists?* No; but He was a Sacrifice to the *Queen* and *Suffolk.*

These Proceedings of the *Queen* and her *Faction* set the Kingdom in a Flame, and drew upon them the universal Hatred of the People; who, *perceiving* (says *Rapin*) *that the Time appointed to procure a* Peace *was spent in vain, loudly murmur'd against the Marquiss of* Suffolk. *They made no Scruple to say openly that he had betray'd the* King *and the* State; *that the* Treaty *he had made with the* French *tended only to a* Truce *destructive of* England, *as it afforded the* Enemy *Time to fortify Himself.*

These Murmurs became at last so publick, that the *Marquiss* thought it necessary to justify himself; and his Method of doing it is so very extraordinary, that it deserves a Place amongst these Remarks; especially since the Author of the *Reflections* seems to have a great Mind to pronounce *this Minister* innocent; for what Reason I need not say. I will transcribe the Account of his *Defence* (as it call'd) from *Rapin*, that I may not be thought to make it more ridiculous and burlesque than it really is.

"These Murmurs, *says he,* were so publick, that the *Marquiss* could not help taking Notice of them. In order therefore to endeavour to silence them, he requested the King that he would be pleased to hear his *Defence,* that he might satisfy him of his Innocence. Whereupon the King set him a Day to come and clear Himself, and heard him in his *own Appartment,* in the Presence of several Lords, *none of whom were come there to refute Him.* He gave an Account of all he had done in *France;* wherein he was at no great Loss to justify Himself; since, before his setting out upon his Embassy, he had taken Care to be provided with the *King's Orders.* Having finished his Discourse, the King declared he was satisfy'd, and gave him *Letters Patents* under the great Seal, whereby he acquitted him from all Imputation of Misdemeanor, and enjoyned all Persons, under Pain of his Displeasure, not to *accuse,* or *speak ill* of Him."—What a summary Method of Tryal and Acquittal is here; which[a] would have been follow'd, no Doubt, by succeeding Ministers, in the same Circumstances, if it had met the desired

---

[a] which | a Method which *B*.

Success? but the *same Author* observes that "this was not capable of putting a Stop to the Murmurs of the People. Nobody question'd that the *King* would be satisfy'd; but that was not thought a Reason sufficient to satisfy the *Nation*."

Soon after This, the *Marquiss of Suffolk* was created *Duke of Suffolk*, at the Intercession of the *Queen*; upon which the *Historian* observes that *one would have thought she intended to brave the People, by showering daily her Favours upon* that Lord, *extremely hated by the whole Nation*.

From hence it appears that the *Murmurs* and *Discontents* of the People did not arise, as the *Reflecter* asserts, from the Intrigues of the *Yorkists*; but that the Intrigues of the *Yorkists* arose from the *Murmurs* and *Discontents* of the People.—*Rapin* says expressly that *the Disposition most People were in, with Regard to the* Queen and Ministry, *inspired the Duke of* York *with Hopes that he should one Day be able to assert his Title to the Crown*; and in another Place, that "the whole Kingdom rung with Complaints against the Duke of *Suffolk*. It was publickly said that he had betray'd the State.— People complained that there were but few Persons of *Parts*, and still fewer of *Honesty* in the *Council.*—That it was the same Thing with Regard to Those in publick Posts; in whom *Honesty* and *Ability* were not so much required as an Attachment to the *Ministry*. They were no less dissatisfied with the *Queen*." I will quote no more.

What! Because the People lost neither their *Privileges*, nor *Patrimonies* in *England*, ought They not to complain, when They had sustain'd so many other national Losses and Dishonours? Ought They to suffer *one Faction* to ruin the Nation, lest *another Faction* should arise? This would be like the Conduct of Those, who kill Themselves *to Day*, for fear of being kill'd *to Morrow*. Such an Argument will hold equally good against all Opposition whatsoever. It would have serv'd the Purposes of King *James the Second's Queen* and her Creatures as well as of *Henry the sixth's Queen* and her Faction. It may be pleaded against all Reformations and Revolutions whatsoever; and the People may be taught to submit to the *greatest Evils*, because an Attempt to remove them may possibly be the Occasion of introducing *worse*,[a] but it is needless to push this Argument into all its Absurdities.

<hr>

[a] *worse,*] *others as bad*; B.

The only good Use, that can be made of this Period of History, is by shewing what might have been done by a *Spirit of Liberty* and what was actually done by a *Spirit of Faction*; the *former* of which ought to be imitated, and the *latter* avoided, if a *Parallel Case* should ever happen in future Times.—Had the *Lancastrian Party* joined heartily and unanimously to *reform*, They would have *preserved* the Government. They would have defeated the Designs of the *York Party*; but They turned into *Faction*. They did what the Author of the *Reflections* recommends. From a fear of giving Strength to the *other Party*, They would not be guilty of any *curious and strict Enquiries into publick Management*. This maintained the *Court Faction* for a while; but gave Strength to the *other Faction* at the same Time, and at last ruined *Henry* and his Family.

Having laid this Foundation, I am ready to allow every Thing, that can be said against the *York Faction*. It is almost all true. *They* meant nothing by opposing the *Administration* of the Government but dethroning the *King*; yet They could not have dethron'd Him, if his *Wife* and his *Minister* had not paved the Way by their ill Conduct—The *Yorkists* oppos'd out of Hatred to the *Lancastrians*. The *Lancastrians* defended out of Hatred to the *Yorkists*—The *National Interest* was sunk in *two private Interests*—We express'd our Dislike of This—The *Reflecter* seems to think it would have been well for *England*, if the *National Interest* had been suffered to be sunk in *one* of them; but surely, it would have been much better if it had been sunk in *neither*.

A true State of the Circumstances, which attended the Reign of *Henry* VI. will demonstrate the Truth of what was said in *Oldcastle*'s first Letter;[4] that a *Spirit of Liberty* will never destroy a free Government; but that a *Spirit of Faction* may.—Had the *Lancastrians* oppos'd the Intrigues of the *Yorkists* with a *Spirit of Liberty* and *Reformation*, *Henry the Sixth* had kept his Crown; but when it came to be *Faction* against *Faction* it is no Wonder that He lost it.

The *Reflecter* concludes with *hoping that the Reader will observe no Attempt, in this Discourse, to make* Parallels *between any particular Characters of* this *and a* former *Age.*—I must desire the same Indulgence and have a Right to insist upon it, at least, in *this Paper*. The Reader sees that I was call'd up to it by the Author of the *Reflections*; and that He charg'd me with *slipping over the Reign of Henry* VI. because it was a Reign of *Faction*, and therefore not fit for my Purpose. I hope I have given him Satisfaction. I flatter my self, at least, that I have satisfy'd the World that the *Discontents* of the People, at that Time, and the Ruin of *Henry* VI. were not owing to the Intrigues of the *York Faction*, but to the Conduct of some *bad Men in Power*, who call'd Themselves the *best Friends* of the *House of Lancaster*, and deluded the *Queen* into their own Measures, under that Pretence—Who the *Factious* at present are, I shall not determine.

But since the *pensionary Writers* are encourag'd to continue their infamous Practice of instructing the People to interpret all *Historical Reasonings*, by *Parallels and Innuendoes*, into Libels upon *Majesty*; I must add a Word or two more upon that Subject.

The real Design of *these Papers* (as I have often declared,) is to shew that it is always necessary to the Preservation of *Liberty*, to keep up a *Spirit of Liberty*, in Opposition to a *Spirit of Faction*; and that the Reigns of almost all our *English* Monarchs have been either fortunate or unhappy, in Proportion as *This*, or *That Spirit* hath prevailed.

In the Prosecution of this Design it was necessary to take a short View of the most remarkable Reigns in the *English* History, and to point out the *Measures*, which render'd Them either *fortunate* or *unhappy*. In the *latter* Case, as well as in the *former*, We were oblig'd to distinguish the *Persons*, from whom those *bad Measures* proceeded; whether They were *weak Princes, ambitious Queens*, or (which is much more often the Case) *rapacious* and *ill-designing Ministers*—Could not We do This for the Sake of *Instruction*, without intending a libellous Parallel to the *present Times*; and is it not a most scandalous Liberty, which some People have taken in forming *such Parallels* out of their own Brains, and publishing Them to the World without any Disguise?

We may, perhaps, take Notice, in the Course of these Papers, that the *next Heir to the Crown* had too much Influence in the Councils of a *certain Reign*, and was the Author of several *violent Proceedings*; from whence *these Authors* may infer that We intend a seditious Parallel between *Him* and the *present Heir to the Crown*, with as much Justice as they have drawn their *other treasonable Parallels*.

As for their *present Majesties*, (whom I mention with Reluctance, upon this Occasion) it is well known that I have taken frequent Opportunities to declare my Attachment to their *illustrious House*; and I was so far from having any such Intention, as hath been laid to my Charge, in these *Historical Abstracts* and *Remarks*, that I have us'd the utmost Precaution (consistent with my *general Design*) to avoid such an Imputation. I could demonstrate This, by producing Multitudes of Passages, which I have suppress'd, not only in the *Reign*, under our present Consideration, but likewise in several *former Reigns*, meerly from an Apprehension that They might give these *licentious Writers* an Opportunity to exercise the malignant Humour of drawing *Parallels*. But I am sensible that even my doing This might be construed into the very *Design*, which I profess to avoid. I must therefore forbear, at present, and be silent; with this Declaration, however, that I shall be ready, at any Time, to produce *those Passages*, when I am call'd upon to do it, under a sufficient Assurance that *no other Design* shall be imputed to me than my *own Justification*.

I can say no more upon this Head—I hope what I have said is sufficient to convince all impartial Men of our *real Design*; and nothing will convince *Those*, who are hired to argue against Conviction—We know *their Views* and the Views of their *Masters* in such *Applications*; but whatever may be the Consequence, We must not suffer our selves to be menac'd out of our most valuable Liberties by such *vile* and *mercenary Prostitutes*.

No. 249.   Saturday, 10 April 1731[a]

The CLOAK.

A *TALE*.

Dear *Caleb*, what the Devil ails ye?
Surely your Understanding fails ye;
Fretting eternally and railing;
Not the least Symptom of prevailing;
Be wise; attend to what I say;
Let every Dog enjoy his Day;
For should you happen This to chase,
Another Dog will have his Place.
I judge you read, as well as write;

[a] The verse appears as part of No. 236, 9 January 1731, in *B*.

No. 252. 1 May 1731

We had a Story t'other Night,
And whether it be new or old.
The *Papers* thus the Story told.

The Night was dark, the Wind was keen;
(The Wind that gives us all the Spleen)[1]
When one discreet, took Care of one,
And on his Back the *Cloak* was thrown;
The *Cloak* was on a sudden gone;
A Rascal took it; soon 'twas dropt,
In Danger He of being stopt;
Another, ('twas a merry Varlet)
Took up and brought again the Scarlet.
The Gentleman presents the Fee,
A *Crown*, and glad at Heart was He,
In humble Guise the Villain spoke,
Good Sir, let me help on the Cloak.
Consent obtain'd, not only That,
The Crown, the Periwig and Hat
Were carried off; You'll ask me why
I thus this *Accident* apply?
My Answer ready is, dear Sir;
You cavil at our *Minister.*
He takes the *Cloak*; but if you chuse
Another, you may chance to lose
Not the *Cloak* only; Hat and Wig
And Crown may dance just such a Jig.—
Says *Caleb*, with contracted Brow,
Why pr'ythee what is doing now?

No. 252. Saturday, 1 May 1731.

His Grace, the late DUKE of MARLBOROUGH hath been often mentioned in this Paper with that Veneration, which his immortal Actions deserve, not only from every *Briton*, but from every Man in *Europe*, who does not wish to see it fall under the Dominion of universal Monarchy.[1] The Duke of *Marlborough* was indeed a *great Man*; as great as This or any former Age hath

121

produc'd; perhaps I may add, as great as human Nature is capable of producing. Nor did his Grandeur consist only in the most important Posts, which He enjoyed; or in the high Titles, which several Monarchs conferr'd upon Him; or even in those higher Honours, which the Voice of his Country decreed to Him in Parliament. These Honours were rather Monuments of Gratitude than Acts of Munificence. They were design'd to inspire others with an Emulation to serve their Country, by making such a publick Acknowledgement of his Services. They could not illustrate his Actions, but were justified by them. They may serve to perpetuate his Titles, but were needless to immortalize his Name.

As He had no Occasion[a] to arrogate to Himself the Merit of any good, or great Action, which did not really belong to Him, or to keep a Set of Mercenaries in regular Pay to extol Him; so it would have been ridiculous to call upon Him for any particular Instance of national Points, which He accomplish'd. The Knowledge of his great and glorious Atchievements was not confined to a little Cabal of his own Creatures. Nations concurr'd, nay vy'd in doing Him Justice; and *Europe*, which ow'd her Deliverance to Him, was the Trumpeter of his Fame.

The following short Enumeration of his unparallel'd Victories and Exploits, which is now inscribing on a monumental Pillar at *Blenheim*, in a plain, elegant, masculine Style, is the only Panegyrick They require. It is founded on Facts, universally known, as all just Panegyricks ought to be; and, to give it the highest Commendation, is worthy of the Memory of the Duke of *Marlborough*.

I was unwilling to let these Papers go forth into the World without *this Piece*, both as an Ornament to the Work and a Testimony of my Regard for the Memory of that *truely great Man*.[b] I am sure it will prove a most agreeable Entertainment to Those of my Readers, who may have no other Opportunity of seeing it. Another Reason had likewise some Weight with me; I mean the late Endeavours of some Hirelings to draw an awkward Parallel between his Grace of *Marlborough* and *another* Gentleman, who hath discover'd a manifest Affectation to vye with Him in Titles and exceed Him in Acquisitions, without the least Similitude of Character, Ability, or Service.

---

[a] Occasion] *B*; Occasions *fol.*   [b] *truely great Man.*] *great Hero. B.*

THE MONUMENTAL INSCRIPTION, &c.

The Castle of *Blenheim* was founded by Q. ANNE,
In the fourth Year of her Reign,
In the Year of the christian *Æra* 1705;
A Monument design'd to perpetuate the Memory of the
signal Victory
Obtained over the *French* and *Bavarians*,
Near the Village of *Blenheim*,
On the Banks of the *Danube*,
By JOHN Duke of MARLBOROUGH;
The Hero not only of his Nation, but his Age;
Whose Glory was equal in the Council and in the Field;
Who by Wisdom, Justice, Candour and Address,
Reconciled various, and even opposite Interests;
Acquired an Influence, which no Rank, no Authority can give,[a]
Nor any Force but That of superior Virtue;
Became the fixed important Center,
Which united in one common Cause
The principal States of *Europe*;
Who by military Knowledge, and irresistible Valour,
In a long Series of uninterrupted Triumphs,
Broke the Power of *France*,
When raised the highest, when exerted the most;
Rescued the *Empire* from Desolation;
Asserted, and confirmed the Liberties of *Europe*.

PHILIP, a Grandson of the House of *France*, united to the Interests, directed by the Policy, supported by the Arms of that Crown, was placed on the Throne of *Spain*. King WILLIAM the third beheld this formidable Union of two great, and once rival, Monarchies. At the End of a Life spent in defending the Liberties of *Europe*, he saw them in their greatest Danger. He provided for their Security in the most effectual Manner. He took the Duke of MARLBOROUGH into his Service.

Ambassador extraordinary and Plenipotentiary
To the STATES-GENERAL of the united Provinces.[b]

The Duke contracted several Alliances before the Death of King

---

[a] give,] *B*; give *fol.*   [b] Provinces.] *B*; Provinces, *fol.*

WILLIAM. He confirmed and improved These. He contracted others, after the Accession of Queen ANNE; and re-united the Confederacy, which had been dissolved at the End of a former War, in a stricter and firmer League.

Captain General and Commander in Chief
Of the Forces of GREAT-BRITAIN,

The Duke led to the Field the Army of the Allies. He took with surprizing Rapidity *Venlo, Ruremonde, Stevenswaert, Liege*. He extended and secured the Frontiers of the *Dutch*. The Enemies, whom he found insulting at the Gates of *Nimeghen*, were driven to seek for Shelter behind their Lines. He forced *Bonne, Huy, Limbourg* in another Campaign. He opened the Communication of the *Rhine*, as well as the *Maes*. He added all the Country between these Rivers to his former Conquests. The Arms of *France*, favoured by the Defection of the Elector of *Bavaria*, had penetrated into the Heart of the *Empire*. This mighty Body lay exposed to immediate Ruin. In that memorable Crisis, the Duke of MARLBOROUGH led his Troops with unexampled Celerity, Secrecy, Order, from the *Ocean* to the *Danube*. He saw; he attacked; nor stopped, but to conquer the Enemy. He forced the *Bavarians*, sustained by the *French*, in their strong Intrenchments at *Schellenberg*. He passed the *Danube*. A second royal Army, composed of the best Troops of *France*, was sent to reinforce the first. That of the Confederates was divided. With one Part of it the Siege of *Ingolstadt* was carried out. With the other the Duke gave Battle to the united Strength of *France* and *Bavaria*. On the second Day of August, 1704, he gained a more glorious Victory than the Histories of any age can boast. The Heaps of Slain were dreadful Proofs of his Valour. A Marshall of *France*, whole Legions of *French*, his Prisoners, proclaimed his Mercy. *Bavaria* was subdued. *Ratisbon, Augsbourg, Ulm, Meminghen*, all the Usurpations of the Enemy, were recovered. The Liberty of the *Diet*, the Peace of the *Empire* were restored. From the *Danube* the Duke turned his victorious Arms towards the *Rhine*, and the *Moselle*. *Landau, Treves, Traerbach* were taken. In the Course of one Campaign the very Nature of the War was changed. The Invaders of other States were reduced to defend their own. The Frontier of *France* was exposed in its weakest Part to[a] the Efforts of the Allies.

[a] to] *B*; of *fol.*

That he might improve this Advantage, that he might push the Sum of Things to a speedy Decision, the Duke of MARLBOROUGH led his Troops early in the following Year once more to the *Moselle*. They, whom he had saved a few Months before, neglected to second him now. They, who might have been his Companions in Conquest, refused to join him. When he saw the generous Designs he had formed frustrated by private Interest, by Pique, by Jealousy, he returned with Speed to the *Maes*. He returned; and Fortune and Victory returned with him. *Liege* was relieved; *Huy* re-taken; the *French*, who had pressed the Army of the *States-General* with superior Numbers, retired behind Intrenchments, which they deemed impregnable. The Duke forced these Intrenchments, with inconsiderable Loss, on the seventh Day of *July* 1705. He defeated a great Part of the Army, which defended them. The rest escaped by a precipitate Retreat. If Advantages proportionable to this Success were not immediately obtained, let the Failure be ascribed to that Misfortune, which attends most Confederacies; a Division of Opinions, where one alone should judge; a Division of Powers, where one alone should command. The Disappointment itself did Honour to the Duke. It became the Wonder of Mankind how he could do so much under those Restraints, which had hindered him from doing more.

Powers more absolute were given him afterwards. The Encrease of his Powers multiplied his Victories. At the opening of the next Campaign, when all his Army was not yet assembled, when it was hardly known that he had taken the Field, the Noise of his Triumphs was heard over *Europe*. On the 12th of *May* 1706, he attacked the *French* at *Ramillies*. In the Space of two Hours their[a] whole Army was put to Flight. The Vigour and Conduct, with which he improved this Success, were equal to Those, with which he gained it. *Louvain, Brussels, Malines, Liere, Ghent, Oudenard, Antwerp, Damme, Bruges, Courtray* surrender'd. *Ostend, Menin, Dendermond, Aeth* were taken. *Brabant* and *Flanders* were recovered. Places, which had resisted the greatest Generals for Months, for Years; Provinces, disputed for Ages, were the Conquests of a Summer. Nor was the Duke content to triumph alone. Solicitous for the general Interest, his Care extended to the remotest Scenes of the War. He chose to lessen his own Army, that

[a] their] the *B*.

he might enable the Leaders of the other Armies to conquer. To This it must be ascribed that *Turin* was relieved; the Duke of *Savoy* re-instated; the *French* driven with Confusion out of *Italy*.

These Victories gave the Confederates an Opportunity of carrying the War on every Side into the Dominions of *France*. But She continued to enjoy a Kind of peaceful Neutrality in *Germany*. From *Italy* She was once alarmed, and had no more to fear. The entire Reduction of this Power, whose Ambition had caused, whose Strength supported the War, seemed reserved for Him alone, who had so triumphantly begun the glorious Work.

The Barrier of *France*, on the Side of the *Low-Countries*, had been forming for more than half a Century. What Art, Power, Expence could do had been done to render it impenetrable. Yet here She was most exposed; for here the Duke of MARLBOROUGH threatened to attack her.

To cover what they had gained by Surprize, or had been yielded to them by Treachery, the *French* marched to the Banks of the *Schelde*. At their Head were the Princes of the Blood, and their most fortunate General, the Duke of *Vendosme*. Thus commanded, thus posted, they hoped to check the Victor in his Course. Vain were their Hopes. The Duke of MARLBOROUGH passed the River in their Sight. He defeated their whole Army. The Approach of Night concealed, the Proximity of *Ghent* favoured their Flight. They neglected nothing to repair their Loss, to defend their Frontier. New Generals, new Armies appeared in the *Netherlands*. All contributed to enhance the Glory, none were able to retard the Progress of the confederate Arms.

Lisle, the Bulwark of this Barrier, was besieged. A numerous Garrison and a Marshall of *France* defended the Place. Prince *Eugene* of *Savoy* commanded, the Duke of MARLBOROUGH covered and sustained the Siege. The Rivers were seized, and the Communication with *Holland* interrupted. The Duke opened new Communications with great Labour and much greater Art. Through Countries, over-run by the Enemy, the necessary Convoys arrived in Safety. One alone was attacked. The Troops, which attacked it, were beat. The Defence of *Lisle* was animated by Assurances of Relief.

The *French* assembled all their Force. They marched towards the Town. The Duke of MARLBOROUGH offered them Battle, without suspending the Siege. They abandoned the Enterprize.

They came to save the Town. They were Spectators of its Fall.

From this Conquest the Duke hastened to others. The Posts taken by the Enemy on the *Schelde* were surprized. That River was passed the second Time; and, notwithstanding the great Preparations made to prevent it, without Opposition.

Brussels, besieged by the Elector of *Bavaria*, was relieved. *Ghent* surrender'd to the Duke in the Middle of a Winter remarkably severe. An Army, little inferior to his own, marched out of the Place.

As soon as the Season of the Year permitted him to open another Campaign, the Duke besieged and took *Tournay*. He invested *Mons*.[2] Near this City the *French* Army, covered by thick Woods, defended by treble Intrenchments, waited to molest, nor presumed to offer Battle. Even This was not attempted by them with Impunity. On the last Day of *August* 1709, the Duke attacked them in their Camp. All was employed, nothing availed against the Resolution of such a General, against the Fury of such Troops. The Battle was bloody. The Event decisive. The Woods were pierced. The Fortifications trampled down. The Enemy fled. The Town was taken. *Doway, Bethune, Aire, St. Venant, Bouchain* underwent the same Fate in two succeeding Years. Their vigorous Resistance could not save them. The Army of *France* durst not attempt to relieve them. It seemed preserved to defend the Capital of the Monarchy.

The Prospect of this extreme Distress was neither distant, nor dubious. The *French* acknowledged their Conqueror, and sued for Peace. These are the Actions of the D. of MARLBOROUGH,[a]

Performed in the Compass of few Years,
Sufficient to adorn the Annals of Ages.
The Admiration of other Nations
Will be conveyed to latest Posterity,
In the Histories even of the Enemies of BRITAIN.
The Sense, which the BRITISH Nation had
Of his transcendent Merit,
Was expressed
In the most solemn, most effectual, most durable Manner.
The ACTS of PARLIAMENT, inscribed on this Pillar,
Shall stand

[a] These . . . MARLBOROUGH,] *new line B.*

No. 264. 24 July 1731

As long as the BRITISH Name and Language last,
Illustrious Monuments
Of MARLBOROUGH's Glory
And
Of BRITAIN's Gratitude.

No. 264. Saturday, 24 July 1731.

Some *late Occurrences* and *Proceedings* have induced me once more to reconsider my own Conduct, and compare it with the Conduct of my Adversaries. Though I have frequently done This upon particular Occasions; yet[a] I apprehend that it will be of Service, at present, to lay the Sum of our Controversies in one View before the Publick. Such a cursory Recapitulation will not only justify my Writings, but naturally bring us back to the great Point in Debate, from which our *Adversaries* have endeavoured to divert us by *personal Abuse*, and *extraordinary Appeals to the Secular Arm*.

The general design of *this Paper* hath been sufficiently explain'd upon several Occasions; particularly in my late *Dedication to the People of England*.[1] What We propos'd to ourselves, in this Undertaking, may be summ'd up in a very few Words. It was *first*, to establish those general Principles of Government, upon which the true Interest, Happiness and Glory of this Nation are founded, and upon which only They can subsist; *secondly*, to give our Countrymen, from Time to Time, a genuine Account and Information of all great Transactions of State, which might occur, while We continued to write.

This was the Design, which we profess'd at our first setting out; which We have hitherto pursued with inflexible Constancy; and which We are still determined to pursue, unless some *Act of Power* should render it absolutely impracticable.—This is a *Design* so honest, so just, so legal, so necessary, and therefore so popular, that even the Men, who are hired to write against us, have not dared directly to attack it; and yet their Attacks have really and in Truth been level'd against the *Design* itself, and not, as They pretend, against our *Manner* of conducting it. They have therefore en-

<hr>

[a] yet] *omitted B.*

128

deavoured to fix *other Designs* upon us, by false Interpretations given to several Parts of our Writings. These Interpretations have been occasionally refuted; and therefore I shall only observe here, that supposing my[a] Design to be what I[b]profess, I cannot see, upon Recollection, how it is possible to carry it on in any other Manner than That, which I[c] have hitherto pursued, and upon which the Objections against me[d] are founded; from whence it follows, by necessary Consequence, that the Objections are made to the *Design* itself, and not to the *Manner* of conducting it.

I will not pretend to say that no particular Expressions have ever fallen from my Pen, or from the Pens of my Correspondents, in the Hurry of writing, or the Warmth of a just Opposition, which may not be wrested to bear some malicious Comments. If there are any such Passages, or Expressions in my Writings, I have often declared my Readiness to explain, or retract them, and am very sorry they should give an Umbrage, which I did not intend. But what I must insist upon is, that the general Tenor of these Writings hath been answerable to the professed, original Design of them. This general Tenor must be preserved, or We must abandon our Design, and Those, who write against us, must be left to give what Accounts they please of publick Affairs, and make what Impressions They are able on the Minds of Men, without Contradiction; the Consequences of which will be immediately explained.

But what is this *Manner* of writing, to which so many Objections have been made; or how is it possible to avoid these Objections, if We pursue our *Design?* We know very well, by Experience, how far our *Adversaries* are willing to allow the *Liberty of Writing*, and to what Bounds they would restrain the Use of it; that is, to Panegyricks and Encomiums on all *ministerial Schemes*. To make any Doubt of the Wisdom of the Design, or the dextrous Management of *these Schemes*, is sufficient, according to these Men, to convert the most decent and well-intended Writings into *seditious*, and even *traiterous Libels.*—If we forewarn our Countrymen against any Measures in Agitation, which We apprehend to be dangerous, it is call'd *furnishing Arguments, to the King's Enemies*— If We chuse to avoid this Imputation, by waiting for the Event of them, and then condemn the Measures, which produced such an Event, We are charg'd with *defaming his Majesty's Government*—

Let me ask now what is to be done in this Case, or what is the plain Meaning of these Objections? Why, that we ought not to write against the Management of publick Affairs at all; for if We do, We must write either before, or after they are transacted; and both, you see, are represented to be criminal.

Another Objection to our *Manner* of writing is, that it is *personal*, and that We always bring our Reflections home to *one Man*. But how, again, can this be avoided, consistently with our *Design*, in the present Circumstances of Affairs? Can We, or ought We to animadvert on Mismanagements in Government; and yet decline taking any Notice of the *Author* of them?—In other Times, We might have found Fault with one Man for the Conduct of *Maritime Affairs*, and with another for the Management of *Land Affairs*. We might have complained of one, for the ill Conduct of *foreign Negotiations*, and of another, for the Misapplication of the *Revenue at home*.—But is This the Case at present?—Is the ministerial Power of the Nation divided?—Is there a mixt Administration of many Persons, in different Departments; or is there more than *one Spring of Action*?—Do not the *Writers against us* seem to take a particular Pleasure in styling *their Patron* the *Prime Minister?*—Hath He not avowedly conducted *all our Affairs at home?*—Hath He not directed, and transacted by *Himself,* or his *Brother, all our Affairs abroad?*—Did not *this very Man* make himself answerable for the Success of *Measures*, which every Body else thought to be wrong at the Time of negotiating them, and which the Event hath since proved to be wrong? Why should *We* therefore be any longer accused of *personal Pique,* or *private Resentment?* Are there not Reasons sufficient, of a publick Nature, to justify our Conduct? If We have frequently reflected on *this Gentleman*, He must accuse his own Ambition, his own Jealousy, his own engrossing Spirit, which have monopolized all Power in *Himself,* and center'd all Complaints in his *single Person.*

In like Manner, when We have enter'd upon the subject of Government in general, We have been charged with a Design of attacking his Majesty's Government in particular, and of undermining the *Protestant Succession;* though nothing is more evident than that We have asserted the very Principles, upon which *his Majesty's Government* is founded, and upon which the *Protestant Succession* must be supported.

Great Pains have been taken to interrupt our Examination of the *present Times*, by reviving the Transactions of a *former Administration*. Our Answer to This shall be very short and plain. If the *Craftsman* had appear'd, as a Writer, in Queen *Anne*'s Reign, We are very free to declare that We should have written against several Measures of her Administration; but, at the same Time, We should have been more impartial than our *Adversaries*. We should not have condemn'd the Measures of her Reign by wholesale, and when We did condemn, We should have fairly assigned to every Man in Power his particular Share of Blame. We should have had the utmost Contempt for the Advocates of that Administration, if They had endeavoured to run us off from the Consideration of present Grievances, by perpetual Declamations on the Mismanagements, real or supposed, of[a] K. *William*'s, or any *former Reign*—If I had written, at that Time, I should, for Instance, have blamed the *Ministers* for not obtaining a proper District of Ground about[b] *Gibraltar*; but when the want of it hath been so fully demonstrated by fatal Experience; when so many favourable Conjunctures have offer'd Themselves; shall We be diverted, by continued Complaints of that Omission, from complaining that nothing hath been done since, to supply that Deficiency? Shall we not rather transfer all our Complaints on *Him*, who hath not only neglected to supply *that Defect*, but hath even brought our *Right* to that important Place, which his Predecessors left indisputable, into the chief Point of Contention?

Let us consider the Folly and Chicanery of this Reasoning in another Instance.—I do not remember that any Objections have been lately made to *those Ministers*, for what They did in the Case of *Dunkirk*. The Demolition of the Fort and Harbour was fully stipulated;[2] and, notwithstanding the affected Delays and Artifices of the Court of *France*, the Stipulation was at last fully executed.— Ought the present State of *Dunkirk* therefore to be overlook'd by us, because We might have been induced at that Time, to have censured some other concurrent Measures of the Administration? Shall our *present Advocates of Power* be suffer'd to draw our Attention, when They declaim eternally against *those Ministers* for being too much in the Hands of *France*, whilst *Dunkirk* is undeniably restored to the Condition of being an *Harbour* again, and We have too much Reason to apprehend that it will be likewise *fortify'd* anew?

[a] of] *B*; by *fol*.   [b] about] round *B*.

But these personal Altercations and mutual Recriminations are of little Consequence to the Publick. What chiefly sticks with me, and what must stick with every Man, who hath any Regard for his Country; what is the fullest Justification of my Writings, and the strongest Condemnation of my Adversaries, does not proceed alone from our different Opinions, concerning particular Transactions; but from the general Principles, which have been maintained on one Side and on the other. What monstrous Propositions have the *Writers against us* been led to assert, in the Course of this Debate?— Though They have been often touch'd upon before, it may be of Use to collect them together, as They lye scatter'd up and down in their Works, that our Readers may be the better able to judge whether *these Men* can be properly said, in any Sense, to be Friends of *Liberty*, or the *British Constitution*.

1. *The Proceedings of the *Star Chamber* and the cruel Punishments inflicted upon *Writers*, in the most arbitrary Reigns, ought to be made Precedents in the same Cases, at present; though my Lord *Clarendon* very justly observes that the Exorbitances of *this Court* raised a general Uneasiness in the Nation, amongst all Degrees of People, and at last occasion'd the Abolition of it by Parliament, in a very extraordinary Manner.

2. The †*corrupt Dependency of the Parliament on the Crown* is necessary to preserve the *Ballance of our Constitution*. We say the *Corrupt Dependency:* because having allowed and even contended for that *Dependency*, which the Constitution forms, of *one Part* of the Legislature on the *others*, these Men, who continue to write against us, must either write for a *Corrupt Dependency*, or for nothing.

3. The Independency of ‡*Country Gentlemen* (who are very decently stiled *Fox-hunters*)[3] ought to disqualify them from being chosen *Representatives of their Country*; for as *Corruption* is necessary to support the Constitution, those Persons ought to be kept out of Parliament, whose *Independency* may place them above *Corruption*.

4. The **People of *England* are no longer fit to be trusted with *Liberty*; for though *standing Armies* have generally been the Destruction of *free Governments*; yet the *British* Constitution being in a *declining Way*, and even near its Dissolution, a *standing Army* is necessary to protract its Date a little longer, in Opposition to the *Levity and Corruption of the People*.

132

5. As *a standing Army in Britain* is necessary to preserve the Constitution of *Britain*; so it is reasonable and expedient to maintain a ††*standing Army abroad*, in order to protect his Majesty's *foreign Dominions*; and because the *Parliament* are not restrain'd from providing for these Troops, what They were once induced to do, upon a particular Occasion, ought to be a Precedent in all succeeding Times.

We could mention several more Positions of the same Tendency; but These are sufficient to our Purpose, and We chuse to mark them out particularly to the Resentment of the Publick, because They are systematical, and depend upon each other in a regular Concatenation.

Now let us suppose, for a Moment, that *these Doctrines* should be generally received by the Nation; what must be the Consequence? Would not our *Constitution* be at once overthrown? Would not the great Work of the *Revolution* be at once undone?—Was not the Restoration of *free Parliaments*, against *Closeting* and all other *indirect Influence*, one of the most prevailing Motives to that glorious Undertaking?—Was not the Apprehension of a *military Government* one of the principal Reasons for deposing King *James*; and hath it not been insinuated, that if He had been less sparing of his Money, (that is, in other Words, if He had procur'd a *corrupt Dependency of the Parliament on the Crown*) his arbitrary Power would have been establish'd, and consequently our Religion and Liberties must have been subverted?

To compleat and secure the Success of this *noble System*, They have not been ashamed to borrow from the *antient Doctors of Slavery*; nay, even from that *modern Doctor*, of it, whom They accused of *casting black and odious Colours on the Revolution*. What else can be the Meaning of their insisting so much, of late, on the long exploded Doctrine of ‡‡*hereditary Right*, and waving, as it were, that much more glorious and stable Title, the Establishment of this Family on the Throne by the *Authority of the People in Parliament*, who nominated Them particularly to succeed, as They had before excluded *Papists*?—Here are pretended *Whigs* arguing for *arbitrary Power, passive Obedience* and *hereditary Right*; Men, who call Themselves *Writers for the Government*, undermining the Foundations, on which it is built; for We shall leave the World to judge whether *Liberty* would not be as effectually destroyed by the Establishment of *these Doctrines*, as it would have been by the

Exercise of the *Prerogative* in the largest Extent and the highest Degree, that was ever claimed, or pleaded for, in any former Reign.

To resume therefore what was said above—If the Dispute turn'd only on *my Opinions*, and the Opinions of *these Writers*, concerning some particular Transactions, (though even in these Opinions I am confirm'd by the concurrent Sense of Mankind) a Dispute, thus confin'd, however the *Craftsman* had written, or whatever the *Craftsman* might have said, would never have raised the publick Clamour, so unjustly complain'd of, nor the private Uneasiness,[a] so imprudently neglected. That, which gives Life and Strength to both, is the abominable System, which I have just now epitomized. Mankind behold with Horror the Propagation of such *Principles of Government*, as are calculated not only to screen the Weakness and sanctify the Guilt of any *present Minister*, but as tend necessarily to destroy the Freedom of our Government, and open a Way to the Exercise of the most lawless and uncontroulable Power.

This Scheme tends, like all Schemes of the same Nature, to reduce us to *Beggary*, as well as *Slavery*; for if We lye under a *Necessity*, as the Writer of the *London Journal* asserts, *of paying Armies and Subsidies abroad*, for the Support of *foreign Dominions*, We may find our selves, at one Time or other, even in a worse Condition than That of a *Province*; since though a *Province* is oblig'd to follow the Interests and Policy of the *Mistress-Country*, she is likewise intitled to her Protection; whereas if We are obliged, at all Times, to support *foreign Dominions*, whose Interests are not immediately and necessarily united with ours, and whose Policy cannot be suppos'd to be directed by ours, We should really act the Part of a *Province* to those Countries, and it would be ludicrous to suppose that They could give us any Protection in Return.

What is the natural Conclusion of all This?—Can *these Writers* charge me with unjust Imputations? Do I put any violent Constructions on their Words? Have I had Recourse to remote Innuendoes? No. These are the *Principles*, which They propagate[b] and endeavour to establish, at the Expence of the *British* Constitution and Interest. They seem fully prepared to give up the Liberties of their Country, in order to preserve their *Patron* from the Hazard of being, one Day, punish'd by the Laws of their Country.

---

[a] Uneasiness,] Uneasinesses, *B*.   [b] propagate] *B*; progatate *fol.*

These are the *Men*, and these are the *Doctrines* I have opposed. It is a Cause, which I have carried on, I hope, with some Success; I am sure with much Approbation. It is a Cause, which I will continue to pursue, at any Hazard, as long as my poor Endeavours may be of any Use. It is a Cause, in which, if I was to be oppress'd, and if Those, who are said to assist and support me, were to fall the Victims of insolent Power, would never want an Assertor, as long as there remain'd in the Hearts of *Britons*, the least Spark of publick Spirit, the least Degree of Zeal for the Laws and Liberties of their Country. I am so fully convinc'd of the Justice of this Cause, that if my Doctrines and the Doctrines of my Adversaries should be brought to the Test of all the *grand Juries* in *England*, where Gentlemen of *Fortune*, *Birth* and *Distinction* attended, I should make no Doubt whose Writings would be presented as *false*, *seditious* and *scandalous Libels*. If nothing of this Kind hath been, or should be done, I am sure it does not proceed from any Want of a *due Sense of that presumptuous and unprecedented Licence, which hath been assumed by some* State Incendiaries, *for a few Years past*, of writing against the *Constitution*, under the Pretence of writing for the *Government*; but from a just and tender Regard for the sacred Liberties of *Britain*, and particularly the *Liberty of the Press*. They look on the Publication of these Doctrines as the bad Effects of a good Cause, and abhor the Thoughts of cutting up *Liberty* by the Roots, because she sometimes produces such mischievous and, I may even say, unnatural Excrescencies.

Having thus given the Publick a short View of the *general Principles*, advanc'd in Opposition to us, We shall take another Opportunity of explaining the Manner, in which They have been apply'd to the State of Affairs, for some Years past.

---

* *The Doctrine of Libels discussed*, &c.
† *The Cambridge Letter published in the* Courant, *on Saturday May 8.*
‡ *A Letter* to Caleb D'Anvers, *Esq; on his* proper Reply, &c. *p.* 48.
** *Some Observations on the present State of Affairs*, &c. *p.*ᵃ
†† *The London Journal, May 15.*   ‡‡ *The Daily Courant, June 24.*

ᵃ p.] *omitted B.*

No. 319.   Saturday, 12 August 1732.

PEDANTRY, as the *Spectator* formerly observ'd, is not confined to *Learning* only, tho' it is commonly understood in that Sense.[1] The *affected Fop*, who ridicules the *Collegiate*, is Himself as proper an Object of Satire; nor can the justest Pursuit, or the most laudable Profession, if carry'd to Excess, shield a Man from the Imputation of this Folly. But of all Sorts of *Pedantry* there is one, which, in my Opinion, far transcends the rest, both as to the Absurdities it leads Men into, and the pernicious Effects it often produces. I mean the *Pedantry of Politicks*; which discovers it self, like other Kinds of *Pedantry*, in a vain and formal Ostentation of Knowledge, without any real Foundation; but as the *Scholastick Pedant* can only make Himself ridiculous by an outward Shew and Grimace of Learning, the *political Pedant* runs the Hazard of ruining his Country, by an Affectation of shewing his Parts; for *Treaties* and *Negotiations*, in which the Interest of a whole People are concerned, are not to be trifled with like meer *Points of Speculation*, or *Systems of Philosophy*.

The Freedom of our Constitution, and the true Interest of this Nation, are Points so obvious and intelligible, that a Man of the plainest Understanding may make Himself a tolerable Master of them with a little Application and an honest Disposition; yet what exorbitant Merit have *some Men* arrogated to Themselves from a little superficial Knowledge of *these Affairs*; and what infinite Mischief have They sometimes brought upon their Country by a dogmatical Adherence to their own *narrow System?*—From a Want of true Knowledge, and Sagacity to discover *real Dangers*, They are continually alarming the Publick with *fictitious*, or *imaginary ones*; and, like *Moon blind Horses*, are apt to startle at every Object, which appears a little odd, or uncommon. This Spirit of *political Pedantry* hath been carried to an extravagant Height in *former Reigns*; and, to speak very moderately, seems to have lost no Ground amongst us, *of late*. One Instance, at least, to what a Pitch of Absurdity it can lead even sober and experienced Persons, in *private Life*, may be seen in the following Letter, which was written a Month or two ago, as appears by the Contents, though it happened not to reach my Hands till last Week. However, the Novelty and Curiosity of the Matter contained in it will, I believe, sufficiently recommend it to the Reader, though the Occasion of it is somewhat antiquated and may, perhaps, be almost forgotten. I have therefore ordered my Bookseller to print it.

To CALEB D'ANVERS, *Esq*;

SIR,

I HAVE for several Years past spent most of my Time in the Country, which I had formerly the Honour of representing in Parliament, and did my Duty there to the utmost of my Power; but having had little Money to spare, since the Year 1720, and less Inclination to be led by any Man it hath neither been for my own Interest, nor any Body's else, to be at the Expence of getting into the *House*. Yet, though I trouble my self but little with any Thing, besides my *farming Affairs*, I come up to *London* now and then to see my old Acquaintance, enquire how Matters go, and divert my self with the Amusements of the Town.

This brought me up, last Week, upon a Friend's having written me Word that some Musick of *Bononcini* was to be perform'd at the *Opera House*, of which He knew I was a great Admirer;[2] but being very much disappointed at the Performance, I went afterwards to pass the Evening with some of my Acquaintance, who were Lovers of *Musick* as well as my self, in order to get some Information about it. I found the Discourse had turn'd upon this Subject, before I came in, and was immediately resumed, as soon as I mentioned my Disappointment. The Company happen'd to be mixt, being compos'd of Gentlemen and Ladies, partly old and partly young, which naturally occasioned a Diversity of Opinions. Some regretted the Loss of the *Entertainment*, and others were concerned for *Bononcini*. A very pretty Lady, whose Features were quite distorted at the very mention of his Name, cry'd out *that though she could not live without* Musick, *she had rather never hear a Tune than that any of* his composing *should be perform'd, or meet with Success; and, for her Part, she was very glad the Creature had met with such a Mortification.* Upon This, several Stories were told for and against the *two late famous Antagonists*, and the Conversation was kept up, for some Time, with a good deal of Warmth. At last, one of the Company had the Curiosity to ask what might have been the Occasion that the *Serenata* was not continued; to which another made Answer that it fell out chiefly by the Means of *Strada*'s *Husband*, who would not suffer his Wife to sing in it; upon which He took out of his Pocket the *Daily Post* of *June* 9, and read an

Advertisement, which *that Gentleman* had caus'd to be inserted there, in the following remarkable Style:

"Whereas Signor *Bononcini* intends, after the *Serenata*, compos'd by Mr. *Handel*, hath been perform'd, to have one of his own at the *Opera House*, and hath desired Signora *Strada* to sing in that Entertainment;

AURELIO DEL PO, Husband of the said Signora *Strada*, thinks it incumbent on Him to acquaint the Nobility and Gentry, that He shall ever think Himself happy in every Opportunity, wherein He can have the Honour to contribute to their Satisfaction; but, with Respect to this particular Request of Signor *Bononcini*, He hopes He shall be permitted to decline complying with it, for Reasons best known to the said *Aurelio del Po* and his Wife; and therefore the said *Aurelio del Po* flatters Himself that the Nobility and Gentry will esteem This a sufficient Cause for his Non-Compliance with Signor *Bononcini*'s Desire, and likewise judge it to be a proper Answer to whatever the Enemies of the said *Aurelio del Po* may object against Him, or his Wife, upon this Occasion."

A *fat, elderly Gentleman*, who had not, till then mix'd in the Discourse, immediately started up with some Emotion. *How is This, Sir*, says He? *Pray, shall I trouble you to read that Paragraph once more?*—The *other Gentleman*, with the Leave of the Company, very readily comply'd. Whilst He was reading, I observed the *fat Gentleman* shake his Head several Times and clap his Hand upon his Knee with great Vehemence, repeating almost at every Word, *Observe! ay, pray observe, Gentlemen!* As soon as it was ended, *Good God!* said He, *When shall I see this poor Country free from such Practices?*—*Why, They are simple enough*, reply'd the other; *and, for my Part, I think some Body ought to apply to this* Aurelio del Po, *not to put a Stop to the publick Diversions, in order to gratify his own private Whims, or Resentments*—*Apply to Him*; said the fat Gentleman! *Why do you know who He is?*—*Know who He is*, cry'd the *other* a little peevishly, *why does not the Advertisement tell you that He is* Strada's *Husband?*—*What!* Aurelio del Po (reply'd the *fat Gentleman)* Strada's *Husband, a singing Woman's Husband? Lord, Sir, where was your Attention? Pray observe the Words, and the Manner, in which this Paragraph is drawn up.*—"He thinks it incumbent upon Him to acquaint the *Nobility* and *Gentry*" (*Dont you mark the Pompousness of the Style?)* "that He shall ever think Himself happy in every Opportunity, wherein He can have the

Honour to contribute to their Satisfaction;" (*pray observe how artfully He introduces it!*) "but hopes He shall be permitted to decline complying with this Request of *Bononcini*, for REASONS BEST KNOWN to the said *Aurelio del Po* and his Wife;" *What Dignity! What Authority discovers itself in every Line? Does This sound like the Style of a poor* Italian, *who lets out his Wife to sing for Hire? No, Sir, you cannot certainly be in Earnest.—I suppose you are not, Sir,* reply'd the other; *but I wish I could understand your Meaning; for I don't take the Joke a Bit.—The Joke, Sir,* reply'd the *elderly Gentleman* warmly! *I don't know what Reason[a] you may have for turning it into a Joke; but I am in very good Earnest. I suppose you would make me believe that it is really* Strada's *Husband. You would have it pass for a very innocent Advertisement. No* Libel, *I warrant you; no Attempt against the Government!—Ay, to be sure!* (interrupted an *old Lady* hastily) *as if every Body did not know who was meant by* Aurelio del Po; *but He should have cloak'd it better, if He design'd it should pass. Every Body knows whose Name begins with a* P. *and every Body knows that it is pronounc'd in the Beginning like those two Letters* P. O.[3] *What! I suppose We shall hear, by and by, that Mr.* P. *is no Enemy to his Country; though all the World knows that He is for suspending the* Habeas Corpus Act; *for* Pensionary Parliaments; *for arbitrary Power in the* Crown; *for* Corruption *and* Taxes; *for a* general Excise, a standing Army, *and all the* bad Things *one can possibly think of.*—Here I took the Liberty of interrupting the *old Lady* a little, and desired to know from whom she received this Information, which I apprehended to be the very Reverse of *that Gentleman's* Character.—*How, Sir,* said she, *have We not the Blessing of a* Whig Ministry; *and are not the* Whig Principles *directly opposite to such Measures? No doubt of it, Madam,* said I; *but how does This prove that Mr.* P. *is for them?*—*Lord, Sir,* reply'd the Lady, *nothing can be plainer; for if He opposes a* Whig Ministry, *must not He of Course be for every Thing, that is contrary to* Whig Principles?—The *fat, elderly Gentleman* seem'd to frown at This, and sav'd me the Trouble of any Reply. *Madam,* said He, *your Zeal hath led you into some Mistakes as to my Meaning. Mr.* P. *must, no doubt, have some Concern in this* Affair, *because it is a vile Thing and against the Government; but I am able to trace it farther still, and will undertake to prove that nobody could pen this Advertisement but the*

---

[a] *Reason*] *Reasons* B.

PRETENDER *Himself.* Upon This, half the Company burst into a loud Laugh; but my Astonishment prevail'd over my risible Faculty. I kept my Eyes fixt on the *elderly Gentleman,* who, without altering his Countenance, continued; *Ay, ay, you may laugh, Gentlemen and Ladies; but it is evident to me that this* Aurelio—*Why, did you never hear of* Marcus Aurelius, *the famous Statue on Horseback; and what, I pray, is a Man on Horseback; but a* CHEVALIER? *Now, We all know who the* Chevalier *is,* and—*Ay, 'tis plain* (cry'd a *sober Fellow,* who sate musing all the while in a Corner) *'tis very plain that* AURELIO *stands for the* PRETENDER, PO *for the* POPE, *and* DEL *for the* DEVIL. *Heaven shield us from such Advertisements!*—*I don't know* (reply'd a *young Lady,* who sate near me) *what Reason the* Devil *may have for expressing so much Kindness to this Nation; but I am sure the* Pope *and the* Pretender *have very little*—*Well,* (quoth the *elderly Gentleman) say what you will, They are obliged, at least, to some People, for screening their Design; but does not every Word shew it? Who could write with that* Elegance, *that* Art, *which I observ'd to you, but the* Pretender? *Who could assume so much* Dignity *and* Majesty *but one, who calls Himself a* Monarch.— *For Reasons best known to the said* Aurelio del Po *and his Wife!*—*Is not This the Style of a* King *and his* Ministers? *When vast Sums of Money have been granted, in* former Times, *by the Wisdom of Parliament, hath it not been for* Reasons best known to the *King* and his *Ministers? When the* Liberty of the People *hath been given up into their Hands, at certain Seasons, hath it not been* for Reasons best known to the *King* and his *Ministers? When* Votes of Credit *have been desired, which have so often saved this Nation from Ruin; when naval Armaments have been fitted out at a*[a] *vast Expence, without any apparent Necessity at that Time; when* foreign Fleets *have been destroyed, without any* Declaration of War, *or* legal Orders *for so doing; and when* our own *have suffer'd infinite Damages and Insults, without any Power of redressing Themselves; when various* Treaties and Allyances *have been made within a short space of Time, not altogether consistent with each other, or seemingly agreeable to the Interest of the Nation; have not all these Things, I say, been done* for Reasons best known to the *King* and his *Ministers? Hath not that* sacred Stamp *been often thought sufficient to induce the* publick Approbation? *And would an* Italian, *would a* singing Woman's

[a] *at a]* at B.

Husband *presume to make Use of such a Stile, or have the Insolence* to offer Terms, *in this Manner, to the* Nobility *and* Gentry *of* Great Britain? *No, no, it must be the* Pretender, *who hath endeavoured to impose upon the Nation, under this Disguise, and to open a Correspondence with the* Royal Academy of Musick.—*Why, I vow now I never should have guess'd This;* (said *the* warm Lady) *and yet how plain is it, now you,* Sir, *have found it out? What an happy Thing it is to be Master of so much Penetration?*—*The* Gentleman *hath proved it by many undeniable Arguments,* said *another Person* with a Sneer, *but there is one farther Argument,* continued He; *that occurs to me and must, I think, confirm every Body in the Belief of this infamous Design. I mean that Part of the* Advertisement, *where the* Person, *who calls Himself* Strada's Husband, *makes his Acknowledgments to the* Nobility *and* Gentry, *without so much as once mentioning the* COURT, *as a Man, who was really in the Character He personates, would certainly have done;* such Persons *always depending very much upon the Bounty and Generosity of Princes. This, I say, is a plain Proof that it must be the* Pretender. *Besides, I should be glad to know who are the* ENEMIES *of this* Aurelio del Po *and his Wife, mentioned in the* Advertisement. *For my Part, I never heard of any, nor even of his Name, before it was signaliz'd in this Manner; but we all know that the* Pretender *hath Millions of* Enemies *in this Nation.*—*Ay, ay, the Thing is plain,* reply'd the *same elderly Person, and if People won't see* Plots *till they feel Them, I can't help it; but it is plain that They only pretend not to see Them, because They wish them Success.*

Here he lost all Temper; call'd every Body in the Room *Jacobites,* who did not agree with Him, and having quite spoilt the Conversation, I took an Opportunity of withdrawing, very little satisfy'd with my Visit, and less with my Journey to Town, which I found so much alter'd for the worse, since I was last in it.

I send you this Account, Mr. *D'Anvers,* and leave it to your Judgment how to expose such a strange Way of forcing Constructions; for I am really afraid, if this Practice continues, that I shall be charg'd, in a little Time, with a Design of introducing the famous *Constitution unigenitus,*[4] if I do but write a Letter to my Salesman about sending up my *Bulls* to market.

I am, Sir, Yours, &c.

No. 346.   Saturday, 17 February 1733.

To CALEB D'ANVERS, *Esq;*

Mr. D'ANVERS,

AS the *Landholders* are the only Persons, pretended to be eas'd by the present Project of *excising* WINE and TOBACCO, I beg Leave by your Means to offer Them some Considerations upon that Subject.

Gentlemen,

I can't help observing that it hath always been the Method of ill-designing Men to endeavour to *divide the People*, whom They would enslave; and therefore am not surpriz'd to hear reviv'd, upon this Occasion, the invidious Distinction of the *landed* and *trading Interest*, which in Reality are always united; the *annual Rent* of Lands and the *Number of Years Purchase* having generally increas'd, or decreas'd, as *Trade* hath been more, or less flourishing. For this Reason I desire to lay before you some Considerations on the *present Scheme, for collecting the Duties on* WINE *and* TOBACCO.

Gentlemen, I shall *first* consider what immediate Advantage is proposed to you by it; and *secondly*, if there should be any, whether it will be for your Interest, upon a slight Advantage, to consent to the incommoding, if not inslaving, so great a Number of your Fellow Subjects.

As to the *first*, it is said that, by collecting the present Duties on *Wine* and *Tobacco*, by Way of *Excise*, a Surplus beyond what they now produce may be raised, sufficient to answer *one Shilling in the Pound upon Land*.

In Answer to This, I am credibly inform'd, as you may upon Enquiry, that the whole Duties upon *these Commodities*, at present, do not amount to near such a Sum; and it is very improbable that *this Method* should more than double it; since I have not heard of any Frauds prov'd to be committed by the Dealers in *those bulky Commodities*, or so much as mentioned before now; though You must have heard of several in *Tea* and *Coffee*, since the Duties on *those Commodities* have been collected *this Way*.

But if it should be design'd to give *these Duties for a Number of Years to come*, as was done in the *Salt-Tax*, to answer the *Land-Tax of one Shilling in the Pound for one Year*; I wish, *Gentlemen,* You would consider whether it will[a] be for your Advantage to run in Debt, and mortgage your Estates to the Publick, on that Account; for You must pay your Proportion of the *Tax*, as *Consumers*, as well as your Share of the *Charge of Collection*, and the additional Profit of the *Trader*, who will expect it for his additional Trouble and Servitude.

I wish likewise You would consider, that if there should be a *Deficiency*, (a Thing by no Means unlikely) it may, in a Year or two, occasion *one Shilling in the Pound extraordinary upon Land*, to make it good.

You would also do well to compute your Savings by the *Salt Duty*. A Gentleman of 500 *l. per Ann.* who pays the *full Tax*, hath this Year paid 25 *l.* less to the Government; but He hath paid 3 *s.* 4 *d. per* Bushel on all the *Salt* consumed in his Family, and all *salted Commodities* used in it, besides the additional Duty laid on Him by the *Retailer*, and is to pay it for *two Years to come*; nay, He is liable to make good the[b] *Deficiency*, that may happen at the End of that Term; and not only This, but his *Tenants*, by this additional Expence in the Support of their Families and Labourers, may find it necessary to ask for an *Abatement of Rent*.

Another Reason, urg'd for *this Alteration*, is the Care of our *Health*, and the Concern They have that We should drink *better Wine*, by preventing *Mixtures* to be sold for *Wine*.

This *over-Tenderness for us* is much to be suspected; and I am afraid the *Project* will not answer the End; for *those Mixtures* may be certainly afforded cheaper than *neat Wine* can be imported, even though they should pay the Duty on *Wines*.

Besides, if it should produce this Effect, it ought to be maturely weigh'd whether *good Wine*, as it is call'd, may not do more Harm to the Publick than *bad*, by tempting People to *Excess*, as well as occasioning a larger Importation of *that Commodity*, consequently a larger Ballance, in Favour of *Foreigners*, and less Consumption of *Malt Spirits*, *Cyder* and *Perry*, which are Home-Manufactures, generally supposed to be used in *such Mixtures*, made from the Produce of your Lands, already subjected to a *large Duty*; which Branch of the Revenue may become deficient by *these Means*, and You be called upon to supply *that Deficiency*.

---

[a] will] would *B.*   [b] the] any *B.*

It is urg'd likewise, in Defence of *this Scheme*, that *many Duties* are collected this Way already. I am sorry, there are so many Instances of it; but it is but a small Consolation, that the *Dealers in these Commodities* will have a great many Fellow-Sufferers; and it is a very insolent Way of Reasoning, that because a *great Number of People are already oppress'd*, therefore it will be no Grievance *to increase the Number.*

I hope, *Gentlemen,* that this very Argument will Convince you it is Time to put a Stop to *this grievous Method of collecting the publick Revenues*; since the farther it extends, the better Argument it will be, according to the Logick of *these Gentlemen,* for extending it still farther, and may in Time reach to *Yourselves.*

There is already a large Body of People liable to have *Soldiers* quarter'd upon Them; but I hope it will never be thought a good Argument for making more People liable to the same Burthen.

That *this Method of Collection* is grievous, I appeal to the Experience of all Traders, subject to the *Laws of Excise*; and to the impartial Judgment of every disinterested Gentleman.

Some *shallow Coxcombs* (Compositions of Ignorance, Idleness and Insolence[a]) have attempted to ridicule the People, liable to be aggrieved by *this Method,* as Persons of no Consequence, and unworthy of any Regard.

I am sorry, *Gentlemen,* that They should be so considerable for their Numbers; and believe, if *this Project* succeeds, the Traders, subject to the *Laws of Excise,* will be a very large Proportion of the *Burgesses* of this Kingdom, and no small Part of the *Freeholders*; which leads me to the *second Thing* I propos'd to your Consideration, *viz.* whether you will find it your Interest, for any present Advantage, to consent to the Grievance of so considerable a Number of your Fellow-Subjects.
Gentlemen,

We have, in Conjunction, been at the Expence of above *two hundred Millions,* in Support of our common Liberties, since the *Revolution*; and I hope you will never consent to the Loss of so considerable a Branch of them, as the quiet and undisturb'd Possession of our own Houses, for the Sum of *three, or four hundred thousand Pounds a Year*; the utmost Convenience propos'd by this Abridgment of them.

---

[a] Insolence] Indolence *B.*

Should you come into *such a Scheme*, wicked Men hereafter may make Use of this Argument with the *Burgesses of England* to consent to the Abridgment, or Invasion of *your Liberties*; an Handle, which I hope you will never give Them; since People, who are Themselves oppress'd, are apt to lose all generous Concern for the Liberty of others, and their Oppression may pave the Way to your own.

What Tenderness the *Projectors of this Scheme* have for your Interest, may be collected from the vast Quantities of *French Brandy*, permitted to be imported from *Dunkirk* at the *Flemish Duty*; by which a very considerable Part of the Produce of your Estates sells at so low a Price.

But I hope that *People of Education*, such as Gentlemen, living upon their Estates, are supposed to be, should be wrought upon by Motives far more generous; and that a Concern for the *Liberties of Mankind* should animate you above any mean Considerations of *private Interest*.

> I am, Gentlemen,
> Your most affectionate Fellow-Subject,
> and Countryman, S. S.

No. 350. Saturday, 17 March 1733.

At the Request of my Correspondents, I shall this Week entertain the Publick with some Remarks on the Writings of two very silly Creatures; the *occasional Financer* and *Teague-Carus*.[1]

To CALEB D'ANVERS, *Esq*;

Mr. D'Anvers,

AS the *occasional Financer* hath thought fit to write what He calls an Answer to my Address to the *Landholders*, I shall just make a few Remarks on his Paper for the Satisfaction of all impartial Readers.

1st.[a] I must appeal to the Ears and Eyes of Mankind, who it was that first revived the invidious Distinction of the *landed* and *trading Interest*; which I shall be glad to hear of no more; for I agree with Him that our present Enquiry ought to be what is for the Interest of the whole; and I thought it obvious to every Body, that I did not

---

[a] 1st.] First B.

object to this Project for excising *Wine* and *Tobacco*, as an additional Tax upon *Trade*, but to the grievous Method of collecting it. What Necessity there is for increasing the publick Revenues, at this Time, I shall not inquire; but must observe, that the Traders do not object to any Taxes, which are not collected in this grievous Manner; nor, indeed, are They more interested than the *Landholder*; since all Taxes laid on Commodities must be paid by the *Consumer*.

The *Financer* then insinuates, that the Number of Purchases, made since the *Revolution*, is owing to the large *Land-Tax*, which has obliged the *Landholder* to sell, and to the Exemption from Taxes, which the *Traders* have enjoyed, and which has enabled Them to buy. Upon these Topicks, I must again appeal to general Experience, whether the *Purchasers* of late Years have been principally People, who have got their Money by *Trade*, or such as have raised large Fortunes by the *publick Funds*; to which this Method of laying Taxes, and borrowing Sums upon the Produce, will give a larger Scope; or whether the Gentlemen, who have sold, have been obliged to it by the large *Land-Tax*, or by other Causes; principally by their coming to Town, and living expensively, in Hopes of getting *Places*, or *Pensions*. I must observe likewise, that this Reduction of *one Shilling in the Pound* will be a farther Advantage to the *late Purchasers*, who have included a *Land-Tax* of *two Shillings in the Pound* in all their Computations ever since the *Revolution*, and *this Excise* a further[a] Grievance to those unfortunate Gentlemen, who have been obliged to *sell their Estates*, and engage in some Branch of *Trade*.

The *Financer* then affects not to understand these Words; *that this Project will not answer the End, because* such Mixtures *may be sold cheaper than* neat Wine, *even though They should pay the Duty*; which I believe every Body but himself will understand thus; that the *Wine-Brewers* will still have a Temptation to brew, notwithstanding the *Excise*, such Liquors as will afford Them the most Profit. The *Letter from a Member of Parliament*, lately published, amongst a great many Propositions of equal Truth says, that I allow the Advantage to the Publick, from collecting the present Duties on *Wine* and *Tobacco*, by Way of *Excise*, to amount to 3 or 400,000 *l.* whereas I did not pretend to guess at the Amount; but only proposed, if it did amount to as much as the *Projectors* pretended, whether it

[a] further] farther *B.*

would be for our *Interest*, even upon such a Consideration, to sacrifice the Liberty of so large a Number of our Fellow-Subjects.

I must once more beg the *landed Gentlemen* to consider the Danger to their own Liberties and Estates from this farther Extension of the *Laws of Excise*.

Consider, *Gentlemen*, how large a Number of the Burgesses and Freeholders of this Kingdom are already liable to be aw'd and influenced by the *Commissioners of Excise*; who do not as yet use their Power to the utmost, lest it should prevent the Extension of it. Consider that every new Article of Trade made subject to the *Laws of Excise* is one Step nearer to a *general Excise*, which the *Projector* as yet pretends to abhor; and if a *general Excise* be a formidable Evil, every Step towards it is in Proportion formidable, and renders it more practicable.

Consider, *Gentlemen*, that the Majority of the *House of Commons* are sent from *Boroughs*, and that a large Proportion of *Burgesses* and *Freeholders* will be Dealers in *Exciseable Commodities*; whose Houses and Shops will consequently be open to *Excise Officers*, appointed by the *Crown*, and themselves liable to severe Penalties, on Account of any Blunders, or Omissions of their Servants; that, upon any publick Struggle, some through Hopes of Favour or Connivance, some through Fear of Trouble, and some perhaps from Guilt, may be induced to sacrifice the Liberty and Welfare of their Country to the Care of their private Families.

I am your sincere Well-wisher, S. S.

No. 351. Saturday, 24 March 1733.

To CALEB D'ANVERS, *Esq*;

SIR,

THE Author of *a Letter from a Member of Parliament to his Friends*[a] *in the Country*, speaking of a *general Excise* and *imaginary Terrors*, (p. 7.) hath these remarkable Words; "Such was the *Danger* of the *Church*, in the Days of Queen *Anne*; such was the *Danger* of *Gibraltar*, in the Days of the *late good King*, and of the *present Father of our Country*; such was the *Danger* of *universal War*, by blundering

---

[a] *Friends*] *Friend* B.

Counsels, which have ended in *universal Peace*; such was, and is, the *Danger* of the *Liberty of the Press*, &c."[1]

What, *Sir*, can we think of the *Author of this Pamphlet*, or of his Director and Supervisor? How unguarded is He, and how great an Advantage does he give the *Tories*, by ranking the *Danger of the Church*, in the Days of Queen *Anne*, with those *real, certain, notorious Dangers*, which make up the following Part of the Paragraph?

For I desire to ask him, was *Gibraltar* in no Danger from the *late King's Letter?*—Had his Parliament refused Him so many things, that there was *no Danger of their Consent*, if He had requested This from them?—Were there no Instructions given to the Obedient, to declaim upon the *little Importance* of *Gibraltar*, and that the Charge of its *Maintenance* exceeded its *Worth?*—Was not the *Spirit*, rais'd by some seasonable Writings, the most probable Reason why that Affair was carried no farther?—Or was it in no *Danger*, when it was actually besieged by a *strong Force*, and defended by a Garrison, at first *small and weak?*—Nay, can we even now be so well satisfied of its *Safety* as we should have been, if the King of *Spain*, in the late Treaties, had *explicitly renounc'd his Pretensions to it?*

Next, let me ask, is it a good Proof that there was no Danger of an *universal War*, because those Measures, which naturally might have produced it, have accidentally ended in *universal Peace?*—Is it just reasoning to argue, from the *Event*; or where is the Security, or Advantage of *such a Peace*, as requires a Continuance, if not an Increase, of our *Taxes and military Forces*, because it *affords Ambition more Leisure to look round?*

As to the *Liberty of the Press*, was That in no Danger, when Men were tamper'd with to give it up; when some were encourag'd to abuse that Liberty, with regard to *Morality* and *Religion*, that others might the more readily submit to a *Restraint* of it? And is not its present Security more to be ascribed to *Those*, who will not concur in bringing so great a Load of Slavery upon us, than to *Those*, who have spared no secret Pains to lay it upon our Shoulders?

It is possible that a *ministerial Writer* may have the Boldness to answer *no* to each of these Questions; but it is not possible that he should meet with Belief, or have so much Folly as to expect it.

I am, Sir, your humble Servant, X.

No. 353. Saturday, 7 April 1733.

To CALEB D'ANVERS, *Esq*;

SIR,

I AM always rejoiced, when I see a *Spirit of Liberty* exert itself among any Sett, or Denomination of my Countrymen. I please my self with the Hopes that it will grow more diffusive; some Time or other become fashionable; and at last useful to the Publick. As I know your Zeal for Liberty, I thought I could not address better than to you the following exact Account of the noble Stand, lately made by the polite Part of the World, in Defence of their Liberties and Properties, against the open Attacks and bold Attempts of Mr. *H————l* upon both. I shall singly relate the Fact, and leave you, who are better able than I am, to make what Inferences, or Applications may be proper.

The Rise and Progress of Mr. *H————l's* Power and Fortune are too well known for me now to relate. Let it suffice to say that he was grown so insolent upon the sudden and undeserved Increase of both, that he thought nothing ought to oppose his imperious and extravagant Will. He had, for some Time, governed the *Opera's*, and modell'd the *Orchestre*, without the least Controul. No *Voices*, no *Instruments* were admitted, but such as flatter'd his Ears, though they shock'd those of the Audience. *Wretched Scrapers* were put above the *best Hands* in the *Orchestre*. No Musick but *his own* was to be allowed, though every Body was weary of it; and he had the Impudence to assert, *that there was no Composer in* England *but Himself*. Even *Kings* and *Queens* were to be content with whatever low Characters he was pleased to assign them, as is evident in the Case of Signior *Montagnana*; who, though a *King*, is always obliged to act (except an angry, rumbling Song, or two) the most insignificant Part of the whole Drama. This Excess and Abuse of Power soon disgusted the Town; his Government grew odious; and his *Opera's* grew empty. However this Degree of Unpopularity and general Hatred, instead of humbling him, only made him more furious and desperate. He resolved to make one last Effort to establish his Power and Fortune by Force, since he found it now impossible to hope for it from the good Will of Mankind. In order to This, He form'd a *Plan*, without consulting any of his *Friends*, (if he has any) and declared that at a proper Season he would com-

149

municate it to the Publick; assuring us, at the same Time, that it would be very much for the Advantage of the Publick in general, and of *Opera's* in particular. Some People suspect that he had settled it previously with Signora *Strada del Po*, who is much in his Favour; but all, that I can advance with certainty, is, that he had concerted it with a *Brother of his own*, in whom he places a most undeserved Confidence. In this Brother of his, *Heat* and *Dulness* are miraculously united. The *former* prompts him to any Thing new and violent; while the *latter* hinders him from seeing any of the Inconveniencies of it. As Mr. *H————l's Brother*, he thought it was necessary he should be a *Musician* too; but all he could arrive at, after a very laborious Application for many Years, was a moderate Performance upon the *Jew's Trump*. He had, for some Time, play'd a *parte buffa abroad*, and had entangled his *Brother* in several troublesome and dangerous Engagements, in the Commissions he had given him to contract with *foreign Performers*; and from which (by the Way) Mr. *H————l* did not disengage Himself with much Honour. Notwithstanding all these and many more Objections, Mr. *H————l*, by and with the Advice of *this Brother*, at last produces his *Project*; resolves to cram it down the Throats of the Town; prostitutes *great* and *awful Names*, as the Patrons of it; and even does not scruple to insinuate that they are to be Sharers of the Profit. His *Scheme* set forth in Substance, that the late Decay of *Opera's* was owing to their *Cheapness*, and to the great *Frauds* committed by the *Doorkeepers*; that the *annual Subscribers* were a Parcel of *Rogues*, and made an ill Use of their Tickets, by often *running* two into the Gallery; that to obviate these Abuses he had contrived a Thing, that was better than an *Opera*, call'd an *Oratorio*; to which none should be admitted, but by *printed Permits*, or Tickets of one Guinea each, which should be distributed out of *Warehouses of his own*, and by *Officers of his own naming*; which *Officers* could not so reasonably be supposed to cheat in the Collection of *Guineas*, as the *Door-keepers* in the Collection of *half Guineas*; and lastly, that as the very being of *Opera's* depended upon *Him singly*, it was just that the Profit arising from hence should be for his *own Benefit*. He added, indeed, one Condition, to varnish the whole a little; which was, that if any Person should think himself aggriev'd, and that the *Oratorio* was not worth the Price of the *Permit*, he should be at Liberty to appeal to *three Judges of Musick*, who should be oblig'd, within the Space of seven Years at farthest, finally to determine the same; provided always that the said *Judges* should be of his Nomination, and known to like no other Musick but his.

The Absurdity, Extravagancy, and Oppression of *this Scheme* disgusted the whole Town. Many of the most constant Attenders of the *Opera's* resolv'd absolutely to renounce them, rather than go to them under such Extortion and Vexation. They exclaim'd against the *insolent and rapacious Projector of this Plan*. The King's old and sworn Servants, of the two Theatres of *Drury-Lane* and *Covent-Garden*, reap'd the Benefit of this general Discontent, and were resorted to in Crowds, by way of Opposition to the *Oratorio*. Even the fairest Breasts were fir'd with Indignation against this *new Imposition*. Assemblies, Cards, Tea, Coffee, and all other Female Batteries were vigorously employ'd to defeat the *Project*, and destroy the *Projector*. These joint Endeavours of all Ranks and Sexes succeeded so well, that the *Projector* had the Mortification to see but a very thin Audience at his *Oratorio*: and of about two hundred and sixty odd, that it consisted of, it is notorious that not ten paid for their *Permits*, but, on the contrary, had them given them, and Money into the Bargain for coming to keep him in Countenance.[1]

This Accident, they say, has thrown Him into a *deep Melancholy*, interrupted sometimes by *raving Fits*; in which he fancies he sees ten thousand *Opera* Devils coming to tear Him to Pieces; then he breaks out into frantick, incoherent Speeches; muttering *sturdy Beggars, Assassination*, &c. In these delirious Moments, he discovers a particular Aversion for the *City*. He calls them all a Parcel of *Rogues*,[2] and asserts that the *honestest Trader among them deserves to be hang'd*—It is much question'd whether he will recover; at least, if he does, it is not doubted but he will seek for a Retreat in his *own Country* from the general Resentment of the Town.

I am, Sir, your very humble Servant,
P--LO R--LI.

P. S. Having seen a little Epigram, lately handed about Town, which seems to allude to the same Subject, I believe it will not be unwelcome to your Readers.

EPIGRAM.

QUoth *W----e* to *H----l*, shall We Two agree,
And *excise* the whole Nation?
                    H. si, Caro, si.
Of what Use are *Sheep*, if the *Shepherd* can't shear them?
At the *Hay-Market* I, you at *Westminster*—
                    W. Hear Him!
  Call'd to Order, their *Seconds* appear in their Place;
One fam'd for his *Morals*, and one for his *Face*.[3]
In half They succeeded, in half They were crost.
The EXCISE was obtain'd, but poor DEBORAH lost.[4]

No. 375. Saturday, 8 September 1733.

To CALEB D'ANVERS, *Esq*;
SIR,
IT is pleasant to observe a Set of Writers charging others with
forming *Republican Schemes*, when They themselves are the
Persons, who in Effect and by the necessary Consequence of their
Way of Reasoning, have been placing our *excellent Constitution* in a
most ridiculous and contemptible Light. According to Them, it is
no better than a Jumble of incompatible Powers, which would
separate and fall to Pieces of Themselves, unless restrained and
upheld by such honourable Methods as Those of *Bribery* and
Corruption; for how is it possible for any Man, under any other
Notion, to plead for the Necessity, or for the Fitness of *Places*, and
Pensions, or any *pecuniary Influence* among the Members of the
House of Commons? If any *Dependence*, or *Biass*, created by *such
Motives*, were really necessary, it would prove that the *Form* of our
Government it self was defective to a Degree of Ridiculousness;
that it was a *Constitution*, having a *Representative of the People*,
which must be engaged *not to represent them*; not[a] to vote and act, as
They would vote and act, if uninfluenced by *private Interest*, or
corrupt Motives. Now, if such an *Influence*, or *Dependance*, was
universal and unlimited throughout the *whole House*, the Monarchy
would be *absolute*; and whenever *this Influence* prevails in any

---

[a] not | nor *B*.

Degree, it tends to *arbitrary Power*. For this Reason, the true Friends of *Liberty* must perpetually guard against *such Influences*; which is not setting up a *new Form of Government*, but preserving the *old*.

Our *Constitution* may, in some Sense, be said to be a fleeting Thing, which at different Times hath differ'd from itself, as Men differ from Themselves in Age and Youth, or in Sickness and Health; but still it is the same, and it is our Duty to preserve it, as far as We are able, in its full Strength and Vigour. I don't know a more useful Turn of Mind, and what will contribute more to this End, than That, which disposeth us to observe the several *Changes* in our *Constitution*; the *Causes*, which have produced them; and the *Consequences* attending them. I don't pretend, for my Part, to enter far into this Subject; but will only offer some few Observations on what hath happened of that Kind, during the Reigns of King WILLIAM and Queen ANNE; and I leave it to other Pens to remark farther back, or to continue such Remarks farther on.

At the Time of the *Revolution*, our *Constitution* received a considerable Strength by *that Act*, which is call'd the *Declaration of Rights*; by which, we hope, an End is put to the dangerous Claims and Practices of some *former Reigns*; such as That of a Power in the Crown to *dispense with the Execution of the Laws*; as also That of keeping up a *standing Army in Time of Peace, without Consent of Parliament*; and some other Particulars, which are contained in *that Act*. I don't reckon that we obtained any Thing *new* by it; any Thing, that was not our just Right before; nor does it provide such *Remedies* for us, or such *Penalties* for the Offenders against it, as might have been contrived; yet it is an Advantage to have That expresly declared and acknowledged to be *our Right*, which had once been brought, how unjustly soever, into Dispute.

About five or six Years after This, We obtain'd the *Triennial Act*;[1] which was an additional Security to our *Liberties*; for tho'[a] it may seem, from the Reason of Things and ancient Usage, that *Parliaments* ought to have been either *annual*, or to continue no longer than till the *particular Business*, for which They were summoned, was finished; yet, by the Precedents made of the *long Continuance of the same Parliament*, in the Reigns of *Charles* the *first* and *second*, it was become fit and requisite to enact, by an express

---

[a] tho'] though *B*.

Law, that there should be a *new one*, at least, once in *three Years*. It may, perhaps, be wondered that This was not taken Care of in the *Declaration of Rights*; for though it is there declared that *Parliaments ought to be held frequently*; (by which might not improperly be understood *new Parliaments*) yet in a Matter of such Importance, one might have expected more clear and positive Expressions. The only Reason I can assign for This is, that *that Declaration* was chiefly intended to assert and assure to us *those Rights*, which had been invaded by King *James*. Now, That of holding the *same Parliament for a long Term*, was no Part of the Complaints against his Government; since during his short Reign He called but *one Parliament*, and That He dissolved abruptly at their *second Session*.

But I proceed to mention those *other Acts*, which King *William* passed, for securing to us *free Parliaments*, and consequently our *Constitution* and *Liberties*. There was one, to prevent *double* and *false Returns*; another to prevent *Bribery*; another to prohibit *Commissioners of the Excise sitting in the House*; and by a Clause in an *Act* of the 12th of his Reign, which is the *Act of Settlement*, it was provided that after his Decease, and the Decease of the then Princess *Anne*, no Person, who had *any Office, or Place of Profit, under the King, or received any Pension from the Crown, should be capable of serving as a Member of the House of Commons*. The passing *those Laws* was certainly giving Strength and Security to our *Liberties*, in the most important and essential Article; for the Freedom and Independency of *this Assembly* is undeniably the Support of them all, and upon which the Fabrick of our whole Constitution depends. The *Members of this House* are the Trustees and Guardians of all we have, and of all our Posterity.

I will add one Instance more of the Advantage, accruing to the Cause of *Liberty*, under the Reign of that *glorious Deliverer of our Country*. What I mean is, his complying with the Desire of his *People* and *Parliament*, in reducing the Number of the *standing Forces in England* to about 7000 Men. Thus we see that as by the coming in of King *William* our *Religion* and *Liberties* were preserved from the Designs and Projects then on Foot to destroy *both*; so by his succeeding Reign He further[a] strengthened and secured them to us by *good Laws*. I cannot help thinking, that whenever it shall be thought proper to set up an Equestrian Statue

---

[a] further] farther *B*.

to the Memory of *that Prince*, an Inscription ought to be engraven on the Pedestal in these, or such like Words.—*To the immortal Memory of King* WILLIAM *the Third, who by an hazardous and glorious Enterprize preserved the* British *Nation from the imminent Danger of* Popery *and* Slavery; *and afterwards with more Glory, as securing us for the future is doing a far greater Good than only once preventing a present Danger, He confirmed and strengthened its Liberties by such excellent Laws as the* TRIENNIAL ACT, *and That of the* 12 *th of his Reign, entitled an Act for the* FARTHER LIMITATION *of the Crown; and better securing* THE RIGHTS *and* LIBERTIES *of the Subject.*

It can be no Objection against setting up such a Memorial of *those Laws*, that the *first* of them is repealed, and that the *Clause above-mentioned in the other* is repealed likewise; for though, in Deference to the Wisdom of the *Legislature*, we suppose that the *Repeal* was for *good Reasons*, with Regard to the Time, in which they were repealed; yet we may affirm that the *enacting of them*, at the Time they were enacted, was for *good Reasons* too, and such as arise from a Consideration of the Nature of *Government*, the Principles of *Liberty*, and Precedents in *free States*.

I was induced to mention these Things at present, because *some Persons* are often calling upon and defying People to instance any *one Article of Liberty*, or *Security for Liberty*, which we once had, and do not still hold and enjoy. I desire Leave to ask Them, whether *long Parliaments* are the same Thing as having *frequent Elections*.— Is the Circumstance of having *almost two hundred Members of the House of Commons* vested with Offices or Places, under the Crown, the same Thing as having a *Law*, that would have *excluded all Persons, who hold Places, from sitting there?*—Is an Army of above 17,000 Men, at the Expence of 850,000 *per Ann.* for the Service of *Great Britain*, the same Thing as an Army of 7000 Men, at the Expence of 350,000 *l. per Annum* for *England*; and I will suppose there might be about 3000 Men more for *Scotland?*—Is the *Riot-Act*, which establishes *Passive-Obedience* and *Non-Resistance* by a Law, even in Cases of the utmost Extremity, the same Thing as leaving the People at Liberty to redress Themselves, when They are grievously oppress'd, and thereby oblige the Prince, in some Measure, to depend on *their Affections?*

But to return from whence I have digress'd, and pass to the next Reign. In That of Queen *Anne* a very expensive War against *France* involved the Nation in a heavy Debt, (which I hope will be a Warning to us from engaging hastily in another) and occasion'd the granting several *Duties* and *Taxes*, which are received by the *Crown*, and charged as Funds to pay Interest on several great Sums, that have been borrowed. This Circumstance is certainly of no Advantage to the Cause of *Liberty*, as it makes the *Crown* the immediate Steward and Receiver of the annual Income of near *fifty Millions of the People's Property*; besides increasing its Influence and Weight by the vast Number of *Officers*, employed in collecting, overseeing and paying *these Funds and Revenues*. I must farther add, that there was a *Clause in an Act of Parliament* repealed in this Reign, which till then had been highly valued, as what would tend very much to the Security of our *Liberties*. I mean *that Clause of the 12th of King William* above-mentioned, by Virtue of which, after the Decease of the *Queen*, no Person having any *Place* could sit in the *House of Commons*. I mention This without any Design to cast the least Reflection on *that excellent Princess*, who pass'd many *good Laws* for the Security of *Liberty*, as will appear from what I am going to mention; for by the same *Act*, in which *that Clause* was repealed, there was *another* inserted, by which all Persons, holding the several *Offices* therein specify'd, were incapacitated from sitting in the *House of Commons*; as well as all Persons, holding any *new Places*, created since 1705. By the same Act all Persons, who, after their Election into Parliament, shall accept any *Office of Profit* whatsoever under the *Crown*, (except in the *Army* or *Navy)* are declared incapable of sitting in the House, unless *Re-elected*.[a]—In consenting to *these* Clauses, her Majesty gave us immediate Possession of the Benefit of Them; whereas That of the 12th of King *William*, though it was more extensive, yet was not to take Place till a Time remote, and so was repealed before it came in Force. In the 5th Year of her Reign, she passed the *Qualification Act*, which requires that every Member for a Borough shall have 300 *l. per Annum*, and for a County 600 *l. per Annum*;[2] a Law, which was intended to confine the Election to such Persons as are *independent in their Circumstances*; have a valuable Stake in the *Land*; and must therefore be the most strongly engaged to consult the *publick Good*, and least liable to *Corruption*. *This Law* has been of great Service to us, and is so still; though far from being effectual;

---

[a] *Re-elected.*] B; *Re-elected fol.*

but it would be, in a great Measure needless, if we were once made secure against *Bribery at Elections* and *Corruption after Elections*; because the People, when left to Themselves, would naturally chuse the chief and best Sort of the Gentry to represent Them.

But I purpose,[a] as I said before, to pursue these Kind of Remarks no farther than those two Reigns. I will only add, that if any Part of these *good Laws*, which still subsist, and were formed for the Preservation of the *Freedom of Parliaments*, have not their due Force, by Reason of some *concealed Evasions*, which in length of Time may have been found out; what can be more reasonable than to apply an effectual Remedy? Is it not of a hundred Times more Consequence to prevent *such Evasions* than any *little Frauds in the Customs?* If the Laws formerly contrived for securing to us *free Parliaments* and *frequent Elections* have been repealed; it is natural to desire that a proper Opportunity may offer itself for recovering what we once enjoy'd by *express Law*, as well as by the Nature of our *Constitution.* And farther, if the *publick Debts* are such an Incumbrance and Embarassment to us, that we could not engage with Vigour in a War, even upon *our own Account* and for *our own immediate Interests*, if Occasion required; or if They are so circumstanced, that They may render our *Liberties* less secure; what can be more fit and reasonable than to make Use of the Means we have in our Hands to lessen these Debts, by managing the national Expence with all possible Frugality, and shunning all Occasions of increasing it.[b] Sure, no *good Ally* can expect that we should act for *his Interest*, with less Caution than we use for *our own*; or that we should be more quick in making Reprisals upon the Aggressors against *Him*, than we are upon Those against *our selves!*

If the *ministerial Advocates* would be thought to have any Sense of *Liberty*, or *Revolution-Principles*, left unextinguished in their Breasts, let Them come fairly to *these Points*, without Sophistry, or Prevarication; but if, instead of This, They are resolved to drudge on in their old Road of calling *Jacobite* and *Republican*, They must expect to continue in the same Contempt They are at present, and only make their *Patron* ridiculous, as well as Themselves.

I am, SIR, &c.

[a] purpose] propose *B*.   [b] it] them *B*.

No. 377. Saturday, 22 September 1733.

I Have lately read a little Piece, intitled *the Freeholder's political Catechism*; and as the Duty to our Country is next to our Duty to God, I think it ought to be spread into as many Hands as possible, at this Juncture. I shall therefore present my Country Readers with those Parts of it, which relate immediately to the *British Constitution* and the *Liberty of the Subject*.[1]

Extracts from the FREEHOLDER's POLITICAL CATECHISM.

QUESTION.

"*WHO are you?*

Answer, I am *T. M.* a Freeholder of *Great Britain*.

  Q. *What Privilege enjoy'st thou by being a Freeholder of* Great Britain?

  A. By being a Freeholder of *Great Britain*, I am a greater Man in my civil Capacity, than the greatest Subject of an arbitrary Prince; because I am governed by Laws, to which I give my Consent; and my Life, Liberty, and Goods cannot be taken from me, but according to those Laws. I am a Freeman.

  Q. *Who gave Thee this Liberty?*

  A. No Man gave it me. *Liberty* is the natural Right of every human Creature. He is born to the Exercise of it, as soon as he has attain'd to That of his Reason; but that my *Liberty* is preserved to Me, when lost to a great Part of Mankind, is owing under God to the Wisdom and Valour of my Ancestors, Freeholders of this Realm.

  Q. *Wherein does this* Liberty, *which thou enjoyest, consist?*

  A. In *Laws* made by the Consent of the People, and the due Execution of *those Laws*. I am free not *from the Law*, but *by the Law*.

  Q. *Wilt thou stand fast in* this Liberty, *whereunto thou art born and entitled by the Laws of thy Country?*

  A. Yes, verily, by God's Grace, I will; and I thank his good Providence that I am born a Member of a Community governed by *Laws*, and not by *arbitrary Power*.

158

Q. *What do'st thou think incumbent upon Thee, to secure this Blessing to thy self and Posterity?*

A. As I am a *Freeholder*, I think it incumbent upon Me to believe aright concerning the fundamental Articles of the Government, to which I am subject; to write, speak, and act on all Occasions conformably to this orthodox Faith; to oppose, with all the Powers of my Body and Mind, such as are Enemies of our good Constitution, together with all their secret and open Abettors, and to be obedient to the King, the supreme Magistrate of the Society.

Q. *Rehearse unto me the Articles of thy political Creed?*

A. I believe that the supreme, or legislative Power of this Realm resides in the *King, Lords*, and *Commons*; that his Majesty King *George* the second is sovereign, or supreme Executor of the Law; to whom, upon that Account, all Loyalty is due; that *each of the three Members of the Legislature* are endowed with their particular Rights, and Offices; that the *King*, by his royal Prerogative, has the Power of determining and appointing the Time and Place of the Meeting of Parliaments; that the Consent of *King, Lords*, and *Commons* is necessary to the Being of a Law, and all the *three* make but *one Lawgiver*; that as to the Freedom of Consent in making of Laws, those *three Powers are independent*, and that each and all the Three are bound to observe the Laws that are made.

Q. *Why is the Legislative Power supreme?*

A. Because what gives Law to all, must be supreme.

Q. *What mean'st thou by Loyalty to the King?*

A. I have heard that *Loy* signifies Law; and Loyalty *Obedience*, according to *Law*; therefore He who pays this Obedience, is a loyal Subject; and He, who executes the King's Commands, when contrary to *Law*, is disloyal and a Traytor.

Q. *Is it not a Maxim in the Law, that the King can do no Wrong?*

A. It is; for since *Kings* do not act immediately by themselves, but mediately by their *Officers*, and *inferior Magistrates*; the Wisdom of the Law provides sufficiently against any undue Exercise of their Power, by charging all illegal Acts, and all Kinds of Male-Administration upon their *Ministers*; by the great Regard, which is paid to the *King* by this Maxim, laying him under an indisputable Obligation, not to skreen his *Ministers* from publick Justice, or publick Enquiry.

Q. *What do'st thou mean by the* royal Prerogative?

A. A discretionary Power in the *King* to act for the *Good of the People*, where the *Laws* are silent, never *contrary to Law*, and always subject to the *Limitations of the Law*.

Q. *Is not then the* King above the Laws?

A. By no Means; for the Intention of Government being the Security of the Lives, Liberties and Properties of the Members of the Community, they never can be supposed by the Law of Nature, to give an *arbitrary Power* over their Persons and Estates. *King* is a Title, which, translated into several Languages, signifies a Magistrate with as many different Degrees of Power, as there are Kingdoms in the World; and he can have no Power but what is given him by *Law*; yea, even the *supreme*, or *legislative Power* is bound, by the Rules of Equity, to govern by *Laws* enacted, and published in due Form; for what is not *legal* is *arbitrary*.

Q. *How comes it that Those, who endeavour to destroy the Authority and Independance of any of the Branches of the Legislature, subvert the Constitution?*

A. By the fundamental Laws of the Constitution, the free and impartial Consent of *each of the three Members* is necessary to the Being of a Law; therefore if the Consent of any of the *Three* is wilfully omitted; or obtained by *Terror* or *Corruption*, the Legislature is violated; and instead of *Three* there may be really and effectually but *one Branch of the Legislature*.

Q. *Can'st Thou illustrate This by any Example?*

A. The royal Authority and That of the House of Peers were both destroyed by the House of Commons, and by a small Part of That, in the late civil War; so that the very Form of Government was annihilated.

Q. *Can you give me an Instance, where the* Form of Government *may be kept, and yet the* Constitution *destroyed?*

A. Yes. The Forms of the free Government of *Rome* were preserved under the arbitrary Government of the *Emperors*.

There was a *Senate, Consuls,* and *Tribunes of the People*; as one might say *King, Lords* and *Commons*; and yet the Government under the Emperors was always *despotick,* and often *tyrannical*; and indeed the worst of all Governments is *Tyranny* sanctify'd by the Appearance of *Law*.

Q. *By what Means fell* that great People *into this State of Slavery?*

A. I have read the *Roman* History, and by what I can judge, it was by *Faction, Corruption,* and *standing Armies.*

Q. *All That*[a] *might happen to* Romans; *but did ever* any Parliament of this Nation *give up the Liberty of the People?*

A. Yes. A pack'd Parliament, in *Richard* the second's Time, establish'd by a Law the *King's arbitrary Power,* and with Leave to name a *Commission with Parliamentary Authority.* Parliaments in *Henry* the eighth's Time were Slaves to his Passions, and One gave the King a *legislative Authority.* And there are many Instances of *Parliaments* making dangerous Steps towards the Destruction of the Liberty of the People.

Q. *Who were the English Monarchs, who were most indulgent to the Liberties of the People?*

A. The great King *Alfred,* who declar'd *that the* English *Nation was as free as the Thoughts of Man*; the glorious Monarchs *Edward* the first, *Edward* the third, and *Henry* the fifth, who would not let his People swear to him till he had an Opportunity of swearing to them, at his Coronation. And the immortal Queen *Elizabeth,* who declar'd it by Law *High Treason,* during her Life, and a *Premunire* afterwards, *to deny the Power of* Parliament *in limiting and binding the Descent or Inheritance of the Crown, or the Claim to it.*

Q. *When were those slavish Maxims* of hereditary, indefeazable Right *and* Prerogative, *superior to* Law, *first introduced?*

A. In the Time of *James* the first; who, by endeavouring to establish them, laid the Foundation of all the Miseries, which have since happened to his Family; and it is the greatest Security to the present Branch of it, that *such Doctrines,*

---

[a] *That*] *these Things* B.

161

which sow the Seeds of Jealousy between the *King* and his *People*, are by the present Establishment quite exploded.

Q. *What do'st thou learn from those Histories?*

A. That a *King* of this Realm, in the full Possession of the *Affections of his People*, is greater than any *arbitrary Prince*; and that the Nation can never be effectually undone but by a *wicked Parliament*; and lastly, to be thankful to God that, under our present most gracious King, our *Constitution* is preserved entire, tho' at the same Time there are many Circumstances, which call loudly for Vigilance.

Q. *What are Those?*

A. Such as have been the Fore-runners and Causes of the Loss of Liberty in other Countries; Decay of *Virtue* and *publick Spirit*, *Luxury* and *Extravagance in Expence*, *Venality* and *Corruption*, in private and publick Affairs.

Q. *How comes there to be a Decay of* publick Spirit, *when there is more than usual a Desire* to serve the Publick?

A. If a Desire to *live upon the Publick* be a *publick Spirit*, there is enough of it at this Time; when *Extravagance* makes People crave more, and the Administration of a *publick Revenue* (perhaps treble what it was before the *Revolution)* enables the *Crown* to give more than formerly.

Q. *What do'st thou fear from This?*

A. That such as serve the Crown for *Reward* may in Time sacrifice the Interest of the Country to their *Wants*; that Greediness of *publick Money* may produce a slavish Complaisance, as long as the *Crown* can pay; and Mutiny, when it cannot; and, in general, that Motives of Self-Interest will prove an improper and weak Foundation for our Duty to our King and Country.

Q. *What would'st thou do for thy Country?*

A. I would die to procure its Prosperity; and I would rather that my Posterity were cut off, than that they should be Slaves; but as Providence at present requires none of these Sacrifices, I content myself to discharge the ordinary Duties of my Station, and to exhort my Neighbours to do the same.

No. 377. 22 September 1733

Q. *What are the Duties of your Station?*

A. To endeavour, as far as I am able, to preserve the publick Tranquility; and, as I am a *Freeholder*, to give my Vote for the Candidate whom I judge most worthy to serve his Country; for if for any partial Motive I should give my Vote for one unworthy, I should think myself justly chargeable with his Guilt.

Q. *Thou hast perhaps but one Vote of five hundred, and the Member perhaps one of five hundred more; then your Share of the Guilt is but small?*

A. As He, who assists at a *Murder*, is guilty of *Murder*, so He, who acts the lowest Part in the *enslaving his Country*, is guilty of a much greater Crime than *Murder*.

Q. *Is enslaving one's Country a greater Crime than Murder?*

A. Yes; inasmuch as the Murder of human Nature is a greater Crime than the Murder of a human Creature; or as He, who debaseth and rendereth miserable the Race of Mankind, is more wicked than He, who cutteth off an Individual.

Q. *Why is enslaving Mankind murdering human Nature?*

A. Because Mankind in a State of Slavery and Freedom is a different Sort of Creature; for Proof of This I have read what the *Greeks* were of old, and what they are now in a State of Slavery.

Q. *What is become of the Heroes, Philosophers, Orators, and free Citizens of Greece?*

A. They are now Slaves to the *great Turk*.

Q. *What is become of the* Scipio's *and* Cato's *of* Rome?

A. They sing now on the *English* Stage.

Q. *Does not the Tranquility, occasioned by* absolute Monarchy, *make the Country thrive?*

A. Peace and Plenty are not the genuine Fruits of *absolute Monarchy*; for absolute Monarchies are more subject to Convulsions than *free Governments*, and Slavery turneth the fruitful Plains into a Desart; whereas *Liberty*, like the Dew from Heaven, fructifieth the barren Mountains. This I have learned from Travellers, who have visited Countries in both

Conditions; therefore, as I said before, I should reckon my self guilty of the greatest Crime human Nature is capable of, if I were any ways accessary to the enslaving my Country. Though I have but *one Vote*, many Unites make a Number, and if *every Elector* should reason after the same Manner, that he has but *one*; what must become of the whole? A *Law* of great Consequence and the Election of the *Member*, who voteth for *that Law*, may be both carried by *one Vote*. Great and important Services for the Liberties of their Country have been done by *ordinary Men*. I have read that the Institution of the Tribunes of *Rome*, or the whole Power of the *Commons*, was owing to a Word spoke in Season by a *common Man*.

Q. *Is it not lawful then to take a* Bribe *from a Person otherwise worthy to serve his Country?*

A. No more than for a *Judge* to take a Bribe for a *righteous Sentence*; nor is it any more lawful to *corrupt*, than to *commit Evil that Good may come of it. Corruption* converts a good Action into Wickedness. *Bribery* of all Sorts is contrary to the Law of God; it is a heinous Sin, often punished with the severest Judgments; it involves in it the Sin of Perjury, as the Law stands now; and is besides the greatest Folly and Madness.

Q. *How is it contrary to the Law of God?*

A. The Law of God saith expresly, *Thou shalt not wrest Judgment*; *Thou shalt not take a Gift.* If it is a Sin in a *Judge*, it is much more in a *Lawgiver*, or an *Elector*; because the Mischiefs occasioned by the *first* reach only to Individuals; That of the *last* may affect whole Nations, and even the Generations to come. The Psalmist, describing the Wicked, saith, *his right Hand is full of Bribes.* The Prophet, describing the Righteous, tells us, *he shaketh his Hands from holding a Bribe. Samuel*, justifying his Innocence, appeals to the People, *of whose Hands have I taken a Bribe?* Then as to divine Vengeance, holy *Job* tells us, *that God shall destroy the Tabernacle of Bribery. Achan*'s Avarice, who had appropriated to his own Use the golden Wedge and the *Babylonish* Garment, brought the Judgment of God upon the whole People, so that they fled before their Enemies, till the

Criminal was discovered and stoned to Death. The Leprosy adhered to *Gehazi* (the Servant of *Elisha)* and his House for ever, for taking a Bribe from *Naaman,* a rich Minister of a great Prince. Therefore He, that taketh a Bribe, may justly expect what is threatned in holy Writ; *He shall not prosper in his Way, neither shall his Substance continue; his Silver and Gold shall not be able to deliver him in the Day of the Wrath of the Lord.*[2]

Q. *Why is He, that taketh a* Bribe, *guilty of the Sin of Perjury?*

A. Because he sweareth,

I A. B.* *do swear* (or being one of the People called Quakers, *I* A. B. *do solemnly affirm) I have not received, or had by my Self, or any*[a] *Person whatsoever in Trust for me, or for my Use and Benefit, directly or indirectly, any Sum or Sums of Money, Office, Place or Employment, Gift or Reward, or any Promise or Security for any Money, Office, Imployment or Gift, in order to give my Vote at this Election; and that I have not before been polled at this Election.*

Q. *What thinkest thou of Those, who are bribed by Gluttony and Drunkenness?*

A. That they are viler than *Esau,* who sold his Birth-right for a *Mess of Porridge.*

Q. *Why is taking a* Bribe *Folly or Madness?*

A. Because I must refund Ten-fold in *Taxes* of what I take in *Election;* and the Member, who bought me, has a fair Pretence to sell me; nor can I, in such a Case, have any just Cause of Complaints.[b]

Q. *What wilt thou say then to the Candidate, that offers thee a* Bribe?

A. I will say, *Thy Money perish with Thee! As Thou art now purchasing thy Seat in Parliament, I have just Reason to suspect that thou resolvest to sell thy Vote. What thou offerest and what thou promiseth may be the Price of the* Liberties of my Country. *I will not only reject thy* Bribe *with Disdain, but will vote against Thee.*

---

[a] *any*] *any other B.*   [b] Complaints] Complaint *B.*

Q. *Is not the* Justice of a King *sufficient Security for the* Liberty of a People?

A. The People ought to have more Security for all, that is valuable in the World, than the Will of a *mortal and fallible Man.* A King of *Britain* may make as many Peers, and such, as he pleaseth; therefore the last and best Security for the Liberties of the People, is a *House of Commons genuine and independant.*

Q. *What meanest thou by a genuine House of Commons?*

A. One, that is the lawful Issue of the People, and no Bastard.

Q. *How is a Bastard House of Commons produced?*

A. When the People by *Terror, Corruption,* or *other indirect Means,* chuses such as they otherwise would not chuse; when such as are fairly chosen, are not returned; when such as are returned, are turn'd out by partial Votes in contraverted Elections, and others not fairly chosen set in their Places.

Q. *How may a* House of Commons *become dependant?*

A. When the *Freedom of voting* is destroy'd by Threatnings, Promises, Punishments, and Rewards; by the open Force of the Government, or the Insults of the Populace; but above all by private Influence; for They, who are armed with the Power of the *Crown,* have many Ways of gratifying such as are subservient to their Designs, and many Ways of oppressing such as oppose them, both within the Bounds of the *Law.*

Q. *Can a* King *have a more faithful Council than a* House of Commons, *which speaketh the Sense of the* People?

A. None; for They will not only give him impartial Council, but will powerfully and chearfully assist him to execute what they advise.

Q. *What are the Marks of a* Person, *worthy to serve his Country in Parliament?*

A. The Marks of a *good Ruler* given in Scripture will serve for a *Parliament-man; Such as rule over you shall be Men of Truth, hating Covetousness; They shall not take a Gift; They shall not be afraid of the Face of a Man,* Deut. xvi. therefore I conclude, that the Marks of a *good Parliament-man* are Riches with Frugality; Integrity; Courage; being well-affected to the Constitution; Knowledge of the State of the Country; being prudently frugal of the Money, careful of the Trade, and zealous for the Liberties of the People; having stuck to the Interests of his Country in perilous Times, and being assiduous in Attendance.

Q. *Who is most likely to* take a Bribe?

A. He who *offereth one.*

Q. *Who is likely to be frugal of the People's Money?*

A. He, who puts none of it in his *own Pocket.*

Q. *You seem by This to be averse from chusing such as accept* Places *and* Gratuities from the Crown. *What is your Reason for this Partiality?*

A. I am far from thinking that a Man may not serve his *King* and his *Country* faithfully at the same Time. Nay, their Interests are inseparable, Mr. *Such an one,* my Lord's Steward, is a very honest Man; and yet, if I had any Affairs to settle with my Lord, I would chuse my *Neighbour* for a Referee rather than my *Lord's Steward.*

Q. *Why is* Frugality of the People's Money *so necessary at this Time?*

A. Because They have run out much, and are still much in Debt. My Father and I have paid our Share of *one hundred Millions,* and I have heard there are near *Fifty more to pay.* I grudge not this prodigious Expence, as far as it has been the necessary Price of *Liberty*; but as it would grieve me much to see this Blessing ravish'd from me, which has cost me so dear; so on the other Hand I think it expedient to save, now the Affair is over, and the Government settled.

Q. *Who are Those, who are so careful of the Trade of the Nation?*

A. Such as are willing to keep it from all vexatious Interruptions by *Inspections, entering into Houses, Seizures, Suits,* and the *Oppression of Tax-gatherers,* as much as possible; such as are willing to take off the *burthensome Duties* which encrease the Expence of the Workman, and consequently the Price of the Manufacture.

Q. *But as you have a* Freehold, *would you not be willing to be excus'd from paying* Two Shillings in the Pound, *by laying* Excises *upon other Parts of our Consumption?*

A. No doubt but every *landed Man* would be glad to be free from paying *Two Shillings in the Pound*; but, at the same Time, I would not raise, *by another Tax,* two Shillings in the Pound, *nor* one Shilling in the Pound *for a Perpetuity*; for *Parliaments* who have no more to give, may be disappointed in the Redress of their *Grievances.* Besides, I would not be deluded by an Impossibility; for if my Tenant has any *new Tax* laid upon him, I am afraid he will not pay me so much Rent; so that the *new Tax* must still affect *Land.* Then it is utterly impossible to raise by *Excises* what shall be equivalent to *two Shillings in the Pound*, without the Ruin of *Trade*; for the *Excises*, which are settled already, generally speaking, raise double the Duty upon the *People*, of what they bring in to the Government.

Q. *How can'st Thou prove That?*

A. By Experience of *several Excises*, as of *Leather, Candles, Soap, &c.* Whatever is brought into the Publick by *those Excises* is raised double upon the *People*; therefore if a *Million of Money*, or what is equivalent to *two Shillings in the Pound*, were levy'd by *Excise*, it would be *two Millions* upon the excis'd Commodities, which must destroy every Subject of Trade in *Britain*.

Q. *Why do'st Thou insist that a* Knowledge of the State of the Country *is a necessary Qualification for a Parliament-man?*

A. Because this is a Qualification, of late, very much unheeded. I have heard that there are many Corporations, that never saw their Members.

Q. *Is then a Writ of Parliament only a* Conge d'Elire *for a Bishop, where the King nominates?*

A. God forbid! The *Crown* is never to meddle in an *Election.*

Q. *Why is* assiduous Attendance *so necessary?*

A. Because a *Parliament-man* is entrusted with the Lives, Liberties and Properties of the People, which have often been endangered by the Non Attendance of many Members; because, if *Representatives* do not attend, I may have a Law impos'd upon Me, to which I had no Opportunity of giving my Assent.

Q. *Thou hast prudently and justly resolved to promote, to the utmost of thy Power, the publick Tranquility. What are the Advanatages Thou proposest from That?*

A. All the Advantages resulting from political Society depend upon the *publick Tranquility*. Besides, by publick Tranquility, *Armies*, which are a Mark of Distrust of the Affections of the People, may be disbanded.

Q. *Why do'st Thou not love Armies, in Time of Peace?*

A. Because *Armies* have overturn'd the Liberties of most Countries; and all, who are well-affected to *Liberty*, ever hated them; because they are subject to an *implicit Obedience to their Officers*, and to a *Law of their own*; because they are so many lusty Men taken from *Work*, and maintain'd at an extravagant Expence upon the *Labour of the rest*; because they are many ways burthensome to the People in their *Quarters*, even under the best Discipline, especially in *dear Countries*; because there are so many Preferments in the Hands of *designing Ministers*; and lastly, because the *King* will never be deny'd an *Army* as great as he pleaseth, when it is *necessary*."

---

* *This Oath is enjoin'd by the late glorious Act, for preventing Bribery and Corruption at Elections.*

No. 406. Saturday, 13 April 1734.

To CALEB D'ANVERS, *Esq*;

SIR,

CICERO, in the second Book of his *Offices*, highly commends a wise and handsome Rebuke, which *Philip* of *Macedon* gave his Son *Alexander*, for foolishly attempting to gain the Affections of the *Macedonians* by BRIBERY. He wrote his Son a Letter upon it, in these Words. "Quæ Te, màlum! Ratio in istam spem induxit, ut eos Tibi fideles putares fore, quos pecuniâ corrupisses? An Tu id agis, ut *Macedones* non Te *Regem suum*, sed *ministrum & præbitorem*

sperent *fore?*"—*Tully* makes this Remark upon it.—"Bene ministrum & præbitorem; quia sordidum *Regi.* Melius etiam, quod
Largitionem Corruptelam esse dixit. Fit enim deterior, qui accipit,
atque ad idem semper expectandum paratior."[1]

Philip was undoubtedly the greatest Prince of his Time. He was
wise, artful and fortunate. The Advice of such a King, while he was
forming the Mind of a young Prince, who afterwards gave Law to
the World, deserves our Regard. This wise King had observed in
his Son many noble Principles, the Seeds of Greatness, but ill
conducted through Youth and Inexperience. *Alexander* was young,
valiant and generous; but an Excess, or Misapplication of Valour
and Generosity, often leads to the greatest Inconveniencies. That
his Generosity might take a good and useful Turn, he writes him
this short, but important Epistle. "What Notion is This, *says He*,
that you have got in your Head? Can You imagine the Fidelity and
Affection of the Subject are to be acquired by *Bribery* and
Corruption? Or is This your Motive, that the *Macedonians* may not
consider you as One, who is to be their *Sovereign*, but a Minister to
their *Extravagance* and *Corruption?*"

Tully's Observation is equally fine. " 'Tis sordid and mean, *says
He*, below the Diginity of a *great King*, to court the Affection of his
People with *base Bribes.*" True Love and Esteem are built upon a
quite different Foundation. "*Largesses*, or the giving of Money, as
the *same Author* observes, is *Corruption* itself; for the *Receiver*
becomes a worse Man, and is always apt to increase his
Demands."—This Maxim of *Philip* is certainly one of the wisest in
the whole System of Politicks, and likewise consistent with the
strictest Rules of Morality; that a *King giving Bribes to his own
Subjects* renders Himself mean and sordid; that He never gains the
true Affection of one Person by it; that He subjects Himself to the
arbitrary Will and fantastical Government of *such Prostitutes*; and
that his very Crown is at their Disposal to the * *highest Bidder.*

The Immorality of it is likewise evident; for such Proceedings,
when generally known, debauch the Morals of a whole People. The
same Depravity and Corruption, soon find their Way from a Court to
a Cottage; and in Proportion to the Distance, is to be traced in a
greater or less Degree through every private Family; so that in a
short Time the very Name of Virtue may come to be lost in such
a Kingdom. It is very probable that *Philip* might not regard this
Maxim in the *moral View*; for, if we may credit the *Greek Historians*

and *Orators*, He was not apt to guide his Actions by the Rules of a *nice Morality*. He is generally drawn by Them as *cunning* and *designing*, and though a warlike Prince, no Man knew the Weight of *Money* more than He, as well as how and where to apply it. His usual Method of *Bribery* was to buy an *Enemy's General*, and sometimes a *convenient Town*, or *Fortress*; by which Means He artfully avoided risking his own Glory, and the Lives of his Subjects. He carried it so far, that just before the decisive Victory at *Chæronea*,³ the very Priestess of *Apollo* at *Delphi* was strongly suspected to have been tampered with by *that Prince*; for the confederate Army, who were then going to engage, for the common Liberties of *Greece*, could get no Manner of Encouragement from Her; so that *Demosthenes*, who well knew the Avarice of *Priests* and their juggling Tricks, might easily guess that *Philip* had secured the *Oracle*. At another Time, a grave-looking Demogogue of *Athens*, who had long bawl'd at the exorbitant Power of the King of *Macedon*, was at length prevail'd upon, and took the Reward of his Treachery with great Complaisance.

These were the successful Arts, which He used abroad; and by such Intrigues He often defeated the strongest Confederacies of all *Greece*. His Administration was wise, dreaded abroad, and respected at home. What Occasion could He have to *pension his own Subjects?* Their Love and Esteem was founded upon the real Conviction of the Excellency of his Government, and not upon that slippery Foundation of *Corruption*. He kept them honest, by not tempting them to be otherwise. Even in a *just Cause*, a *Gift* perverts the Mind; and, as *Tully* well observes upon this Place, "the *Receiver* immediately becomes a *bad Man*, and is always expecting *greater Bribes*." The Plunder of a whole People is scarce sufficient. To this Honesty of the *Macedonians*, confirm'd by their *King*, is to be attributed their true Greatness of Mind and personal Courage. The Name of *Barbarians*, which the over-wise *Greeks* were too apt to bestow upon their Neighbours, now left Them, even by the Confession of those very *Greeks*, who, in a general Assembly of their several confederate Republicks, soon after placed *Alexander* at the Head of that grand Alliance, which gave Him and his *Macedonians* the Empire of the World.

From the whole it is clearly evident, that an *unpension'd Subject* will give the wisest Counsel to his *Prince*, and will always continue the most faithful to Him. It is the true Interest of the *Prince* to have such about Him, as will not flatter Him, and be Slaves to his *Passions*, for the Sake of his *Money*. The greatest Danger, that can happen to a *Prince*, will arise from such of his *own Servants*, as from their own *corrupt Principles* would sell Him and his Counsels to the common Enemy. *Treason* is too often the fatal Attendant upon *Corruption*. A Government may be conducted with the greatest Security, without employing these *pecuniary Arts* at home; for a *wise Administration* will always stand upon its own Legs, and support it self without the Assistance of *Gold*. It can raise a whole People, almost from a State of *Barbarity*, to the Heighth of Greatness and heroick Virtue.

I am, SIR, &c.

* *See* Wolfius *and* Grævius *upon this Passage of* Cicero.[2]

No. 430.   Saturday, 28 September 1734.

Salvâ Libertate fidus.[1]

IN all Governments there are, either expresly or tacitly, certain Conditions between the *People* and their *Rulers*, which in Conscience They are both bound to preserve. In the more arbitrary Kingdoms, the Traces of an *original Compact* are less discernible; and by Length of Time, Destruction of Records, or the Artifice of Princes, the Monuments of *antient Liberty* may be destroyed; or, which is worse, the Minds of the People prepared to imagine that either They never had a Right to *Liberty*, or that it hath been cancelled by Prescription. *These Doctrines* have been always inculcated, with great Art, by *designing Princes*; and, upon the Strength of the Invasion of their Predecessors, most Kings afterwards think Themselves justly intitled to the same Powers, which Those, who went before Them, had notoriously usurp'd. In Order to preserve their arbitrary Sway, They are reduced to maintain an Opinion, which draws after it great Danger, and is the strongest Invitation to the Attempts of their ambitious Subjects. This Opinion is, that Princes are in Themselves SACRED, when once They mount the Throne, though the Means, by which They rose to it, were ever so flagitious.

The Princes of Antiquity, particularly the heathen Emperors, used to *deify* Themselves, with a View of obliging the People, from a religious Reverence, to submit patiently to their Extravagancies. The *Jus divinum*, and Sanctity of Person, which some of our late Monarchs have ascribed to Themselves, were but Copies of this Original, and calculated to the same Views; but the People have been wise enough, in these Kingdoms, to explode such dangerous and iniquitous Superstitions. It is, indeed, amazing that they could ever have prevail'd at all amongst us.

Nobody can be so weak, or so wicked, as to deny that the Prosperity of Mankind is the great End of Government. We are all obliged to promote it in our private Capacities; but it is a Duty more peculiarly incumbent on the *Governor of a People*. If He therefore should play the Tyrant, and pervert his Power to the Destruction, or Misery of a whole Nation, his Crime is infinitely great, even much the greatest, that Man is capable of committing; and yet, according to this blasphemous Position, the worst of These is still *sacred and inviolable*.

In whatever Light We look upon *these absurd and dangerous Sentiments*, We may easily discover their weak Foundation, and monstrous Tendency. But it is very happy for us that there is not the same Occasion to explode them, at present, which there hath formerly been; though, at the same Time, they are not so totally eradicated, nor are the Attempts to revive them so inconsiderable, as not to deserve our Attention in some Degree. The *People* in general are grown too wise to entertain Them any longer; but it is with Astonishment We observe that *Princes* have not likewise seen their Error in the Propagation of them.

We have already taken Notice of the Encouragement, which *such Doctrines* have given to the Ambition of private Men. *That Law*, which owed its Rise to the doubtful Title of *Henry* the 7th, is sufficient of its self[a] to stimulate hot Spirits, without the additional Incentive of a *general Conscience* concurring in the *Opinion* there made legal. *This Law* declares in Effect a King *de Facto* to be a King *de Jure*, and instantly annuls the Right of the *precedent Prince* by the Establishment of the *Person*, who obtains his Seat. Upon This was grounded the Advice, given to *Cromwel* by some of his Friends, that He should declare Himself *King*; and upon This likewise is founded

---

[a] its self] itself *B*.

the Opinion of several Writers upon those Times, who imagine that He would have maintain'd the Crown in his Family to this Day, if He had follow'd that Advice.

But there is still a farther Mischief in it, not only to the *People*, (for That is evident enough) but to the *Prince* himself. If He attempts to ground *these Sentiments* in the Minds of his Subjects, He must either fail, or succeed in the Undertaking. If He fails, the Consequence must necessarily be the total Alienation of the Hearts of his People; for the very Cause of his Miscarriage must be a Discovery that, by giving Way to *such Opinions*, They make Themselves his *Slaves*, and at the same Instant that They perceive the Consequence, They will discover the Cause to be an *arbitrary Intention* in Him, which will always make Them jealous of Him.— But if He should succeed, it will only make Him presume too much upon that Success, and lead Him on, by the passive Principles of his Subjects, to push such Measures as will bring Ruin upon his own Head; for Conscience, when hardly press'd, will rebel against Principle; of which We have had Instances enough in our own History.

It was the Dependance upon *these Principles*, strongly inculcated and artfully spread in the Reign of King *James* the First,[a] and propagated with the same Assiduity by his Son, that brought King *Charles* to so tragical an End. It was a Presumption upon the *Patience of the People*, that engaged Him in so violent an Exercise of the *Prerogative*. It was This, which induced Him to govern so long without *Parliaments*; to raise Money upon the People, contrary to *Law*; and to support an *evil Administration*, however odious to the People, from a very wrong Persuasion that They were useful to Himself. Thus, I say, He fell a Sacrifice to *that Principle*, which He had so large a Share in raising Himself, and proved a memorable Example of this great Truth, that *Princes* generally find their Ruin in That, which They fondly think their strongest Security. We cannot but lament the cruel Destiny of that unhappy Prince, and We know how to acknowledge his private Virtues; but it must be confess'd, at the same Time, that He ow'd his Misfortune to his Fault, and that He had never suffer'd, if He had never aspir'd to more than was agreeable to the Constitution, over which He presided. If He had expected the *Allegiance* and *Duty of his Subjects*

---

[a] First] 1st *B*.

from no other Motive than That, from which it is only due, a Return of *Protection* and a *just Administration*, He might have lived and died in Peace. Nay, He might even have gone some Lengths with Safety. But endeavouring to force their Consciences to Submission, He only ripen'd the *popular Discontents*. If these Discontents had been kept under by no other Force than That of Convenience, They would have shewn themselves sooner, and the Causes of them might have been early removed; but the long Forbearance of the People, upon *these Principles*, encouraged Him to proceed farther in the same Steps, till He had sour'd the Minds of the whole Nation; and thus the Poison became universal, at the same Time that the Disease was intolerable.

King *James* the Second[a] had a better Fate, though his Conduct deserved a worse. The Calamities of his *Father* could not deter Him from walking in the same dangerous Path. That desperate Example was too weak to bridle his Lust of Power.—May This be a Lesson to all succeeding Princes not to desire the Temptation!—May it be an everlasting Instruction to all People never to give it to their Prince!—This Temptation was the same, that had undone his *Father*. It was an Adherence to the same *false Opinions*,[b] which his *Brother* and *Himself* had labour'd to encourage from the Restoration to that Time. They were carry'd higher, at that Æra, than they had ever run before. He rely'd so much upon them, that when Those, who were Friends both to Him and the Publick, advised Him, in the Career of his arbitrary Measures, to act with more Caution; He told Them *that He knew the Conscience of the People would keep Them quiet.*—How far He was mistaken, and how fatal his Error hath proved to Himself, if not to the Nation, the Experience of what hath since happened sufficiently demonstrates. It would be unnecessary to bring any other Examples of the Distresses occasion'd to Princes Themselves by a Thirst of unlimited Power. There cannot be a Truth more fully verify'd by a continued Series of Instances, in all Ages. I have here particularly mentioned but one of the Means, which are used to attain that unwholsome Kind of Sovereignty; but the same Hazard attends all other Methods, by which the same End is to be pursued. The Danger lies not so much in the Manner of the Attempt, as in the Attempt it self. It lies in the Manifestation of a Design to invade the

---

^a Second] 2d *B*.   ^b *Opinions,*] *Opinion, B.*

Liberties of the People; and if once They discover such a Design, unless They are sunk into the lowest State of Corruption and Pusillanimity, They will endeavour to shake off an Authority, so plainly levell'd at their antient Rights, and so contrary to its original Design.

Most Princes are inclined to imagine, and taught from the Cradle to believe that *Those*, who argue in this Manner, are Abettors of *Faction* and Enemies to *Them*. No; They are Enemies to the Growth of *Prerogative* and *arbitrary Power*; but, by being so, They prove Themselves the best Friends to the *Constitution of their Country*, and consequently the soundest Subjects to a Prince, who hath no Designs against the Liberties of his People.

The whole Tendency of *these Discourses* is to inculcate a rational Idea of the Nature of our Government into the Minds of my Countrymen, and to prevent the fatal Consequence of those *slavish Principles*, which are industriously propagated through the Kingdom by *wicked and designing Men*. He, that labours to blind the People, and to keep Them from all Instruction, may be justly suspected of bad Intentions; but He, who makes it his Business to open the Understandings of Mankind, cuts up all *Faction* by the Roots; for it is essential to Wisdom and Knowledge to support an *equal* and *just*[a] *Government*.

Having justify'd our Endeavours in this Manner, We may venture to speak with Freedom upon that *original Compact between the* PRINCE *and the* PEOPLE, which we mentioned at the Beginning of this Paper; but to insist much upon that Head would be more necessary in Countries, where *Liberty* is totally lost, and its Footsteps erazed, than in This, where *that Compact* hath been so lately renewed with the present royal Family. Yet it is sometimes proper even here to touch upon *this original Right of the People*, that no Man may think the *late Contract* We have mentioned unjustly framed; but our principal Business is to ground our Arguments upon the known Conditions of our *present Monarchy*.

Our *Constitution*, as now established, is founded on a most excellent Model. We have all the Advantages of a brisk Execution from the *monarchical Part*. From the *Aristocratical* all the Conveniencies, which are to be found in *that Form of Government*; and the Mischiefs, which usually attend it, where it is absolute and

---

[a] *just*] good *B.*

unconfined, are in a great Measure blunted by the Power of the *Commons*. This is the *Democratical Part of our Constitution*. Their Share in the Ballance is vastly great, as it must be in all good Establishments; and thus We partake of all the Benefits and Securities to Liberty, which result from these different Kinds of Government.

It hath been observed, indeed, that our Work was, in some Measure, left imperfect upon the last great Change of Affairs; nor is it surprizing that in a Time of such Confusion, and from the Variety of Opinions upon these Points, some Errors, or Omissions, might have happened. Yet We may with Pleasure affirm that besides the Advantages, then procured, We likewise obtained the Power of redressing any farther[a] Grievances and Abuses, which might be then overlooked, or might hereafter arise in the Administration of Government. Our Princes are now made sensible that They are exalted, not for their *own Convenience only*, but for the Advantage of the *People*, and therefore will never refuse their Consent to any Laws, which may be found necessary for the Happiness and Security of their Subjects. As They know that their *Prerogative* was settled only with that View, there can never again happen a Contest between us, upon that Foot; nor can They entertain the Thought of preserving any Branch of it, which may in future Ages, by various Accidents, be rendered repugnant to the End, for which it was created.

The *Duty of the People* is also now settled upon so clear a Foundation, that no Man can hesitate how far he is to obey, or doubt on what Occasions to resist. Conscience can battle no longer with the Understanding. We know that We are to defend the *Crown* with our Lives and our Fortunes, as long as the *Crown* protects us, and keeps strictly to the Bounds, within which We have confined it. We likewise know that We are to do it no longer. The Part We have all to act, on every publick Occasion, is plainly laid down before us; and as the Blessings of Peace, Plenty, and Liberty will always secure to his Majesty the Allegiance of his Subjects; so, on the other Hand, the Dangers, which constantly attend all Advances to *arbitrary Power*, will I hope preserve us from any such Attempts for the future.—In short, as We have the Happiness to live under an *excellent Constitution*, so it is very much in our own Power, by a

---

[a] farther] *further* B.

proper Conduct, to secure the Enjoyment of it to our selves, and to transmit it to the latest Posterity.

No. 507.   Saturday, 20 March 1736.

To CALEB D'ANVERS, *Esq*;
SIR,

HAVING read the *Observations on the* PRESENT PLAN OF PEACE, *occasioned by two Papers published in the* GAZETTEER, it was natural to have expected an Answer of some Authority to so *essential a Point*; but as yet nothing of that Kind hath appeared, besides some loose and incoherent Nibblings at it, in **four of the same Papers.* A few Remarks therefore upon what They have said will be sufficient, and naturally lead us into *this important Subject*, which hath not yet been so fully discuss'd as a Point of such great Consequence to the Interests of all *Europe*, in the *projected Alteration of the Ballance of Power*, seems to require.

The only Design of *these Papers* is to give the Glory of our *present Prospect of Peace* to the great Weight, Influence, Credit and Dexterity of our *most excellent Ministers*, who have not as yet personally taken it upon Themselves in *any Place*, where They might have received an Answer; but, instead of That, have suffered Assertions directly opposite to pass uncontradicted by Them. All the Credit therefore, which is to be given *these Papers*, depends upon the *Knowledge*, that hath been communicated to the *Authors*; but They are so far from owning any Thing of this Nature, that They sometimes, for Fear of Consequences, absolutely deny any *such Intercourse*; and there could not surely be a more judicious Proof of it than in the following Passage, *viz*. "†It is highly probable therefore *that the Influence of the Crown of* Great Britain, *and the Respect due to this Nation* (to use the Words of his *Majesty's Speech*) had some Share in this prosperous Event; but whatever Share *our Court* had in it, it was perfectly wise that the *King* should say no more, with Respect to *Spain* and *France*, in the present Conjucture; though *publick Writers, without Authority*, may justly insist upon the Weight of the *British Nation*, and the Importance of *British Councils*."—It must be observed, for the Honour of *his Majesty*, that He says no such Thing, in his *Speech*, as is here asserted. His

Words are of a very different Nature; for He says, "IF the Influence
of the Crown of *Great Britain* and the Respect due to *this Nation*
have had any Share in *composing the present Troubles* in *Europe*, or
preventing new ones, I am persuaded You will be of Opinion that it
will be necessary to continue *some extraordinary Expence*, &c."—
The Wisdom of saying so little, with Respect both to *France* and
Spain, is very obvious; especially as it is qualify'd with those Words,
or preventing new ones; for They may, perhaps, allow us to claim
some Merit in the preventing Hostilities between *Spain* and
Portugal; (if there really was a just Apprehension of any, when *our
Fleet* sail'd thither) and the *Continuation*, that is desir'd, *of some
extraordinary Expence*, seems particularly to point out that it was
wholly upon this Account; for our *only extraordinary Expence*, as
some call it, of *this Year*, are the Subsidies granted to the King of
Denmark, upon a *certain Account*, our *Fleet* at *Lisbon*, and the *three
Regiments* at *Gibraltar*. The only Reason given for the *last* was, that
it was evidently necessary to keep up *those Regiments* at *Gibraltar*,
since We continued our *Fleet* at *Lisbon*. His Majesty's Words
therefore can be understood only as relative to *this Transaction*, if
they are design'd to mean any Thing *positive*, in this Case.

If his *Majesty's Mediation* was really received in so kind a
Manner as *these Writers* assert; if his *Plan of Accommodation* was so
highly approv'd, and so justly calculated, that even now there is no
essential Variation from it; nay, if it was brought to an happy
Conclusion by a mutual Intercourse and Communication of
Counsels with *Him*; if This, I say, was the Case, who can conceive
that *his Majesty* might not have rejoiced with his *People*, on the
Success of the *Weight and Influence of the British Nation*, in more
explicit and *direct Terms?* For surely neither *France* nor *Spain* could
have envy'd this Nation the Pleasure of being told by their *King*,
that They were at length recompens'd for the great Expence, to
which They have been put, for many Years past, in restoring *Peace*
to *Europe*, and settling the *Ballance of Power*, upon a more certain
Foundation for the future. But if the Reverse of This is the true
State of the Case, nothing could be more perfectly wise, with
Regard to *those two great Powers*, than that cautious Form of Words,
in which *his Majesty* was advis'd to deliver Himself; nor can any
Credit be given to *such publick Writers, without Authority*; Experience having constantly shewn that their Writings are to serve
but a few Months before they are disavow'd. The Delicacy of their

Patron's present Situation shews plainly enough why *He* says so little, and his *Advocates* so much; for let it be suppos'd *that He knew and conducted the whole Negotiation*; is there no Reason to apprehend that it may prove one of the most fatal of all our *late Treaties?* But if the contrary is to be suppos'd, *that He was intirely a Stranger to it*; is there no Danger that the *whole* is not communicated to Him, or understood by Him? Some Observations of this Nature will occur from the Examination of the *preliminary Articles* themselves.

One of the ‡*Gazeteers*, which You ascribe to Mr. *Walsingham*,[1] hath puzzled me a good deal, in endeavouring to find out the *Author's* Meaning. It is in Answer to that Part of the *Observations*, where it is said "that it appears, from the *List* itself, (*speaking of the* French *Acquisitions*) that some of them were only *Restitutions of Places* taken from Them in *War*, or granted to Them by *Treaty*, in Exchange for *others*."—To which this most enlightening Answer is given, (as if there had been but *one Treaty* mentioned in his Paper of *Jan.* the 15th) *viz.*

"1. ** That by the 3d Article of the Treaty of *Aix la Chappelle*,[2] which lay before *this Gentleman* whilst He was thus misrepresenting it, the *most christian King was to keep and enjoy all those Places, which his Arms had taken, or fortify'd in the last Campaign.*

2. The *French King* was only obliged to withdraw his Troops out of the *Franche Comte*,[3] and to restore *such Places* as He had seiz'd in the War, and as in *this Treaty* had not been specifically yielded to Him."

I believe every common Reader, as well as Myself, would think This was proving that the *French King* was to restore *such Places* as were not specifically yielded to Him by *this Treaty*; but That[a] is called *infamously misrepresenting those choice Papers* of the 15th and 16th of *January*, because *this Paper* says it was expresly to be seen in the *former of those Papers*, speaking of the vast Acquisitions of *France*, "that afterwards, by the *Treaty* of RYSWIC, much was restor'd of what had been taken by the *French* in *Flanders*, and in *Germany*; and that the Weight of our *great Deliverer*, the immortal King *William* the 3d, compell'd *France*, for the first Time, to restore the *Places*, which She had conquer'd."[4]

How Strong the[b] Assertion of the *first Time, that* France *was*

ª That] This *B*.   ᵇ the] is the *B*.

compell'd to restore the Places she had conquer'd; and how severe the Reflection upon the *Observator*, for asserting, "that by the *List* it appear'd that *some of the Places* mention'd *(by the Way, Mr. Walsingham leaves out the Word some, and makes it general of them all)* were only *Restitutions of Places* taken from Them in *War*, or granted to Them by *Treaty*, in Exchange for *others?*" This is so great a Crime, that even Mr. *Walsingham* is at a Loss for *hard Words* to bestow upon it.—"What Names, *says He*, will You find for a Misrepresentation so *profligate*, so *foolish*, so avowedly done in Contempt of *Honesty* and *common Understanding!*"

It is very probable that *this Author* never read the *Treaties* themselves, but contented Himself with *those Articles*, which were sent Him as Materials to write upon. It is not the first Time, as We may remember by the *famous Enquiry*, that such Things have happened; and it is otherwise scarce possible that He should have fallen into so many Mistakes. His Knowledge of the Affairs of *Europe*, for half a Century past, must be extremely scanty, if He imagines that the Weight of the *not-victorious Party* (for so King *William* and his *Allies* certainly were) compell'd the *other* to restore the Places They had conquer'd.

The several Treaties of *Ryswic* speak the Success of *France* against the united Powers of the *Emperor*, *Spain*, *England* and *Holland*. The *considerable Places* she had taken, during that War, in *Spain*, *Flanders*, and *Germany*, appear in the several Articles for the *Restitution of them*; whereas, there does not appear to have been *any Place* taken, by the *other Side*, that was thought worth the mentioning, as being kept, or restor'd to *France*. Let us not forget her vast Power, during *that War*, nor the great Stand she made against Us, in the *last*. The Motives that induc'd Her to *give up so many Places*, and *demolish others*, for the Sake of *Peace*, by the Treaty of *Ryswic*, was not her Dread of the *Allies*, but her Apprehensions of the declining Health of his then *Catholick Majesty*; for had He dyed, during the *War*, it was probable that the Crown of *Spain* would not have been given to the House of *Bourbon*. For this Reason, every Thing, that was ask'd for *Spain*, was readily granted by *France*, as what might be the Means of its coming back to Her again, even with the *Monarchy* itself. Time hath since shewn to the World that This was the only Reason of her acting as she then did; and that, through the Impolicy of *Others*, she succeeded in her Views beyond the Imagination of many, who undesignedly helped them forward. But I shall not enlarge upon this disagreeable Subject, which it was necessary to explain thus far, by Way of Introduction to my next, concerning LORAIN.

* *Gaz. Feb.* 6, 7. 13 *and* 14. † *Gaz. Feb.* 7. ‡ *Feb.* 13. ** *Feb.* 13.ᵃ

No. 508. Saturday, 27 March 1736.

The State of LORRAIN, *and the Importance of it to* France *consider'd.*

To CALEB D'ANVERS, *Esq*;

SIR,

THE Duke of LORRAIN was one of the Parties provided for, in the Treaty of RYSWIC, and was put upon a much better Footing than He was in many of the *former Treaties*; which is the Reason why the *Gazetteers* insist so much upon the Treaties of *Munster, Pyrennees*, and *Nimeguen*,[1] and not one of them hath so much as mention'd *this Treaty*,ᵇ with Regard to *Him*, though He is so essentially concern'd in it, that there are several Articles, relating to *Him* only. * *Lorrain*, with its Dependencies, was to be restor'd to *Him*, as possess'd by his *Uncle* in 1670. The several Places, fortify'd by *France*, were to be demolish'd first; and nothing is reserved to Her but the Fortress of † *Saar Lovis*, with *half a League round it*, and the City of *Longwick*, in Exchange for *some other Town*, of the same Value. The ‡ *High Ways* and *Places*, that his *most Christian Majesty* had reserv'd to Himself, by the Peace of *Nimiguen*, are to return to the Obedience and Jurisdiction of the *Duke, without any Exception*. If therefore the Duke of *Lorrain* and his Country were formerly suppos'd to be under the Guaranty of *Great Britain*, as they certainly were, They must be so by *this Treaty*, tho' not in specifick Words, as well as by the Treaty of *Hanover*, in which We so prudently made Ourselves a Guaranty of the Treaty of *Westphalia*.[2]

Another Insinuation, which runs through most of *these Papers*, is, that nothing but the *Right of Propriety* is given up to *France*, treating the *Dukes of Lorrain* as *Proprietors* only, and as if the *Right*

ᵃ *Feb.* 13] *Ib. B.*
ᵇ not one . . . *this Treaty*,] pass this Treaty so slightly over, *B.*

of Sovereignty was in *France*, because she can and always does seize upon it, when she takes a Resolution of attacking the *Emperor*. But are not the Electorates of *Treves* and *Palatine* in just the same Case? Examine all the *late Wars*, even the *last*, and You will find that whenever *France* began to seize the *one*, she immediately seiz'd as much as she could of the *others*. The Restitution of *Treves*, *Traerbach*, and *some other Places*, are as constantly met with in the *Treaties*, when a *new Peace* is made, as *Lorrain*, and *its Places*. If therefore the Arguments hold to *one*, they are equally good for giving them all to *France*; and, if found successful now, will undoubtedly be hereafter made use of to obtain them; nor can I possibly conceive any Distinction, unless some People may have imagin'd that *Lorrain* is no Part of the *Empire*. Now supposing it to be so, it would be of no Consequence in the *Alteration of the Ballance of Power in Europe*. But the Reverse of it is the true State of the Case; for *Lorrain* hath ever been avow'd and acknowledged to be a Part of the *Empire*, in such a Manner, that the *Emperor* and the *Duke of Lorrain* cannot separate *one* from the *other*, without the Consent of the *Germanick Body*. This is so contrary to the Interests of the Elector of *Bavaria*, *Palatine* and *Cologn*, that if We may believe all the News-Papers, the Way of obtaining their Consent is by an Army of *Germans*, at the old Camp of *Bruchsal*, and another of *French* upon the *Rhine*, as being the *most persuasive Eloquence*, in this Case; and, in all Probability, it will prove more effectual than our *Rhetorick of the same Kind*, some Years ago, in the *West Indies*.

It hath been the constant View of *France*, for many Years past, to extend their[a] Frontier to the *Rhine*; and, upon the breaking out of their several[b] Wars there, They have[c] constantly seized great Numbers of Places, and fortify'd them at a vast Expence. The Return of *Peace* hath generally demolish'd them, and put the *French* under a Necessity of employing large Sums again, upon the Renewal of every War. The Experience of This, and that They may be the more ready, upon any Occasion, hath convinc'd Them, long before now, that *Lorrain*, if not the greatest, is at least one of the most considerable Acquisitions, that They could possibly gain, or desire.

The Treaty of *Ryswic* was follow'd by the *fatal Partition Treaties*,[3] which shall be more fully consider'd, when I come to

---

[a] their] her *B.*   [b] their several] several *B.*   [c] They have] She hath *B.*

speak of the *Alterations made in the* Ballance of Power, *by the present Preliminaries.* The *first of these Treaties* gave *Milan* to the *Arch-Duke;* to the *Electoral Prince of Bavaria* the rest of the *Spanish Dominions*, except the Kingdoms of *Naples* and *Sicily*, the *Tuscan Ports*, (a more intelligible Appellation than the *Stato del Presidii*) the Marquisate of *Final*, and the Province of *Guipuscua*, &c. which were given to *France*. From hence one Observation must arise, even supposing that *this Alteration* was a right Settlement of the *Ballance of Power in Europe*; I mean, that placing the House of *Bavaria* upon the Throne of *Spain* destroy'd all the former Correspondence and mutual Assistance, which had hitherto enabled the *Emperor* and *Spain* to make the small Stand They had done against the growing Power of *France*; and as from hence their Interests would probably be opposite, it suppos'd a sufficient Power left in *Each* to protect and defend itself against *France*; for no other Reason can be assign'd why, in the *second Partition Treaty*, which gave the *Spanish* Dominions, upon the Death of the *Electoral Prince of Bavaria*, to the House of *Austria*; I say, no other Reason can be assign'd why *France* was to have had any *new Acquisitions* added by *that Treaty*, in order to enable Her to ballance the *Union of that whole Power in the House of Austria*. The giving Her *Lorrain* as that *additional Strength* ought to be consider'd now in the same Light it was then. The *Value* and *Importance of it* was discuss'd in several Observations upon that *Treaty*; and as they will serve to strengthen the Opinions of *Those*, who have already look'd upon *this Article*, of giving up *Lorrain* to *France*, as a *dangerous and formidable Alteration of the Ballance of Power in Europe*, I shall give you some Extracts from a Pamphlet, intitled, the *Fable of the* LYON'S *Share verify'd in the* ** TREATY OF PARTITION; a Title not altogether mal-apropos, even in the present case.

"I come now, *says the Author*, to the last Condition of the *Treaty*, which gives the Dutchy of *Milan* to the Duke of *Lorrain*, in Exchange of *his own Dominions*. We are to suppose that the *French*, who know their own Interest, and stop at nothing, which tends to that End, were mov'd by very powerful Reasons to prefer *those Dominions* before a *Dutchy* They have taken so much Pains to obtain formerly.

That *Lorrain* is of great Use to the *French* in the Design They have long since laid, of carrying their Frontier to the *Rhine*, hath been sufficiently seen in the great Advantages They have received by *that Country*, all the Time of their *Usurpation*.

The Union of *Lorrain* with *France* advances their Frontier
FORTY LEAGUES *into the Empire*; for so many there are from the
Extremity of the Dutchy of BAR to the City of STRASBURG; makes
Them Masters of all the Country between the QUEITSCH,
the SAAR, and the MOSELLE; opens a Way into the PALATINATE,
and into the Territories of MENTZ and TRIER.

This Dutchy secures the Communication of *France* with the
County of *Burgundy*, and the *two Alsatia*'s; is situated at the Head
of the *Moselle* and the *Meuse*, and therefore cannot but be extremely
commodious, as well to preserve their *old Conquests*, as to make *new*.
Here They may assemble their Forces, to distribute them in every
Part; make Provision of Corn to fill their Magazines in *Alsatia*; and
keep an Army in Winter Quarters, to be ready to act upon the *Rhine*,
before their Enemies can take the Field. It is hard to imagine greater
Advantages than these; and if We add to all, that out of *this Country*
TWENTY-FIVE THOUSAND MEN are rais'd and paid, We shall find,
that the *French* have Reason, in this Conjuncture, to prefer the
Possession of it before the Dutchy of *Milan*. Besides, if They had
pretended This, in Conjunction with the Kingdoms of *Naples* and
Sicily, They would not only have driven the *Princes* and *States of
Italy* to Despair, but alarm'd the whole Body of the *Switzers*, with
whom They will always keep fair, till They have lock'd Them in, on
all Sides. Thus keeping a steady Eye upon their *Ends*, They affect a
little MODERATION, on *one Side*, and know how to make Themselves Amends with Interest, on the *other*.

In the last Place, We are to enquire whether the *Treaters* could
stipulate *these Exchanges*, without the Consent of the *Emperor* and
Empire, who were not consulted in the Matter. *Lorrain* is under the
Protection of the *Empire*; possesses diverse[a] Lands in Fee from the
Empire; and acknowledges its Majesty in three essential Points;
which are, the Right of *safe Conduct*; the *common Peace*; and
Contributions, in Case of publick Necessity, or a War against the
Turk, one third Part only less than an *Elector*. Now as it is not the
Interest of the *Empire* that *France*, which is already so formidable,
and upon the Point of becoming much more so, should possess *these
Dominions*, which serve for an *Out-Wall* to cover it, and that
Strasburg was yielded to the *French*, by a kind of Equivalent for the
Restitution of *Lorrain*, it is not to be presum'd that the *Empire*
should consent to *this Alienation*."

<hr>

[a] diverse] divers *B*.

I have chosen to explain the Importance of *Lorrain* in the Words of *this Author*,[††] *who was an able Penman, employ'd*, as We are inform'd *by the* IMPERIAL COURT, that I might not be charg'd with starting Objections out of my own Head, and calculating them with a View of obstructing the *present Negotiations of Peace*; for *this Tract* hath been publish'd above *thirty Years*, and the Sentiments contain'd in it were too fatally verify'd by the Conduct of *France*, upon the King of *Spain*'s Death, and the *War*, that ensued.—But to proceed.

One of the great Objections made to the *Plan of Peace*, as communicated by the late Queen *Anne* to her Parliament, on the 6th of *June* 1712, was, *that* France *offered to make the* Rhine *a Barrier to the Empire*; upon which it was observed, "*[†]that This was giving up the *true Barrier of the Empire*, contrary to the Treaty of *Munster*, that *France* might inclose the Duke of *Lorrain* within his Countries, as in a Prison, and keep the *Electors of the Rhine* in perpetual Fear of Her."—If *this Objection* was of any Weight at *that Time*, how much more so is it *at present?* Since his Influence over the *Princes* and *Electors of the Empire* will not certainly be lessened by his obtaining the *actual Possession and Sovereignty of Lorrain*; and it is more than probable that *their Countries* must have the same Fate, being already forced to follow the Example of the antient Possessors of *Lorrain*; for the *same Author* observes, "[†*]that *Charles* the 4th, Duke of *Lorrain*, had no Love for *France*, and indeed no Reason to have any; yet He almost constantly did what she desired, and once carried his Deferences to Her so far, as to give all his Territories to his *most christian Majesty*; for it is a general Maxim that every Prince, who by the Situation of his Country, and his own Weakness, finds Himself unable to resist *another Prince*, ought to attach himself to his Interest, and endeavour by all possible Sacrifices and Complyances to render *such a Prince* favourable to Him."—This hath long been the State of *that Country*; but is nothing of the same Nature perceived, or at least apprehended, for the future, to the Situation of great Part of *Germany?* From whence proceeded the *late Neutralities*, for *some Parts*, and the Desire of extending them? Must not this Desire increase, as the Neighbourhood of *France* advances nearer, and their Dependence is consequently greater? Will not the constant Seizure of *their Dominions*, upon the breaking out of every War, reduce Them to the same deplorable State; and may not the Necessity of submitting to it hereafter be likewise pleaded as a Reason for giving them up to *France?*

That this Cession of *Lorrain* is against the Interest of the *Empire*, and the *Princes* bordering upon it, cannot be better shewn than by the Apprehensions, which have been express'd, that They will not come into it, without the Conviction of *some present Advantages to Themselves*, or the *last Argument of Sovereigns*, from which They have no Appeal.

The Advantage of *Lorrain*'s being one of the *hereditary Dominions of the Emperor* is sufficiently demonstrated by those very Arguments, which have been offer'd to prove that *France* would never suffer the *Pragmatick Sanction* to take Place, whilst it was likely to be attended with *that Consequence*; for, in this Case, it would be the *Barrier of the Empire*, and so well defended, that *France* could not for the future, upon every Rupture, in a great Measure support her Armies by Contributions[a] from the *many States* and *Provinces*, that hitherto have lain open to them.

That it is against the Interest of the *Dutch*, Experience of *former Wars* hath plainly shewn. The *French* possessing Themselves of Posts upon the *Moselle* hath had fatal Consequences to Them, and given Them the strongest Apprehensions. Even the *last great War*, in which *We* were engaged, would have probably ended much sooner, and better, had it not been upon *this Account*; for the Duke of *Marlborough* might have otherwise pursued his Conquests on the *Rhine*, and soon been in *France*. Nay, *their Frontier* is so weak, on that Side, that even last Year it was expected that if the *Imperialists* had gain'd a Battle, They would soon have penetrated into the Bowels of *that Kingdom*. But when *Lorrain* is once their own, and They no longer run any Hazard of having their *expensive Fortifications* demolish'd, upon the Conclusion of every *new Treaty*, it is highly probable that They will make Themselves as strong a Barrier, on *that Side*, as They have in *Flanders*; the Consequences of which are too dreadful to the *Ballance of Power in Europe* to stand in Need of any farther Explanation.

It is well known that the *Dutch* expected, upon[b] the Conclusion of the *last great War*, that *France* should have been obliged to restore to the *Empire* some of those Places, which she had obtain'd by *former Treaties*, whereby *Lorrain* would have been more at Liberty; and the *Author* before-mentioned, who wrote in Favour of

---

[a] Contributions] Contribution *B*.   [b] upon] from *B*.

Holland and the *Empire*, reproaches *this Nation*, upon the Communication of the *Plan of Peace*, in the *late Queen's Speech*, "***
that it was too true there are People in *England*, who have an
extreme Insensibility for all the Affairs of Germany;"—and puts us
in Mind of the 9th and 10th Articles of the *Association of
Nordlingen*, concluded the 22nd of *March* 1702. But as all the World
must now acknowledge that We are come to a much better
Understanding of the *Affairs of Germany* and our *own Interest* in
them, We cannot be suspected of not knowing what was and is the
true Interest of *Holland*, as well as *our own Country*, in the present
Case.

It hath been somewhere hinted as if the *Dutch* thought it contrary
to *their Interest*, that the Duke of *Lorrain* should possess *that
Dutchy*, and be *Emperor* at the same Time. This is founded upon
their Act of Concurrence to the *Vienna Treaty*, in 1731; by which
They provide that no Prince shall be included in the Guaranty of
the *Pragmatick Sanction*, whose *own hereditary Dominions* may
endanger the Liberties of *Europe*. From hence They conclude that
the Cession of *Lorrain* to *France* is agreeable to the Interest of *Great
Britain* and *Holland*, as well as consistent with our Guaranty of the
Pragmatick Sanction. But this deserves a little farther Consideraton.

The universal Monarchy of *Don Carlos*, and all the Arguments,
employ'd in the *Enquiry*, against our coming into any *Guaranties*, of
this Nature, cannot be forgotten, whilst We see and feel the Effects
of the Treaty of *Hanover*. It is observable that when the *States* were
desired, by *our Minister*, to come into *this last Treaty of Vienna*, He
acquainted Them, "††† that his Majesty, as *Elector of Hanover*, had
negotiated separately, with Respect to his *Electoral Interest*;
nevertheless, He could assure Them that, in Quality of *Elector*, He
had guaranty'd the *Pragmatick Sanction*."—The *Dutch* did not
come into *this Treaty* till eleven Months after *Us*; and no Reason
hath been yet[a] offer'd for our changing Opinions, with Relation to
this Guaranty; but the Backwardness of the *Dutch* seems to have
proceeded from their Apprehension of *Don Carlos*, which was not
without Grounds; for the Experience of last Year shews that all
Thoughts of his marrying *one of the Arch-Dutchesses* were not
intirely dropt; and the Jealousy of *France*, on that Head, is plain
enough (how little soever it might affect *Us*) since They did not

---

[a] been yet] yet been *B*.

restore a Place to the *Emperor*, nor guaranty the *Succession*, before the *eldest Arch-Dutchess* was actually married. But I shall leave *this Point* to some future Observations, and return to the separate Article of the *Dutch Act of Concurrence*, which says, "$\ddagger \ddagger \ddagger$ that if the *Arch-Dutchess*, who shall succeed to all the *hereditary Kingdoms* and *Provinces*, which his *Imperial Majesty* actually enjoys, shall marry a *Prince* so powerful, and possessing so many States, that there may arise any just Apprehensions for the *Tranquility* and *Ballance of Power in Europe*, it shall and ought to be permitted to *that Prince*, upon his transferring to his *next of Kin* the States, which belong to Him, to enjoy the Right and Benefit of the *Guaranty* stipulated in the second Article of the *Treaty, &c.*"—Now, if any one can conceive that *this Provision* was design'd against the Duke of *Lorrain*, the Argument will revert with double Force, that *this Country* is of such Consequence, that after all the Losses and Diminutions of the *Imperial Dominions in Italy*, *Lorrain* alone is[a] sufficient to endanger the *Ballance of Power in Europe*; and therefore We ought not to let *his Brother*, or *next of Kin*, have it, but give it to *France*, that she may be enabled to preserve the *Ballance* against the late formidable Increase of Power in the *House of Austria*.

Whoever seriously reflects on the Consequences of *this additional Power to France*, will naturally conclude either that *our Ministers* were not consulted in the Negotiation of the *late Preliminaries*, or that They are apprehensive of some *bad Effects* from it, which They are unwilling to be thought answerable for hereafter.

Whatever Reason *France* might have why *Lorrain* should not be in the *Emperor's* Hands, it will be[b] far from justifying the not giving it to *another Prince of that Family*, rather than to *France*. But let us consider a little what is said to be purchas'd from *France* by it. Is it any Thing more than a *French Guaranty* of a Succession, in a *new Partition Treaty?* Can it ever be forgotten what their Behaviour was, upon a *former Treaty of the same Nature*, when They made that ever-memorable Distinction between the *Spirit* and *Letter of a Treaty?* Can We be insensible that their *late Conduct* is founded in the same righteous Maxims of Policy? What *Treaties* can be more binding to Princes than their *solemn Acts* and *Declarations* to the whole World? Did not *France*, in her *Manifesto against the Emperor*, disclaim "$* \ddagger$ any Acquisitions to Herself by the War, and alledge

---

[a] is] being added to them is *B*.   [b] will be] will, for that very Reason, be *B*.

that the *Emperor* in vain endeavoured to alarm the *Germanick Body* with such Designs"?—Again, in her *Declaration to the Electors* and *Princes of the Empire*, did she not solemnly declare, "⁺* that she had no View to make any Conquest, nor to keep any Settlements, which may affect the Safety of the *Germanick* Territories?"—Can any great Dependance be therefore placed upon the *very Act*, which directly contravenes *these solemn Declarations?* What Effects hath *this Kind of Guaranties* had in *other Countries*, besides bringing Shame and Reproach upon *Those*, who have enter'd into them, without being of any real Use to *Themselves* or *Others?* The present Interest of all Nations is considered, before They fulfil *such Engagements*, as late Experience sufficiently shews; and it will ever be from *these Motives* that They will either support, or depress their Neighbours. The *same Motives* will generally prevail with Princes, whether They are engag'd in *Treaties*, or not. What have most of our *late Treaties* and *Guaranties* signify'd, beyond the temporary Settlement of Things, and the Amusement of Mankind? Was it ever reckon'd true Policy before in the *weaker Party*, to add Strength to the *other*, by giving up Countries *immediately*, and depending upon a *Piece of Parchment* for the *fortuitous Events of an Equivalent*, which must always be esteem'd the more precarious, as the *other Power*^a will be the better enabled to pursue and obtain *new Advantages*, upon such Occurrences; especially since *France* hath never yet been charg'd with slipping any Opportunity of enlarging *her own Dominions?*

I shall not trouble you with any farther Thoughts upon the *Guaranty*, at present. Some Observations of the same Nature and Purport will necessarily occur, in considering the Importance and Consequences of the *Tuscan Ports* being given to *Spain*, or *Don Carlos*, which shall be the Subject of another Letter.

I am, SIR, &c.

---

* *Treaty between the* Emperor *and* France, *Art.* 28, 29, 30 *and* 31.

⁺ *Art.* 32.   [‡] *Art.* 34.

** See *State Tracts of King* William *the* 3d. *Vol.* 3. *p.* 151, *&c.*

^{††} See *the Introduction to* a general Collection of Treaties, *&c.* printed for Mess. Knapton, *p.* 21.

⁺ Les soupirs de L'Europe a la veüe du Projet de Paix, &c. p. 74.   ⁺* 263.

*** *Soupirs de L'Europe, p.* 76.   ⁺⁺⁺ *Rousset, vol.* 6, *p.* 178.

^{‡‡‡} *Rousset, vol.* 6, *p.* 462.   *[‡] Rousset, vol.* 9, *p.* 289.   [‡]* *Id. p.* 310.

^a *Power*] *Powers* B.

No. 510. Saturday, 10 April 1736.

The Examination of the Preliminaries, *or* Plan of Peace, *continued; in which the Case of the* TUSCAN PORTS *is particularly considered.*

To CALEB D'ANVERS, *Esq*;

SIR,

HAVING shewn the Importance of the Dutchies of LORAIN and BAR to FRANCE, the Reason is obvious why the *Gazetteers* have taken so much Pains to depreciate them, and persuade the World that *France* is but an inconsiderable Gainer by the Conclusion of *this War*; as if it were to pass for an establish'd Maxim, that She was always, upon such Occasions, to go on encreasing her Dominions.

But the Business of *these Writers* was to shew, in Support of *their Patron's* Assertion, *that there was no* ESSENTIAL VARIATIQN *between the* LAST YEAR'S PLAN OF ACCOMMODATION, *proposed by* Us, *and the present Preliminaries*; or, as the *States General* have worded it, in their Answer to the *Memorial of the Marquis de Saint* ª *Gilles,* * *that they don't* GREATLY DIFFER. Whether *all the Articles* were then communicated to Them seems to be very doubtful, not only from the cautious Manner of expressing Themselves, upon that Head, but if what the *Gazetteers* said at first, with Regard to *Lorain*, was all that even *our Ministers* knew, it is now plain They were not acquainted with *all the Articles*; for it was asserted, "† that the Cession of *these Dutchies* to *France* was not to take Effect till the Duke of *Lorain* is in full Possession of *Tuscany, Parma* and *Placentia.*—‡But the *former Part of this Argument* was contradicted, as a *late Writer* observ'd, by the *Preliminaries*, as they are publish'd; which say *that King* Stanislaus *shall have the* IMMEDIATE POSSESSION *of the Dutchy of* BAR; and I have been inform'd, *says He, that the whole Dominions of* LORAIN are to be delivered up to *France*, in Consideration of an *Annuity to the Duke*, in Lieu of the *Revenues*, till the *Vacancy of Tuscany* happens."— Every Body is now sensible that *this Information* was too true, though the Substance of it was not in the *Preliminary Articles*, which have been publish'd; and it is said that some Difficulties have already arisen, upon *that Head*.

The *Dutchies of Tuscany, Parma* and *Placentia* were to have been

ª *Saint*] *St. B.*

191

given to the *Emperor*, by the *Plan of Accommodation* last Year, in Exchange for *Naples* and *Sicily* allotted to *Don Carlos*. But how is *this Scheme* altered at present, though without an *essential Variation?* Why, the Duke of *Lorain* is to have *Tuscany*, in Exchange for the Cession of *Lorain* and *Bar* to *France*, which must therefore be reckoned a very *inconsiderable Acquisition*. But as *that Point* hath been sufficiently explain'd already, let us now consider the *Variation* in another Light.

If it may be supposed that the *present, eldest Arch-Dutchess* should die without Issue, the Duke of *Lorain* and *his Family* will be the Possessors of *those Dutchies*[a] given in Exchange for *his own*, and consequently the Power of the *House of Austria*, in the *second Daughter*, will be so far weaken'd, as to be render'd unable, even upon the Supposition of a *right Ballance of Power* by this Treaty, to preserve it upon that Foundation. Now This would have been prevented, if the Dominions of *Lorain* had been given to the *next of Kin in that Family*. But, in the present Case, where shall We look for a *Power*, capable of making a Stand against *France?* Have not the Riches of the *Italian Dominions* always cast such a Splendor over the Poverty of the *German ones*, that People have been so far deluded with it, of late, as to entertain dreadful Apprehensions from the exorbitant Power of the House of *Austria?* Was it not even thought necessary for *Us* to give our Assistance in reducing it, by very *extraordinary Expences*, and too frequent *Votes of Credit?* But no sooner had the *Emperor* lost *these Provinces* than all *Europe* was sensible of his Weakness, and justly alarm'd for *Themselves*.

In the *Plan of Accommodation*, no Notice was taken, as I remember, of the TUSCAN PORTS; but the giving of them to *Don Carlos*, by the *Preliminaries*, is certainly of a dangerous Tendency; for though they may have been consider'd, at present, in Point of *Revenue* only, and therefore thought an inconsiderable Sacrifice, for the Sake of *Peace*, they have been formerly look'd upon as Places of great Importance, and all the Arguments upon *that Subject* being much stronger now than they were then, I must trouble You with some of them.

In *both the Partition Treaties*, *France* was to have had *Naples*, *Sicily*, the *Tuscan Ports*, and the Marquisate of *Final;* "**and were so much afraid of mistaking, that after They had comprehended

---

[a] *Dutchies*] *Dutchies*, or *Tuscany* alone, if That only is *B*.

them in general Terms, They specify each under its proper Name. *These same Ports*, which have formerly been call'd the MANACLES OF ITALY, in Hatred to the *Spaniards*, will become really so in the Hands of *France*, who doubtless will use them with Dexterity enough to enslave *all the rest of that Continent*; for being *Masters at Sea*, nothing will be more easy than to attack *Tuscany* by that Way, whilst their *Land Armies* possess Themselves of the *Ecclesiastical State*, on one Side, and of *Piedmont* and *Lombardy*, on the other.

If the *French* pretend the *Tuscan Ports* (as accessional to the *two Kingdoms*, that are to be incorporated) are necessary to preserve a *mutual Communication*, no Man ought to be surpriz'd; for they are of great Use to them. But if They have *no other View*, why do They not leave the Marquisate of *Final* to the Duke of *Lorain*, being a Part of the State of *Milan*, which They have stipulated for Him by the *Treaty*; since the *little Port*, or rather *Road*, which belongs to *that Place*, is of no Consideration to secure the Command of *that Sea?* The Reason is evident; for They look upon *Milan* only as a Thing deposited in the Hands of the *Duke*, which They may take when They will, and therefore resolve to keep the *Keys*, that They may enter when it is convenient." Every Body must see that the eventual Succession stipulated for the Duke of *Lorain* is much more precarious *now*, than it was, in the *other Case*, when *both Parties* were to enter into Possession of their respective Shares at one and the same Time. But I will not make any farther Observations upon *this Head*, till We have seen what was the Opinion of *Great Britain* and her *Allies*, upon it.

In the *second grand Allyance*, Art. 5, it is particularly stipulated, "that the *Confederates* shall use their utmost Endeavours to recover the Kingdoms of *Naples* and *Sicily*, and the LANDS and ISLANDS on the Coasts of *Tuscany*, in the *Mediterranean*, that belong to the *Spanish* Dominions, and may serve to the *same Purpose*, (*That is, securing the* Emperor's *hereditary Countries*) and will also be of Advantage to the Navigation and Commerce of the Subjects of the King of GREAT BRITAIN, and of the UNITED PROVINCES."

Negotiations for a *Peace* were set on Foot, in the Year 1709; but not succeeding then, they were renew'd the following Year at *Gertruydenberg*, and the *French* made several Propositions for giving Part of the *Spanish Dominions* to the Duke of *Anjou*. I cannot state this Affair in a shorter Way than from the following Paragraph of the Declaration of Count *Sinzendorf*, the *Imperial Minister*, upon the *Propositions* made there on the 21st and 22nd of *March* 1710.

"††As to the Discourses and Propositions of the *said Ministers, (i.e. the* French *Ministers,)* one need only observe how they have been made by Degrees, to see that they would be the Ruin of the *House of Austria*, as well as of the *Allies*, and consequently of all *Europe*; for as to what concerns the Kingdoms of *Naples* and *Sicily*, or *one of these Kingdoms in particular*, I have already shewn, by a†† separate Writing, how the Proposition, for giving up *both*, or *one of these Kingdoms*, to the Duke of *Anjou*, is unjust, captious, and not to be accepted by the *House of Austria*; and it is the same, with Regard to the Proposition for giving Him *Naples, Sardinia*, and the PLACES situated on the Coasts of *Tuscany*; or *Sicily, Sardinia*, and the *said Places*; and as, in all these Propositions, *one of the two Kingdoms*, either of *Naples*, or *Sicily*, is brought in, and They have join'd by Degrees *Sardinia*, and the *four Places of Tuscany*, it is surprizing that *France* will return to the *same Propositions*, in different Shapes, and with *Places more hurtful*, as the PORTS OF TUSCANY and SARDINIA. The whole, together and separate, tend only to make *France* Mistress of the Commerce of the MEDITERRANEAN and the LEVANT, and to aggrandize Her by *new Conquests*."—This was not only the Opinion of the *Imperialists*; for the Progress of *that Negotiation* shews that it was likewise *ours*, and That of our *Allies*, with Regard to the TUSCAN PORTS. *France* had long insisted upon *Naples, Sicily, &c.* for the Duke of *Anjou*; *†"but their last Demand was only *Sicily, Sardinia*, and the *Tuscan Ports.*—There was no Disposition in any of the *Allies* to give up *those Places*; her *late Majesty* having before made it known that she would not consent to it. *Several other Princes* amongst the *Allies* were of the same Opinion; and the Minister of *Savoy* appeared the most against it."—From hence We may judge of the Importance of *those Places*; since it appears from the *above Memorial* that when only *four of them* were demanded, *We* and *our Allies* thought the Cession of them to be of such a dangerous Nature to our Interest, and the growing Power of *France*, (though given to *another Prince of the House of Bourbon*, with *Sicily* and *Sardinia* only) that We refus'd to comply with it at a Time, when *France* offer'd to restore all the rest of the *Spanish Dominions* to the House of *Austria*. There cannot be a stronger Proof that the Importance of *these Places* was well consider'd and understood, at that Time, since so high a Value was put upon them by *both Sides*. Can therefore the giving *all six of them* now, with the *Isle of Elbe*, to the *same Branch of the House of Bourbon* (because the fine Kingdom of *Naples* is substituted in the Room of the poor Island of *Sardinia)* be less detrimental to the *Trade of this Nation*, or less dangerous to the *Ballance of Power in Europe?*

But, perhaps, a more particular Enquiry into the Reasons, which induc'd *this Nation* to consider them in such an important Light as We have ever done, may be the best Way of shewing how much it is against *our Interest* that they should ever be given to any of the *Bourbon* Family.

By the *Partition Treaties*, the Crown of *France* was to have been put in Possession of *these Ports*, with *Naples* and *Sicily*; the natural Consequence of which must have been that the *French*, in a few Years, would have been *Masters of all Italy*; for there would have been no Prince left there, able of Himself to make any Opposition; nor, considering their Situation, and the Possessions of *France*, would They be capable of receiving any Succour from the *maritime Powers*, or from any others; so disjointed and incommunicable would They have been render'd to the rest of *Europe*.

The Apprehension of This, and the Danger of *France's* becoming Mistress of the *Levant Trade*, made the Importance of *these Ports* so much consider'd at the Treaty of *Gertruydenberg*; though they were then to be plac'd in the Hands of a *separate Prince of that Family*, as they are at present, with *less Dominions in Italy*; whilst the House of *Austria* was to keep Possession of as much Power and Territory there, as is now left Them, with the Crown of *Spain* into the Bargain. As *that Disposition* would have therefore given Us the Advantage of the *Spanish Ports* in the *Mediterranean*, We should not have been liable to so much Dependence upon the Goodwill of *France*, or the *House of Bourbon*, for our *Mediterranean* and *Levant Trade*, as We must be at present, when all these Countries are in the Hands of the *same Family*.

The View of *France* in all her Endeavours to obtain *these Ports* hath been, not only for the Sake of a Communication between *Them* and *Naples*, &c. but as Places, that gave Them a Power of entering into the very Bowels of *Italy*, at any Time. Nor must it be forgot how much They had it at Heart, in a former War with *Spain*, to get Possession of *these Places*; by Means of which They would then, as They may hereafter, transport their Forces, and assemble them wherever They please, with all imaginable Safety, upon a Coast in a Manner intirely made their own.

The Dukes of *Savoy* (those shifting Princes, who have gain'd on all Sides, by possessing the Barrier between *France* and *Italy)* might well apprehend their Insignificancy, as well as Danger, if *France* had another way of coming there; nor were They wanting to express their Fears, upon the Cession of *Tuscany* to *Don Carlos*.

As to *Great Britain, Leghorn* will be of little Use to Us, in Times of War, without *these Ports*, which will make it absolutely unsafe to carry on any Trade but by *Squadrons of Men of War*; so beset will *that Coast* be by the *Enemy's Ports*; and, at such a Time, to what other Parts of the *Levant* can We possibly trade with any Security, when We consider that our *Enemies* will be in Possession of all the Ports of *Naples* and *Sicily* too.—But That is too melancholy a Consideration to be dwelt upon any longer.

It is true, We shall have the Port of *Leghorn* open to assist the *Emperor*, if Occasion should require. But is it to be suppos'd that We shall always have such early Notice, as to be able to send a *Fleet* there, to interrupt their Communication and Entrance into *Italy?* Ought not the Alacrity of the *French* to give Us equal Apprehensions with the Slowness of the *Germans*, upon those Occasions; and may not the Blow be struck, as well as our Trade destroy'd, before We can possibly send the *Emperor* any Assistance?

Some Persons have flattered Themselves with a Notion that giving *these Dominions in Italy* to a *Prince of Spain* will renew the antient Friendship, which subsisted between *that Nation* and *Us*, when They formerly possess'd *Italy*, as being a necessary Support for maintaining Them there; and from hence the *same Persons* reason that our keeping *Gibraltar* would be the Interest of *Spain*. I heartily wish it may prove so, and am sorry it is not more probable; for what could be the Reason, that induced *France* to stipulate the *Tuscan Ports* for *Don Carlos?* They were not wanted, nor are They of any Use, for the Communication between *Spain, Naples* and *Sicily*; but are of the greatest Importance for the Communication between *Italy* and *France*; which is one of the Reasons why the *latter* have so earnestly insisted upon them, in *former Treaties*, as I have already shewn. This of Course must make the *Prince*, who possesses them, dependent upon *France*, who can easily and readily assist Him, at any Time, whereas *our Aid* must always be distant and precarious. Let us likewise consider, from the Nature of *that Prince's* Situation, against *whom* it is, that We are suppos'd to assist Him. Can it ever be necessary against any but the *Emperor*; and can

We possibly conceive a Conjuncture of that Nature to arise, in which it will not be the more immediate Interest of *France* to do it, as well as of *Us* to support the *Emperor*, as far at least as good Wishes? If it can be suppos'd that *France* and the *Emperor* should ever join against *Don Carlos*, what Imagination can be form'd of our being able to protect Him against *those united Powers?* The Mistake of this Opinion arises from not reflecting that at the Time, when *Spain* had such a Dependance upon *Us* on Account of their *Italian*[a] Dominions, *both of them* were in the Hands of the *House of Austria*, whose whole united Force was not sufficient to defend Them against the overgrown Power of *France*. How much Things are altered for the better since, by our *late wise Treaties*, and how long they are like to continue so, does not here require any farther Explanation.

Whilst *France* hath the Command of *these Ports*, the Duke of *Savoy*'s Barrier will be almost intirely useless; for she may invade *Italy* with more Ease, by the commodious Situation of *these Places*, than by passing the *Alps*. Here They may make their Preparations, and be ready, upon the Death of the present Duke of *Tuscany*, to take immediate Possession of *that Dutchy*; nor can any Thing else be expected, if so imprudent a Thing should be done as to give the immediate Possession of *Lorain* to *France*, and leave the Exchange of *this Dutchy* for it to a future Contingency, when the Execution of it may depend on their remarkable *good Faith* only.

But it may be imagined that *this Point*[b] will be effectually secured by the *Guaranty of the maritime Powers*. Yet who, that reflects upon *this last War*, can have any great Dependance upon *such Cobwebs?*[c] *We* and the *Dutch* were Guaranties of the *Emperor*'s Dominions before the Treaty of *Vienna* in 1731, by which We guaranty'd the *Pragmatick Sanction* ; yet as the War arose between *France* and the *Emperor*, upon the Affair of *Poland*, it became Matter of Dispute who was the *Aggressor*, and consequently was made a Doubt whether it was a *Casus Fœderis.*[1] For this Reason, *Time was taken to examine into it.* But *Naples* and *Sicily* were attack'd by the *Spanish Troops* alone, who had nothing to do in the Broils of *Poland*, and made a barefac'd War upon the *Emperor*, for the Sake of *Conquest* only. Yet what Assistance was given Him even *there?* Was it so

---

[a] *Italian*] *Italian* and other *B*.
[b] *Point*] *Point*, as well as the Rest of the *Imperial* Dominions, *B*.
[c] *Cobwebs?*] *B*; *Cobwebs. fol.*

much as consider'd as a separate Case from the Quarrel of *Poland*, though distinct in itself, and of more immediate Consequence to *Us?* Our Case then was, as it probably will always be, when We are call'd upon to fulfil *such sort of Guaranties*; which is one good Reason why We ought never to delude *ourselves* or *our Friends*, by entering into them.

What hath happened, and always will happen, with Respect to *our Guaranty* there, was long ago foreseen, in this Case; for in the Reasons alledg'd by Count *Sinzendorf* against giving *Sicily* to the Duke of *Anjou*, in 1710, He says, "†* that the *Guaranty of the Allies*, however it may be made, will not protect the *House of Austria* from the Enterprizes of *France* upon the Kingdom of *Naples*, by the Party, which the *Duke of Anjou* hath there at present, and which will be increas'd by his being in their Neighbourhood; so that *before it can be debated amongst the* Allies, *whether the* Case of Guaranty *subsists, or shall have agreed upon the* Succours *to be given, the Blow will be struck*; and how can They flatter Themselves with it, for the Time to come, after the Examples of what is past, which have fully shewn that *Guaranties* have never been of any immediate Use, but only given *France* Time to arrive at that Height, in which We have seen Her?

As This hath been so lately the Case, and is now scarce possible to be otherwise, considering how much *Italy* will be put under the Power of the *Bourbons*, by this Treaty, *our Guaranty* would be of very little Avail there, should We be never so willing and ready to make it good. Why therefore should We enter into so useless an Engagement, which can only throw Us under Difficulties, but not make us more able or willing to assist Those, to whom we plight our Faith, than We should be without it, if We find it for our Interest, and are in a proper Condition?ᵃ Late Experience shews Us that it serves only to deceive our *Allies*, by making Them depend upon false Hopes and Securities, for the Preservation of *those Places*, which They would have better provided for and defended, had it not been for such vain Amusements. The *Emperor* had Notice, long enough before the Rupture with *France*, to have been better prepar'd in *Italy*; and it is not improbable, considering of how much greater Advantage *those Provinces* are to Him than the *Dominions of the Empire*, that He would have taken more Care of them, had He not fondly imagin'd that the *maritime Powers* would

---

ᵃ Condition?] *B*; Condition. *fol.*

have thought the *Case of Guaranty* did exist there, and that it was more essentially their Interest to preserve *those Dominions* to Him, than their entering into the Broils of *Germany*, occasion'd by the Election of a King of *Poland*, which had therefore induc'd Him to draw his Forces together for his Defence in *Germany*.

Guaranties, in the present Form, are of a modern Invention. Their Original was owing to the Imagination of *weak Princes*, that They should be able to support Themselves by *these Means*, and tye up the Hands of the *stronger* with Paper Chains. But will dear-bought Experience never teach Them otherwise? This *general Method of negotiating* arose from the Time of leaving off the Custom of *swearing* to the Observation of Treaties, in the most solemn Manner. *Power* and *Interest* having shew'd how insignificant the Tyes of *Oaths* were, in that Case, the Custom was laid aside, and this ridiculous one of *Guaranties* hath been substituted in its Room, as more binding. There was, at least, one Use in the *former Method* more than in the *present*; for Princes then knew the *Treaties* and *Obligations* They laid Themselves under, which may now be sometimes conceal'd from Them by their *Ministers*.

Upon the whole, as it can never be prudent for this Nation to enter into *such sort of Obligations*, so it can never be necessary, and therefore by all possible Means ought to be avoided.

I shall trouble You with but one Letter more, shewing from the Alterations in *Italy*, that *France* and *Spain* would be sufficient Gainers by *this Treaty*, without *Lorrain* and the *Tuscan Ports*; to which I shall add my Reasons for writing, at present, upon *these Subjects*.

I am, SIR, &c.

---

* *Gazetteer, March* 16. † *Gazetteer, Jan.* 16.
‡ *Some Observations on the present Plan of Peace, &c. p.* 27.
** *State Tracts, vol.* 3, *p.* 147. †† *Lamberty, vol.* 6, *p.* 42.
‡‡ *Id. vol.* 6, *p.* 37. *† *Lamberty, vol.* 6, *p.* 54, 55.
†* *Lamberty, vol.* 6, *p.* 39.

No. 511. Saturday, 17 April 1736.

The Examination of the PRELIMINARIES *concluded.*

To CALEB D'ANVERS, *Esq;*

SIR,

I Believe a short, historical State of Facts will best shew the *Height of Power*, to which the *House of Bourbon* is arrived, the vast Extent of their *Acquisitions*, and the Effects of the *present Alterations in* ITALY; which will of themselves furnish more and better Observations to many than I am either willing, or able to make.

France, after the Acquisition of *Brittany*, (since which she hath, at no one Time, made any so considerable as LORAIN will be to Her) began to struggle for an absolute Power in *Europe*, and made such a Stand against the Emperor, *Charles* the 5th, (possess'd as He was of all the *Spanish, Italian*, and *Imperial Dominions)* as gave sufficient Evidence of her rising Power, and how little We should ever have to apprehend from the *House of Austria*, whilst it should have the unenriching Countries of the *Netherlands*, with the *Italian* and *Imperial* ones only, at the same time that *France* was even increas'd in Part of[a] her Dominions. The Treaty of *Munster* shew'd her Superiority. The *Pyrenean Treaty* enlarg'd Her so much, that she set no Bounds to her Ambition and made Her wantonly insult over several Powers of *Europe*. Nor were *We*, or more properly *our Governors*, wanting in our Assistance to that End; for even *Cromwel* help'd it forward, allur'd by *Dunkirk*, the View of *personal Security*, and getting Possession of some Part of the *Indies* for this Nation. *Charles* the 2d, from much different and worse Motives, did the same; which at last gave this Nation such an Alarm, that the *House of Commons*, in their Address to his Majesty, upon the Marriage of the Prince of *Orange*, observ'd, "They could grant no Supplies for the War, unless his *Majesty* and his *Allies* would engage not to lay down their Arms till the *Treaty of the Pyrennees* was perform'd, and the *French King* reduc'd to the Condition He was then in."

The Power of *France*, which had been so impolitickly nurs'd up, had like to have been fatal to our Liberties; but the *Revolution* and

---

[a] at the same . . . in Part of] and especially if *France* at the same Time should be greatly increased in *B*.

the *grand Allyance* between the *Emperor*, the *States General*, and *Us*, was our Preservation at that Time, and enabled Us to make the Stand We did. By *that Treaty* We promis'd and engag'd to assist the *Emperor* with all our Forces in taking Possession of the *Spanish Monarchy*, &c. in Case the King of *Spain* should die without Issue; but, instead of This, We were fatally drawn into *Partitioning*, and the War, which follow'd it, brought us to *another grand Allyance*, for the Preservation of the *Ballance of Europe*. We were then so sensible of our Error, in giving *Lorain* by Way of Exchange to *France*, with *Naples, Sicily*, and the *Tuscan Ports*, that * *They* and the *Lands and Islands on the Coasts of Tuscany* are the only Things, which We absolutely engag'd to obtain for the *Emperor* by War, as a Satisfaction for his Right to the *whole Spanish Monarchy*; of such great Importance were *these Places* then thought. Some Alterations were made in *this Treaty* by another with *Portugal* in 1703; in which We engag'd to place the *present Emperor* on the Throne of *Spain*. But as the *Italian Dominions* are the Point now in Dispute, I shall not trouble You with any Thing upon that Head; and having already shewn what pass'd concerning *them*, at the Time of the *Gertruydenberg* Negotiation, let us next enquire what was done in Consequence of the Treaty of *Utrecht*.

The *Italian Dominions*, with the Island of *Sardinia*, were given to the *Emperor*, and *Sicily* to the Duke of *Savoy.—This Treaty* was highly blam'd by the *Whigs*; and, upon the Accession of the present Royal Family, the *Ministers* concern'd in it were impeach'd. I need not mention the *Person*, who then charg'd the Cession of *Sicily* to the Duke of *Savoy*, and thereby leaving the *Emperor* too weak in *Italy*, as a criminal Matter upon *those Ministers*. This, no Doubt, was founded upon our Engagement with the *Emperor*, at our Entrance into the War, and the visible Interest of *this Nation*, in Point of *Trade* there. The *same Hand* afterwards sign'd a Treaty, in 1716, between the *Emperor* and his *late Majesty*, in which They promise "†mutually to defend each other, and to preserve Themselves in the Possession of the *Kingdoms, Provinces* and *Rights*, in the Condition they now are, which either of Them *actually hath* and *enjoys*—or which, during the Continuance of *this League*, They shall by mutual Consent *acquire*."—It may be here proper to forget *some Acquisitions*, which were lately made in the *North*, together with the Deduction, that might be drawn from thence of the *Causes*, which have brought *Europe* to the present, melancholy Crisis.—But to our present Point.

Sicily was soon after attack'd by *Spain*, and *We* engag'd in the Quarrel. Whether We did it for our *own Interest*, or in Consequence of the *Treaty*, or *both*, as they are above stated, is not now the Consideration; but in Justice to the *honourable Person*, who had so great an Hand in *that Affair*, his consistent Behaviour, when out of Place, in the Year 1718, ought never to be forgotten.

By this Step We broke Measures with *Spain*; and to set us right again, the eventual Succession of *Don Carlos* to *Tuscany*, *Parma* and *Placentia* was secur'd by the *Quadruple Allyance*. Yet Peace was not restor'd between the *two Nations* till 1721, by the famous, *private Treaty of Madrid*, whilst We were Mediators between *Spain* and the *Emperor*. The Year before, several *Treaties* and *Partitions* were made in the *North*, for the Sake of *Peace* only; and the *Emperor* gave Uneasiness to a *certain great Power*, by not readily concurring in *some Views*, that were thought to be founded on the Treaty of 1716. *This Treaty* of 1721, between *Spain* and *Us*, had an Article for the *Secrecy* of it. From *whom* could it be necessary to be kept secret, but from the *Emperor*, or the PEOPLE *of this Nation?*

This was the Situation of *Europe*, when the Incident of *France*'s sending back the *Infanta of Spain* gave a new Turn to Affairs; and from thence the wildest Imagination immediately arose of an *universal Monarchy in* DON CARLOS, which could be counter-ballanced by nothing but the ever-memorable Treaty of *Hanover*, so happily calculated, and by Experience found so effectual, for clipping the Wings of *that young Prince*. Nay, We were even told that what had been already stipulated for Him, by *former Treaties*, was against the Interest of *all the Powers in Europe*, and put in Mind of the *Consequences*, that would attend it; in which the Predictions of a *Court Writer*, for once, proved too true. As for *Great Britain*, in particular, He told us, " ‡ that if *Don Carlos* should ever succeed to *Tuscany*, LEGHORN, the Mart of our *Mediterranean Trade* would be in his Possession.—And that We might as well give up *Gibraltar* and *Portmahon*, which would be of little Service to Us, in that Case.—Notwithstanding This, a Treaty was soon afterwards made to carry Him thither; the natural Effects of which were more attentively consider'd by his *Imperial Majesty*; and therefore not complying with it more readily than He had done with *some former Views*, the Seeds of Dissention between the *two Courts* were now ripen'd to such a Degree, that a *Plan* was laid for attacking Him in *Italy* and upon the *Rhine*, which hath since been so fatally executed.

Not contented with taking these Steps to force the *Emperor* to a Compliance with the very Thing, that had been declared so detrimental to *Us*, the contracting Parties in the Treaty of *Seville* would not, in Return, guaranty the *Pragmatick Sanction* to Him any farther than "** with Relation to the *States of Italy*, and with their free Consent; or to *one of his Daughters* only, whom He should chuse to succeed Him in *those Dominions*, with the Consent of the *said States*."—These two Propositions were so limited, that the *Emperor* justly express'd his Surprize at them; and in his Answer to them says, "†† that it was having Views very opposite to *Peace*, and the *Ballance of Europe*, to restrain the *Guaranty* in Question in this Manner."—Who can be surpriz'd that *France* should contend for thus dividing the Power of the *House of Austria?* But that *We* and the *Dutch* should be so far deluded (by *Her*, at least) as to join in making This the *Ultimatum of the Allies of Seville*, is what will scarce be believ'd, or comprehended, in future Times. It is, and ever will be a Question what was to have become of *Flanders*, and the rest of the *hereditary Dominions in Germany*. Were they to be canton'd out amongst several Pretenders; or was it imagined that after weakening the *Imperial Family* by this Division, the Remainder might have been preserv'd united? Yet even then was it possible to conceive that This could have been settled, without future Broils, or a sufficient Power left in *Germany* to preserve *Flanders* for a Barrier to *Us* and the *Dutch*, or even *Germany* itself against *France?* Does not every Diminution and Division of the Power of the *House of Austria* increase That of *France*, though none of the Dominions thus taken from it should fall to her Share? The less able *one* is to oppose the more able the *other* will be to oppress.

This Guaranty, as proposed by the *Allies of Seville* in their *Ultimatum*, was of such a Nature as shew'd the World that We thought *the Ballance of Power in Europe* would be in no Danger, if the *Italian Dominions* were separated from the rest of the *Imperial ones*. But hath not This, with our former Design of attacking the *Emperor* there, been one Reason why He hath been so attack'd? Hath it not convinc'd Him that We do not look upon *Italy* in the same Light as We were wont to do; and that We should be more unlikely to engage in its Defence, since our only Consideration in this Case, could have been to throw the *Prince*, who was to have possess'd *those Dominions*, an *Arch-Dutchess* into the Bargain?[a]

---

[a] Bargain?] *B*; Bargain. *fol.*

No. 511. 17 April 1736

It is true that, in the Treaty of *Vienna* 1731, We guaranty'd the *Emperor*'s *Succession*, for very good Reasons, in a different Manner, and obtain'd the Honour of transporting *Don Carlos* to *Leghorn*; though We were formerly so apprehensive of Him for *Ourselves*, and *all Europe*. Yet of such Importance is *Leghorn* now, that it is thought fit to take it out of his Hands again, at the Expence of *Naples*, *Sicily*, and the *Tuscan Ports*.

Ever since the Notion of an *over-grown Power in the House of Austria* hath arisen, there have been such continual Fluctuations in all our Measures, that it is scarce possible, from outward Appearances, to reconcile the Motives of our Transactions, for two Years, with one another; but nobody can wonder that *Those*, who made the Treaty of *Hanover*, the Treaty of *Seville*, and the *Ultimatum of the Allies* upon it, should approve of the *present Preliminaries*, which all tend alike to weaken the *Emperor*, as *those Persons* may lay in a Claim to some Merit in the *late Negotiations*; and the only Thing They can dislike in them (though not ESSENTIALLY *varying from their own Plan of Accommodation*) is, that the *Emperor* and *his Family*[a] are now left better compacted together than They were formerly design'd to have been.[b]

This Nation hath been long us'd to consider the *Affairs of Italy* in a very different Manner; and though from the Situation, to which We are reduc'd, We must give into *some Alterations* there; yet surely it is to be wish'd that they may be such as will the least affect our *Trade*, and not render us totally unable to support the *present*, *design'd Ballance of Power in Europe*.

The *Tuscan Ports* and *Lorain* ought, if possible, to be sav'd. The King of *Sardinia*'s Share of *Milan*, and the Cession of *Naples* and *Sicily* to *Don Carlos*, are Things of such Importance to the weakening of the *Emperor*, that *France* and *her Allies* ought to be satisfy'd with them. Let it be considered how much more powerful the *House of Bourbon* is now made, than They were left even by the Treaty of *Utrecht*. Hath not Experience shewn us that *France* can be Friends with *Spain*, whenever She will?[c] The Quarrel with *Spain* in the *late Regent's* Time, in 1718, nay even That about sending back the *Infanta* were of but small Duration, when They had a Desire of being Friends again; and the Dupes a *certain Nation*

[a] *Emperor* and *his Family*] *Emperor's* Dominions *B*.   [b] been.] been, by *Them*. *B*.
[c] will?] *B*; will. *fol*.

were made in it should never be forgot. Their *late*, or *present Difference*, if it may be now called so, is easily reconcileable again, whenever *France* shall find it her Interest; for what hath given Occasion to it but the Queen of *Spain*'s unwearied Attempts to aggrandize her *Son*, at any Rate? Nor is it the first Check of this Nature, which she hath met with, by too precipitate Haste. *France*, forever desirous of diminishing the Dominions of the *House of Austria*, will always find a Prince ready to accept them in *Don Carlos*; which will not give the rest of *Europe* so much Alarm as if *France* took them to Herself; and yet will as effectually weaken the *Emperor*. It is justly to be apprehended that This may soon be the Case again, upon the Death of the Duke of *Tuscany*; for as *France* can be no longer jealous, from the Marriage of *Don Carlos* with the *eldest Arch-Dutchess*, that *this Branch of the House of Bourbon* will be superior in Honour, and equal in Power to Herself, He may be again play'd off by Her, to serve farther Purposes.

It was certainly a Stroke of good Policy in the *French*, though it might not have been one of the *Preliminary Articles*, that the Duke of *Lorain* should be marry'd before the *Treaty* was finished, or any Thing restor'd; for by these Means, all Hopes of future Negotiations between *Spain* and the *Emperor*, about such a Match, are stopt, and the *Emperor* will be forc'd to be more complying in the Execution of the *Preliminaries*; some Effects of which are already seen.

Having thus taken a short View of what hath passed, in Relation to *Italy*, as well as what may be justly apprehended for the future, it is easy to perceive that one Reason for writing *these Papers* was to put Us upon our Guard in that Respect, and not imprudently, or unnecessarily, suffer Ourselves to be drawn into a GUARANTY, which is in its own Nature so directly opposite to the true Interest of *this Nation*.

Another Reason was, that the *Ministers*, who communicated the *Preliminaries* both *here* and at the *Hague*, were said, in most of the News-Papers, to declare, "that the *secret Articles* related solely to the Method to be taken for removing all Impediments to the Execution of *this Treaty*, and no Ways concern'd the *maritime Powers*, in any Point whatever."—Notwithstanding which, and what hath been already said, the *Gazetteers* apply'd the whole and every Part to the Conduct and Knowledge of *their Patron*. *Those*

Papers were answered, and very strong Arguments alledg'd against
our entering into any new *Guaranties*, upon that Account.

As no Man could ever charge *our Minister* with being the Author
of the *Preliminaries*, (to *some Articles* of which He was utterly a
Stranger) it was hoped, at least, that nobody would make Himself
answerable for them, by *guarantying* them. But Time hath
discover'd that Hopes were given from *Us* and the *Dutch* of *such a
Guaranty*; which call'd upon Those, who wish well to their
Country, to shew the Consequences of what was doing, before it
was too late; and since the writing of my *other Letters*, upon this
Subject, I have the Pleasure to find the following Article from the
Hague, viz. "‡‡It is assured that Mr. *Trevor*, who is charged with the
Management of the *British* Affairs here, hath declared to their
High-Mightinesses, that when his Britannick Majesty *approv'd the*
Preliminaries, *and consented to give Hopes of his* Guaranty, *He by no
Means design'd that the* Powers interested *should conceive Expec-
tations that He would engage for any Thing* NOT ACTUALLY
STIPULATED IN THE SAID PRELIMINARIES; and that, for his own
Part, in Case any DEVIATIONS *were made from the* LETTER *of
them, He could not but think Himself at Liberty to do as He pleas'd.*—It is
said that *this Answer* hath given great Satisfaction to their *High-
Mightinesses*, who would be glad to quit their Hands of
Engagements, which can never do Them any *Good*, but may
Harm."—I am very glad to find myself prevented, in this Manner,
from urging any farther Arguments to shew that the *Alterations in
the Preliminaries*, now on the Carpet, give us both an Opportunity,
and more Reason than ever, not to enter into the *Guaranty* of them;
and I hope what hath been said will rather tend to strengthen *that
Opinion* than in any wise alter it.

We all see the Effects of our *late Negotiations*, for twenty Years
past, and that, for the Sake of getting over the *present Difficulty*, We
have constantly plunged our selves into a *greater*; which, as it hath
prevented the Payment of *our Debts*, hath likewise exhausted Us, at
the same Time, to such a Degree, that We were not in a Condition
to do much, at the late terrible Crisis of Affairs. It must therefore be
the Desire of every Man, who hath the Interest of *this Nation* at
Heart, and who sees the Poverty of the *Country*, that We should
keep Ourselves out of *new Engagements*, and take all Opportunities,
by saving *unnecessary Expences*, to pay off *our Debts*, and ease the
People of their *Taxes*, that We may be able to prevent the farther

Extension of *those Mischiefs*, which We have at present so much Reason to dread.

I am, SIR, &c.

---

* *Art.* 5. *of the grand Allyance in* 1701.   † *Art.* 2.
‡ *British Journal, Jan.* 4, 1728–9.   ** *Rousset, vol.* 5, *p.*131.[a]
†† *Ib. p.* 137.   ‡‡ *Daily Advertiser, March* 22, 1735–6.

[a] vol. 5, p. 131.] *B; vol.* 6, p. 130. *fol.*

EXPLANATORY NOTES

No. 25. 3 March 1727.

1. Caleb D'Anvers declared in No. 1, 5 December 1726: 'I design to lay open the frauds, abuses, and secret iniquities of all professions, not excepting those of my own, which is at present notoriously adulterated with pernicious mixtures of craft, and several scandalous prostitutions. The same malignant contagion has infected the other learned faculties and polite professions; it has crept into the camp as well as the court; prevailed in the church as well as the state; has vitiated the country in the same manner that it has poison'd the City, and work'd it self into every part of our constitution, from the highest offices of life, down to the lowest occupations, in a regular and gradual descent.

    It is my design, in this paper, to detect and animadvert upon all these corruptions . . . it shall . . . be my chief business to unravel the dark secrets of *political Craft*, and trace it through all its various windings and intricate recesses.'

2. Philip V of Spain, grandson of Louis XIV and uncle to Louis XV.

3. Louis XV's grandfather was actually Louis the Dauphin, who had died in 1711: Bolingbroke can hardly have meant to refer to him as 'all his Life at *Law* with his *Neighbours*' since the legal metaphor usually implies war. He presumably means Louis XIV, actually Louis XV's great grandfather.

No. 30. 20 March 1727.

1. Such an account, promised in No. 1, eventually appeared in the prefatory material to volume i of the 1731 edition (i. 28–32), and was borrowed from the *Country Gentleman*, No. 37, 15 July 1726, from which 'The Design of the *Craftsman*' is said to come.

2. The address to which letters should be sent changed several times in the early weeks, probably because the proprietors of Ballard's Coffee-House in Albemarle Street, and the Cocoa Tree Chocolate House, found the *Craftsman* too dangerous to handle. Fear of prosecution for libel must have been likely, but the first *Craftsman* had been illegal for a quite different reason: it had been printed on unstamped paper, and 'it was not thought safe to sell any of these papers, which were inadvertently printed in this Manner' (No. 2). In fact, only twelve copies of No. 1 were sold (C (H) MS P74, f.28), and I know of only one copy that has survived—it is now in the Bond Collection of Periodicals at the Kenneth Spencer Research Library, University of Kansas.

3. Piracy by Spanish ships. 'Philipeaux' is Philip V.
4. 'Dr. King' and his remedies had become a source of amusement in Nos. 3 and 6, and later appeared in a series of mock advertisements.

No. 35. 7 April 1727.

1. The merchants of Algiers and Salé, then a busy port and pirate headquarters on the west coast of Morocco.

No. 52. 1 July 1727.

1. Adapted from Eccles. 9: 11: 'I returned, and saw under the sun, that the race is not to the swift, nor the battle to the strong, neither yet bread to the wise, nor yet riches to men of understanding, nor yet favour to men of skill; but time and chance happeneth to them all.'
2. Bolingbroke translates freely, but not injudiciously, passages from Jean Luis Guez de Balzac's *Aristippe, ou de la Cour* (Paris, 1658), pp. 49–71.
3. Sir Positive Atall is a character in Shadwell's *The Sullen Lovers* (1668).

No. 54. 15 July 1727.

1. Lechmere died suddenly on 18 June 1727. Notice of the death of 'that great Lawyer and true lover of his Country' appeared in No. 51 on 24 June, and No. 52 contained an acknowledgement of receipt of the letter published in this issue. Lechmere, although an Opposition Whig, had little to do with Bolingbroke.
2. Addison's obituary of Somers was published in *Freeholder* No. 39, 4 May 1715; and the *True Briton* No. 40, 18 October 1723, contained the Duke of Wharton's obituary of Cowper.
3. 'Patriotism takes precedence.'
4. The Septennial Act had been passed by the Court Whigs in 1716.

No. 61. 2 September 1727.

1. For Bolingbroke's assessment of the terms of the Assiento Contract, see Nos. 68 and 71. The Assientos were trading concessions granted by Spain to Britain in the Utrecht settlement in 1713, but Philip V's disregard of them rendered the Assiento trade hopelessly unprofitable.

No. 68. 21 October 1727.

1. Used here in the sense of shelter or protection.

No. 71. 11 November 1727.

1. *Some Considerations of the Lowering of Interest, and Raising the Value of Money* (1691), reprinted in Locke's *Works* (1714), ii. 8.

No. 91. 30 March 1728.

1. Garraway's was frequented by bankers and goldsmiths.

No. 96. 4 May 1728.

1. Captain Henry Johnson was employed by the South Sea Company. In 1714 the House of Lords ordered the directors of the company to produce an account of all proceedings relating to the Assiento trade. The directors themselves were examined on 8 July, as was Johnson, 'late Commander of Her Majesty's Ship the *Anglesea . . .* concerning any Proposal made to him for taking Goods on Board the said Ship for *The South Seas.*' (*Journals of the House of Lords*, xix. 733, 737, 755.)

2. The principal point of contention at the Congress of Soissons, which opened on 14 June 1728, was the proposed succession of Elizabeth Farnese's son, Don Carlos, to Parma and Piacenza. At the Congress of Cambrai, four years earlier, every participant power opposed his succession in Italy, for reasons mostly concerning the undesirable control which Spain would establish over the Mediterranean.

No. 111. 17 August 1728.

1. 'For a bribe he has enacted laws and abrogated them.' (*Aeneid*, vi. 622.)

2. On 21 May 1728 the Commons debated the right to vote in Flint. An election took place in Montgomery in May. (*Journals of the House of Commons*, xxi. 173–6; see also *The Parliamentary Diary of Sir Edward Knatchbull 1722–1730*, ed. A. N. Newman, Camden Society Third Series, xciv (1963), 75–6.)

3. Temple's 'Essay' was published in his *Miscellanea* (1680), from which Bolingbroke quotes pp. 82–5.

No. 123. 9 November 1728.

1. From the opening of *Discourses*, Book I, ch. vii.

No. 130. 28 December 1728.

1. i.e. the Hanseatic League, whose last general assembly took place in 1669, though the name was continued by the commercial union of Lubeck, Hamburg, and Bremen.

No. 131. 4 January 1729.

1. i.e. Bolingbroke's 'Answer to the London Journal of Saturday 21 December 1728', an essay directed at Benjamin Hoadly, and evidently very popular despite its being twice the usual length and, at fourpence, twice the usual price.

2. 'Publicola' was a pseudonymous contributor to the *London Journal*, whose editor was James Pitt.

No. 133. 18 January 1729.

1. i.e. No. 130.

2. Plenipotentiary.

3. 'Letters of Marque' were documents authorizing a ship to be armed for the purpose of what, without such letters, would amount to acts of piracy.

No. 134. 25 January 1729.

1. The Mississippi scheme, John Law's Parisian equivalent of the South Sea scheme, collapsed in May 1720. The demand for land during the periods of speculation was great.

2. A certificate showing that customs duty had been paid.

3. Perpetuana, a woolen fabric.

4. Moidores were gold coins originating from Portugal and in circulation in England. They were worth about 27 shillings.

No. 142. 22 March 1729.

1. Wolsey had been mentioned in the *Craftsman* seven times, Sejanus twice, and Buckingham once, as obvious parallels to Walpole.

2. See n.2 to No. 131.

3. Johan de Witt was shot, and his brother Cornelius battered to death, before their bodies were left to the disposition of a mob, which tore them to pieces.

No. 147. 20 April 1729.

1. Part of a speech in which Sir Francis Winnington had opposed the methods used by Charles II's Treasurer, Danby, was printed in No. 101, 8 June 1728, as the climax of an essay on Danby's character and his method of bribery.

No. 149. 10 May 1729.

1. 'Dare some deed to merit scanty Gyaros and the gaol.' (Juvenal, *Satires*, i. 73.) Gyaros was a barren island in the Aegean, used as a place of exile for state offenders.

2. In February, Bambridge lodged Sir William Rich on the common side of the prison until he agreed to pay a baronet's fee of £5. Rich said he had already paid, and stabbed Bambridge with a knife. The enterprising gaoler brought an action before the Court of Common Pleas.

3. The Spanish satirist Francisco de Quevedo y Villegas (1580–1645), whose works include *Sueños* (Barcelona, 1627), translated as *Visions* by Roger L'Estrange (1667).

4. Bambridge, held in Newgate at this time, was tried on 21 May for the murder of a Fleet prisoner, Robert Castell. He was acquitted.
5. Falstaff is ordered to the Fleet at the end of *2 Henry IV* but does not (in *Henry V*) die there.
6. 'Advice bearer'.

No. 161. 2 August 1729.

1. 'We have come to the peak of fortune.' (*Epistles*, II. i. 32.)
2. Bolingbroke refers to Lord Chancellor Macclesfield's impeachment in 1725 for selling masterships in chancery. The masters recovered the large sums (paid to Macclesfield) from litigants who lodged money with them. For '*Keepers of our Prisons*' see No. 149.
3. 'A wrangler and encourager of law suits' (Johnson's *Dictionary*).

No. 167. 13 September 1729.

1. Chapter 3 of 'Lilliput' in *Gulliver's Travels* describes how men jump over sticks and coloured threads held by the Emperor. Bolingbroke appears to conflate this episode with an echo of 'Verses on the Revival of the Order of the Bath', lines 11–12, attributed to Swift:

> And he who will leap over a Stick for a King
> Is qualified best for a Dog in a String.

(*The Poems of Jonathan Swift*, ed. Harold Williams (2nd edn., Oxford, 1958, ii. 389.)
2. 'Dog lover'.

No. 181. 20 December 1729.

1. Francklin, the *Craftsman*'s printer, was acquitted on 3 December, after a trial for alleged libel (in No. 140). The decision was greeted with public rejoicing, and William Pulteney celebrated the occasion with a ballad, *The Honest Jury: or, Caleb Triumphant* (printed in the *Craftsman* of 1731, v. 337–9.)
2. The Dutch adventurer Jan Willem Ripperdá went in September 1729 to live at Turnham Green, formerly the seat of the Countess of Gainsborough.
3. This much used proverb is perfectly explained by John Ray: 'If we once conceive a good opinion of a man, we will not be perswaded he doth any thing amiss; but him whom we have a prejudice against, we are ready to suspect on the sleightest occasion.' (*A Collection of English Proverbs* (1670), p. 128.)
4. This cryptic comment appears to mean 'Ictus the fisherman is wise.'

No. 182. 27 December 1729.

1. Referring to *Craftsman* No. 178, 29 November 1729.
2. Here used in the sense of compromise of agreement. (Cf. *Antony and Cleopatra*, II. vi. 58.)

No. 185. 17 January 1730.

1. The Treaty of Seville was formally concluded on 9 November 1729.

No. 186. 24 January 1730.

1. i.e. No. 185.
2. Reduction.

No. 225. 24 October 1730.

1. 'A circuit of words; a multiplicity of words' (Johnson's *Dictionary*).
2. Bolingbroke included a very brief survey of Henry VI's reign in No. 219, 12 September 1730, as a part of his sequence of *Remarks on the History of England*.
3. Paul de Rapin-Thoyras's *Histoire d'Angleterre* was a standard Whig history: it was translated by Nicholas Tindal, *The History of England* (15 vols., 1726–31), which he continued to the accession of George II in thirteen additional volumes (1744–7).
4. 'Oldcastle's first Letter' was printed in No. 206, 13 June 1730, the first of the *Remarks on the History of England*.

No. 249. 10 April 1731.

1. Voltaire made the curious observation that easterly winds were a source of melancholy to the English. Also, in several places in the Old Testament, east winds are associated with disasters, plagues, blight, and menace.

No. 252. 1 May 1731.

1. William Pulteney wrote to Sarah, Duchess of Marlborough, enclosing Bolingbroke's 'Draught of the Inscription' and a letter to Pulteney, who hoped they would 'convince your Grace with how just and sincere a Regard for the memory of the Duke of Marlborough my Lord undertook it'. Pulteney might have been remembering Bolingbroke's earlier attitude to the Duke, whom he abandoned and prompted Swift to vilify (in 1711) after a period of virtual hero-worship.

Pulteney thought the inscription a fine piece, 'formed on the model of ancient Inscriptions', and he was confident that Sarah would like it because it was 'not writ by an Able Hand only but that it was done with a good Heart also . . . I send this by a very safe hand, for it is the

Craftsman will have the Honour of Delivering it your Grace.'
(Blenheim Palace, Long Library Portfolio, quoted by David Green,
Blenheim Palace (1951), p. 174.)

2. i.e. besieged Mons.

No. 264. 24 July 1731.

1. An address prefixed to the *Craftsman* (1731), i. A similar dedication was prefixed to vol. viii (1737).

2. The demolition of the Dunkirk fortifications was a condition, which France was slow to fulfil, demanded by the Peace of Utrecht in 1713.

3. In Addison's political periodical the *Freeholder* (1715), Nos. 22, 44, and 47, the typical country gentleman is styled the foxhunter; and Bolingbroke spoke in his *Letter to Sir William Windham* of the House of Commons as an assembly whose members 'grow, like hounds, fond of the man who shows them game, and by whose halloo they are used to be encouraged'. (*Works* (1844, reprinted 1967), i. 117.)

No. 319. 12 August 1732.

1. *Spectator*, No. 286, 28 January 1712 (*The Spectator*, ed. Donald F. Bond (Oxford, 1965), iii, 15).

2. Giovanni Battista Bononcini was enjoying considerable popularity in London as a composer of opera, and was, for a time, Handel's most serious rival.

3. This indicates 'Pulteney' or, as the name was often pronounced and spelled, 'Poultney'.

4. 'Only-begotten constitution'.

No. 350. 17 March 1733.

1. 'The Occasional Financer' and 'Teague Carus' were pseudonyms used by writers in *The Daily Courant.*

No. 351. 24 March 1733.

1. *A Letter from a Member of Parliament to his Friends in the Country concerning the Duties on Wine and Tobacco* (1733) attacked the basis of the *Craftsman*'s opposition to the Excise Bill, commenting on 'this *chimæra* of a *General Excise*' (p. 7), and defending the scheme's ability to remove frauds and impositions on the public. The pamphlet is attributed to Walpole.

No. 353. 7 April 1733.

1. At the first performance of *Deborah* on 17 March 1733, only 120 people paid, but hundreds broke in.

2. Handel was apparently subject to fits of raving about the treatment *Deborah* received, and to complete the parallel, Walpole had long feared assassination, actually coming near to danger during the Excise crisis (Paul Langford, *The Excise Crisis: Society and Politics in the Age of Walpole* (Oxford, 1975), p. 91). Further, it was known that Walpole hated the City merchants and called the traders rogues (Hervey, *Memoirs*, p. 138). Walpole was also said to have revived the phrase 'sturdy beggars' from a medieval statute, though in 1714 there had been passed 'An Act for reducing the Laws relating to Rogues, Vagabonds, Sturdy Beggars, and Vagrants, into One Act of Parliament' (*Journals of the House of Lords*, xix. 738). The phrase was quoted in numerous arguments against excise, as an example of the contempt in which Walpole held the common populace.

3. A copy of this paper in the Cambridge University Library is annotated by a contemporary hand, identifying 'One fam'd for his *Morals*' as Sir William Yonge (author of *Sedition and Defamation Display'd*, 1731, a somewhat violent attack on Pulteney), and 'one for his *Face*' as Heidegger, whose ugly appearance was famous.

4. Paolo Rolli may possibly have been the author of an Italian version of this entire paper. An Italian manuscript, addressed to 'Sigr. Calebi d'Anversa', survives among the Senesino papers in the Bibliotheca Comunale, Siena. The manuscript is possibly, but not definitely, in Rolli's hand: he, or somebody, may have written an original which Bolingbroke translated into English. For this view see George E. Dorris, *Paolo Rolli and the Italian Circle in London 1715–1744* (The Hague, 1967), pp. 102–12.

No. 375. 8 September 1733.

1. An Act for the frequent meeting and calling of Parliaments, known as the Triennial Act, was passed in 1694.

2. This was a measure which Bolingbroke sponsored and vociferously supported. See Peter Wentworth to Lord Raby, 21 December 1710, *The Wentworth Papers 1705–1739*, ed. James J. Cartwright (London, 1883), p. 167.

No. 377. 22 September 1733.

1. This paper prints about two thirds of the whole pamphlet.

2. '*Thou shalt not wrest Judgment*': Exod. 23: 6, 8. '*His right Hand is full of Bribes*': Ps. 26: 10. '*He shaketh his Hands from holding a Bribe*': Isa. 33: 15. '*Of whose Hands have I taken a Bribe?*: 1 Sam. 12: 3. '*God shall destroy the Tabernacle of Bribery*': Job 15: 34. Achan's story is told in Josh. 7: 1, 18, and 22: 20. The story of Gehazi and Naaman is told in 2 Kgs. 5: 20–7. '*He shall not prosper . . .*': Job 15: 29.

No. 406. 13 April 1734.

1. Cicero, *De Officiis*, II. xv.
2. Hieronymus Wolfius edited *De Officiis* in 1569 (2nd edn.: I am unable to trace the first), Johannes Graevius in 1688.
3. A town in north Boeotia where Philip's forces defeated the Athenians and Thebans in 338 BC.

No. 430. 28 September 1734.

1. 'Safe without violation of liberty.'

No. 507. 20 March 1736.

1. A pseudonym used by William Arnall, former editor of the *Free Briton*, and from 1735 editor of the *Daily Gazetteer*.
2. The Treaty of Aix la Chapelle, concluded on 29 May 1668 between France and Spain, put a temporary end to the War of the Spanish Succession. Under the terms of the Treaty, Louis XIV returned Franche-Comté, which had been occupied the previous winter by his troops, but he received Charleroi, Binche, Aeth, Douai, Tournai, Oudenaarde, Lille, Armentieres, Kortrijk, Bergues, and Veurne.
3. Franche-Comté was formally ceded by Spain to France at the Peace of Nijmegen (1678–9), together with Cambrai, Valenciennes, St. Omer, Ypres, Conde, Bouchain, and Maubeuge, among other places.
4. By the treaty of Rijswijk (1697) France surrendered all towns captured since the Treaty of Nijmegen, with the exception of Strasbourg, and agreed that the main frontier posts of the Netherlands should be fortified, to secure the barrier. Louis recognized William III as the rightful king of England, thereby losing face as well as power.

No. 508. 27 March 1736.

1. The Treaty of Munster was a part of the Treaty of Westphalia (see n. 2). By the Pyrenean Treaty of 1659, Spain ceded to France dominions in Flanders, Artois, Hainaut, and Luxembourg, and it was through this treaty that Louis XIV married the Infanta, Maria Theresa.
2. The Treaty of Westphalia consisted of two treaties, those of Osnabruck and Munster. It marked the end of the Thirty Years' War in 1648.
3. Two treaties made between France, England, and the Netherlands in 1698 and 1700 for the settlement of the Spanish Succession.

No. 510. 10 April 1736.

1. Casus fœderis: whatever comes under the terms of a treaty.

APPENDIX

A Memoir of the Duke of Berwick (from the *Craftsman Extraordinary*, 30 June 1734).

Portrait du M^{al.} de Berwick; par Milord Bolingbroke, tiré d'une feuille extraordinaire du Craftsman, du 30 Juin (vieux style) 1734.

LES lettres de Paris nous apprennent que le Maréchal de Berwick a été tué d'un coup de canon, le matin du 12 Juin (*nouveau style*), étant a la tranchée devant Philisbourg, où son intrépidité peu commune & sa vigilance ordinaire ne le portoient que trop souvent. Il étoit fils du feu Roi Jacques II, & de Demoiselle Arabelle Churchill, (qui a été depuis Madame Godfrey) sœur du feu Duc de Marlborough.

Sa patrie le perdit bientôt, n'ayant que dix-sept ans* lors de la dernière révolution, & la France, qui devint dès-lors son refuge, ne tardera pas sans doute à s'appercevoir que l'armée qu'il commandoit, & le Royaume entier le perdent trop tôt aujourd'hui. C'est véritablement une perte pour l'humanité, à laquelle on peut bien dire qu'il faisoit honneur, comme on l'a dit du Grand Turenne.

Il a eu tant de part aux affaires de son temps, qu'il tiendra une grande place dans l'Histoire de ce siècle; & sans doute que quelque bonne plume célébrera particuliérement une vie digne du meilleur Ecrivain. L'étendue de cette Feuille ne me permet que de marquer quelques-uns des principaux traits d'un si excellent tableau.

Il se montra de bonne heure dans la profession qu'il a illustrée depuis. A l'âge de quatorze ans† il se trouva au siege de Bude, & fit deux campagnes en Hongrie, où il fut élevé au grade de Général Major. Depuis ce temps, l'Irlande, la Flandre, l'Espagne, la Savoie, l'Allemagne, ont été successivement le théâtre de ses grands talens pour la guerre. Il se signala dans les commandemens inférieurs, durant la guerre de 1688; lorsqu'il parvint à avoir le commandement en Chef des armées, ce qui fut, si je ne me trompe, en 1702,‡ de dix-huit** campagnes qu'il a faites depuis, il n'y en a pas une qui n'ait été marquée par des succès extraordinaires; & cela, dans des temps où la Fortune sembloit avoir abandonné le parti dans lequel il étoit engagé, comme si la Victoire, n'ayant que l'indifférence pour les Nations qui se faisoient la guerre, eût réservé ses faveurs, pour les répandre uniquement sur deux hommes, dans les veines desquels couloit le même

217

sang, les Ducs de Marlborough & de Berwick. Il avoit un talent particulier pour les sieges, & pour ce qu'on appelle le detail d'une armée; mais les champs d'Almanza attestent que, si les occasions s'en étoient aussi souvent présentées, il n'auroit pas montré moins de capacité pour les batailles, sur lesquelles le commun des hommes, peut-être injustement, mesure la gloire des Généraux, quoique le succès n'en soit souvent dû qu'à des événemens imprévus, & que ce ne soient que les grandes suites d'une victoire qui frappent les imaginations des hommes & enlevent leur admiration. Il étoit particuliérement attentif à ménager la vie du Soldat, soit en pourvoyant avec le plus grand soin à sa subsistance, soit en ne l'exposant qu'à des dangers inévitables qu'on lui voyoit affronter le premier. Il étoit avec cela très-exact à maintenir la discipline. En un mot, il fut généralement regardé comme l'égal des plus grands Généraux de son temps, & dans un pays de Guerriers il vécut assez pour se voir reconnu le premier de tous. Ses talens ne se bornoient pas a cet unique genre de grandeur; il étoit également grand dans le gouvernement civil, & dans le cabinet. L'honneur qu'il eut d'être admis aux plus importans Conseils par Louis XIV, & par le Régent de France, les deux plus sages & les deux plus grands Princes de leur temps, le prouvent suffisament, aussi bien que l'estime & l'affection générale que lui porte une grande Province, la Guienne, dont il eut, durant plusieurs années, le commandement. Tout le monde sait que l'on doit à ses soins & aux sages mesures qu'il prit, que la peste qui menaçoit toute l'Europe ait été contenue dans le lieu où elle avoit pris naissance.

Il connoissoit très-bien les Cours; mais il ne se servoit de cette connoissance, que pour éviter de se laisser entraîner par les factieux, & pour se garantir des artifices & des trahisons de ce pays.

Pour en venir aux qualités de l'homme privé, le Maréchal de Berwick étoit au dessus de l'argent, & son désintéressement, déjà bien connu par nombre de traits, éclatera davantage, quand le Public sera instruit de plusieurs faits que la modestie lui avoit fait céler. Il étoit exact observateur de la justice, & si fidèle ami de la vérité, qu'il avoit coutume de garder un profond silence sur les affaires dont l'importance demandoit le secret; & aucun motif d'intérêt ou autre ne pouvoit l'engager à violer la loi qu'il s'étoit prescrite à lui-même. Personne n'avoit plus d'humanité que lui; il étoit naturellement affable & s'il ne le paroissoit pas au premier abord, cela ne provenoit que de la réserve que l'élévation de son rang lui avoit imposée, & de ce qu'il craignoit de se trop livrer à la familiarité d'une nation souvent portée à en abuser. Quand il ne traitoit point d'affaires, & qu'il se trouvoit parmi ses amis, il étoit familier & parfaitement à son aise. On a toujours remarqué en lui l'humeur la plus égale, ce qui sembloit être une qualité acquise; car il étoit naturellement vif & porté à la colere. Il fut dès sa jeunesse exempt des vices, qui ne sont guère regardés comme des taches à cet âge, & dans les personnes de sa profession. Son penchant pour la vertu le porta bientôt à la Religion, & la Religion à la piété, dans laquelle il persévéra inviolablement. Elle fut en lui si douce, qu'elle n'imposa jamais la moindre contrainte à ceux qui vivoient avec lui.

On s'attend peut-être, que, pour rendre tout ce que je viens de dire plus croyable, je ferai mention de ses défauts; mais dans le vrai ils étoient si légers & si passagers, qu'on avoit peine à les appercevoir. Je suis sûr d'avoir omis plusieurs de ses vertus, & que ses plus grands ennemis, si tant est qu'il en eut, ne sauroient lui imputer aucun vice.

Pour reprendre en peu de mots son caractère, on peut dire de lui, avec quelques additions, ce qui a été dit de son grand-père le Roi Charles I, qu'il étoit le fils le plus soumis, le meilleur père, le mari le plus tendre, l'ami le plus sincère, le maître le plus compatissant, & le sujet le plus fidèle qui ait paru de son temps; & sa mémoire sera chère à tous ceux qui ont eu le bonheur de le bien connoître, comme du *meilleur Grand Homme*, qui ait jamais existé.

> *Multis ille bonis flebilis occidit,*
> *Nulli flebilior quam mihi.*[1]

---

* Il en avoit dix-huit.   † Il en avoit quinze   ‡ C'étoit en 1704.
** De quinze.

NOTE TO APPENDIX

1. Adapted from Horace, *Odes*, I. xxiv. 9–10: 'multis ille bonis flebilis occidit, nulli flebilior quam tibi, Vergili.' (Many are the good who mourn his death, but no one more than you, Virgil.)

INDEX

Acts of Parliament: Navigation 38–42, 44; Qualification 156; Septennial 21, 209; Triennial 153–5, 215.

Aislabie, John xix.

Alexander the Great 169–70.

Algiers and Algerians 10–11, 209.

Amhurst, Nicholas xv, xvi, xviii, xxiii, xxvi, xxx, xxxv.

Anne, Queen 156.

Arbuthnot, John xix, xxi, xxii, xxvi.

Army 62–3, 106–7, 108–9, 133, 153, 154, 155, 169.

Assiento trade 26, 28–31, 35–6, 37, 42–3, 45–6, 65, 209, 210.

Aurelio del Po 138–41.

Austria 184, 189, 192, 194, 195, 197–8, 200, 203, 204–5.

Balzac, Jean-Luis Guez de 13, 209.

Bambridge, Thomas 90–5, 211, 212.

Bavaria 124.

Berwick, James Fitz-James, Duke of xxv, xxxiv, 217–19.

Blenheim Palace xxiv–xxv, 122–3, 214.

Bolingbroke, Henry St John, Viscount: founds *Craftsman* xiii; contributes to *Craftsman* xvi, xxi, xxii, xxiv–xxv, xxvii; asks Swift to contribute xx.
—— *A Collection of Political Tracts* xxv; *A Dissertation upon Parties* xxiv; *The Idea of a Patriot King* xxv; *A Letter to Sir William Windham* 214; *Remarks on the History of England* xxiv, xxvii, xxix, 114, 118, 213.

Bononcini, Giovanni 137–8, 214.

Bramston, James xxii.

Bribery 88–9, 97–9, 152, 157, 164–5, 167, 169–72.

British Journal xviii, xx, 72–3.

Budgell, Eustace xvii–xviii, xxi, xxii, xxxi.

Carlos, Don 110–13, 188, 192, 196–7, 202, 205, 210.

Carteret, John, Lord xvii, xxx.

Castell, Robert 93, 212.

Chesterfield, Philip Dormer Stanhope, 4th Earl of xvii, xxx.

Cibber, Theophilus (pseudonym) xvii, xxvii.

Cicero 169–70.

Coke, Edward, Lord 50.

Common Sense xvii.

Constitution, British 49–53, 59–60, 99, 132, 134, 152–4, 158–62, 172, 176–7.

Cooke, Thomas xiv, xvi, xxx.

Corruption xxvii, 50–1, 57–8, 88–9, 95, 97, 132, 152, 156–7, 170–2.

Country Gentleman 208.

Craftsman, appearance xiii, xx, xxviii; circulation and distribution xiii–xiv, xxix; printers xxix; purpose 128, 134, 208; reprints xiv–xv; reputation xxvii–xxviii; signatory letters in xxii–xxviii.

Credit 74–6, 80.

Customs and custom-houses 38, 44, 76–7.

Daily Courant xxxiv, 113–14, 214.

Daily Gazetteer xiv, xviii, xxv, 178, 180, 191, 205–6.

Daily Journal 73.

Daily Post 137.

D'Anvers, Caleb, pseudonymous editor of the *Craftsman* xiii, xvi, xxi–xxii, xxviii, 8, 103.

Davenant, Charles 64, 66.

Deborah (Handel) 152, 214.

Debts, public 47–8, 74–5, 81.

Declaration of Rights 153–4.

Dogs 100–2, 120.

Dunkirk 131, 214.

Dutch East India Company 57.

Elections 49–53, 60–1, 157.

d'Estrades, Count: letters cited 84–8.

Exchange rate 67–9, 79–80.

Excise 142–5, 146–8, 152, 168, 214, 215.

Faction 118.

Fielding, Henry xxi–xxii, xxxii.

Fleet Prison 90–5, 97.

Flying Post xxii.

Fog's Weekly Journal xxi, xxix, xxxii.

France and the French 10, 12, 35, 66, 69, 70–1, 83–8, 124–6, 131, 178–81, 182–9, 191, 193–9, 200–5, 216.
Francklin, Richard xiii, xiv, xv–xvi, xxiii, xxix, xxxiii, 102–3, 212.
Free Briton xxxiv, 216.
Freeholder 18, 209, 214.
Freeport, Sir Andrew 27–8.

Gay, John xix, xxvi, xxxi.
Germany 188, 189–90, 199, 203.
Gibraltar 9–13, 47–9, 148.

Haines, Henry xv, xxv.
Handel, George Frederick 149–52, 215.
Hanseatic League 64, 210.
Heidegger, John James 215.
Henley, John, 'Orator' xxi.
Henry VI 113–20, 213.
Hervey, John, Baron Hervey of Ickworth xvii, xxvii.
History of the Norfolk Steward xxi, xxvi.
Hoadly, Benjamin 210.

Insurance 11, 23.
Italy 192, 194, 195, 196–8, 200–3; *see also* Tuscany.

James II 175.
Johnson, Capt. Henry 45, 210.
Johnston, Gabriel xxxi.

Kings and kingship 14–17, 160, 173–7.

Land Tax 142–3, 146, 168.
Lechmere, Nicholas, Baron Lechmere 18–22, 209.
Letter from a Member of Parliament to his Friends in the Country, a 146, 147, 214.
Letters 3, 6, 208.
Liberty 59–61, 118, 129, 132, 133, 135, 145, 147, 148, 149, 153–7, 158, 161, 163, 172, 176.
Locke, John 37, 209.
London Journal xxxiv, 134, 210.
Lorraine 182–9, 197, 201, 204.
Louis XIV 208, 216.
Louis XV 208.
Luxury 74, 96.
Lyttelton, George, 1st Baron Lyttelton xvii.

Macclesfield, Lord Chancellor 212.
Machiavelli, Niccolo 60.

Mallet, David xxiii, xxiv.
Margaret of Anjou 115–19.
Marlborough, John Churchill, 1st Duke of 121–8, 213.
Marlborough, Sarah, Duchess of 213.
Mawbey, Sir Joseph xvi.
Ministers of state 14–17, 22, 51–3, 114, 129–31, 134, 148, 178, 179, 191, 206; can corrupt Parliament 59; curbed by a free Parliament 60–3; former, cited as warning to present 83, 115; interfere with trade 57–8, 77; weak and evil 98–9.
Mississippi Scheme 75, 211.
Money 74–5, 80–1, 109, 167; *see also* Credit, Exchange Rate.
Monopolies 38, 54.
Montgomery 49, 59, 210.
Murphy, Arthur xiv, xvi.

Netherlands and the Dutch 29, 35, 44, 55, 64–5, 66, 67–8, 69–70, 79, 83–8, 125–6, 181, 187–9, 200–1, 203, 216.
Newton, Thomas xxiii–xxiv, xxvi, xxvii.

Occasional Financer (pseudonym) 145–6, 214.
Occasional Writer xx.
Onslow, Arthur xvii.
Opera 138, 150–2.

Parallels (as satirical device) 82, 87, 118–20, 130–1.
Parliament 49–53, 60, 97, 99, 105, 132, 152–7, 159, 166–8, 174.
Patriotism 18–22.
Peace, Negotiations for 178–9, 183, 186.
Pedantry 136.
Pensions 89, 152, 154, 156.
Philip V 208, 209.
Philip of Macedon 169–71.
Phillimore, Robert xvii.
Piracy 67, 71–2, 209.
Poland 197–8.
Pope, Alexander xx–xxi, xxii, xxiv, xxvi.
Post Office xxix, 6.
Prosperity, National 73–82, 162.
Publicola (pseudonym) 67, 83, 210.
Pulteney, Daniel xvii, xxvi.
Pulteney, William, Earl of Bath xiii, xvi, xvii, xxii, xxiii–xxiv, xxvi, xxxii, 139, 212, 213, 214.

Quadruple Alliance 110–11.

Index

Quevedo y Villegas, Francisco de 92, 211.

Ralph, James xxiv.
Rapin, Paul de 115, 116, 117, 213.
Richlieu, Armand Jean du Plessis, Cardinal 66.
Ripperdá, Jan Willem de 104, 212.
Rolli, Paolo 151, 215.

Salé 10, 209.
Sedley, Sir Charles 89.
Shippen, William xvii.
South Sea Company 22–7, 28–31, 32, 35–6, 42–3, 45–7, 56–7, 74–5, 210.
Spain and the Spanish 10, 33–4, 36, 103, 108, 110, 178–9, 181, 184, 195–6, 199, 201–2, 204, 209, 210, 216.
Spectator xvi, xxxii, 28, 136, 214.
Steward 4, 7.
Stockjobbers and stockjobbing 34, 57.
Strada del Po 137–41, 150.
Strutt, Samuel xviii.
Suffolk, William, Earl (later Duke) of 115–19.
Swift, Jonathan xx, xxi, xxii, 212, 213.

Teague Carus (pseudonym) 145, 214.
Temple, Sir William 51–2, 83–7, 210.
Tooley, Thomas xviii.
Trade 44, 63, 65, 107, 146–7; cloth 76–9; contraband 38, 44, 46–7, 56; decay of 57–8, 74, 80–1, 96; freedom of, the basis of wealth and liberty 37–8, 42, 54, 66, 72; importance of Gibraltar for 10–11, 47–9; influence of politicians on 58; negro, *see* Assiento trade; South Sea 26–7, 28–31, 33–4.
Treaties: Aix la Chappelle 180, 216; Hanover 182, 188, 204; London 111, 112; Munster 182, 200, 216; Nijmegen 182, 216; Partition 183, 184, 216; Pyrenees 182, 200, 216; Rijswijk 180–1, 182–3, 216; Seville 106, 110–11, 203, 204, 213; Vienna 111, 188, 197, 204; Westphalia 182, 216.
Troops, foreign 108, 109.
True Briton 18, 209.
Tuscany 110, 191, 196, 197, 201, 204.

Venality, in public offices 96–7.
Voltaire, François-Marie Arouet de 213.

Walpole, Horatio 110.
Walpole, Sir Robert xix, xxi, xxii, xxv, xxvii, 6, 8, 134, 152, 214, 215; *see also* Ministers of state.
Walsingham, Francis (pseudonym) 180–1, 216.
West Indian Plantations 3–6, 7, 37, 56, 64–5, 69.
William III 89, 123–4, 153, 154–5, 156, 216.
de Wit, Johan 83–8, 211.
Wyndham, Sir William xvii, xxx.

Yonge, Sir William 215.